PLAYERS' CHOICE

PLAYERS' CHOICE

Eugene V. McCaffrey
and
Roger A. McCaffrey

Facts On File Publications
New York, New York ● Oxford, England

Library of Congress Cataloging-in-Publication Data

McCaffrey, Eugene V.
    Players' choice.

    Includes index.
    1. Baseball players—United States—Biography.
2. Baseball—United States—Records. I. McCaffrey,
Roger A. II. Title.
GV865.A1M36 1987   796.357'092'2 [B]   86-19705
ISBN 0-8160-1362-4

Designed by Anne Scatto/Levavi & Levavi
Composition by Facts On File/Maxwell Photographics
Printed in the United States of America

10 9 8 7 6 5 4 3 2

To Vicki and Priscilla

"All men who have ever lived and achieved success in this world had lived in vain if they knew not baseball."
—Senator Chauncey Depew
(1834–1928)

Contents

Vice President George Bush springs out of the batter's box after singling off Milt Pappas in an oldtimer's game.

Foreword
by Vice President George Bush

Who am I to be taking part in a survey of baseball players and experts?

Well, for one thing, I currently lead the majors in opening-day pitches by Vice Presidents, and modestly claim to be the highest elected official ever to play in an Old-Timers' game (going one for two—a pop-up off Warren Spahn and a single off Milt Pappas, in 1984).

I also happen to be an avid fan, and the father of four avid fans. I love the game, and consider it one of the biggest rewards of my present office that I've been able to meet and get to know some of the finest athletes in the country. It wasn't long ago, for example, that I was with two of my favorite ball players, Nolan Ryan and Gary Carter—how's that for a dream battery?—on a goodwill visit to Honduras. I reminded Gary that I threw him a steaming fastball to open the New York Mets' 1985 season. At least, that's how I recalled the occasion, but he didn't quite remember it the same way.

I grew up loving big-league baseball. I knew all the averages, and prided myself on a great card collection of my favorite players. My love for the game peaked when I became first baseman and, in my senior year, captain of the Yale team in the late 1940s. We didn't keep exact statistics in those days, but for the record book (if anyone's interested) my "lifetime" batting average was about .250—"Good field, no hit," was the way I was described.

Here then is my reply to the McCaffrey All-Star survey. Or at least to those questions I feel qualified to answer. Disagree with me? Fine. To paraphrase Mark Twain, that's what makes baseball great—differences of opinion.

ALL-TIME ALL-STAR TEAM 1

OUTFIELD: Ted Williams, Joe DiMaggio, Babe Ruth **3B:** George Brett **2B:** Joe Morgan **1B:** Lou Gehrig **SS:** Phil Rizzuto **RH PITCHER:** Nolan Ryan **LH PITCHER:** Sandy Koufax **CATCHER:** Johnny Bench **RELIEF PITCHER:** Hoyt Wilhelm

ALL-TIME ALL-STAR TEAM 2

OUTFIELD: Mickey Mantle, Willie Mays, Hank Aaron **3B:** Bobby Brown **2B:** Charlie Gehringer **1B:** Willie McCovey or Ernie Banks **SS:** Lou Aparicio **RH PITCHER:** Tom Seaver **LH PITCHER:** Lefty Grove **CATCHER:** Bill Dickey **RELIEF PITCHER:** Rich Gossage

HONORABLE MENTIONS: Pete Rose, Dwight Gooden, Roberto Clemente, Jimmie Foxx, Ty Cobb

BEST FASTBALL: Nolan Ryan, Dwight Gooden, Bob Feller **BEST CURVE:** Catfish Hunter, Warren Spahn **BEST PICKOFF MOVE:** Mike Cuellar **BEST BASE-STEALER OF ALL TIME:** Lou Brock **BEST BUNTER:** Honus Wagner **BEST THROWING ARM OF ALL TIME:** Roberto Clemente **TOUGHEST PITCHER YOU EVER BATTED AGAINST:** Warren Spahn or Milt Pappas **PLAYERS WHO DID THE MOST TO INSPIRE THEIR TEAMS:** Ty Cobb, Joe DiMaggio, Ted Williams, Leo Durocher **BEST CLUTCH HITTER OF ALL TIME:** Ted Williams, Joe DiMaggio, George Brett **THE BEST TEAM:** 1927 Yankees **DESIGNATED HITTER:** Oppose **7TH GAME WORLD SERIES PITCHER:** Carl Hubbell

ACKNOWLEDGMENTS

The two gentlemen most responsible for *Players' Choice* seeing the light of day are Paul Aron and Gerry Helferich. Mr. Aron, then with Doubleday, gave us guidance and ideas, helping to reshape the book. Mr. Helferich, executive editor with Facts On File, liked our proposal, helped it along, and edited the manuscript. Nelson Doubleday, appropriately enough, got the ball rolling by sending our first proposal into the Doubleday pipeline. Although they didn't accept the book, Paul Aron was good enough to give us his time and thoughts.

Our father, Neil McCaffrey, contributed a couple of survey questions and provided advice from inception to completion. Thanks, Dad. A multitalented man of ideas named Vic Gold—maybe you've read some of his articles or magazine pieces, or one of his books—gave us encouragement and key support from the very first. As did Maureen McCaffrey, and brother Neil III, both savvy in the ways of the book world.

Others who went out of their way to help: Marvin Nagourney, Barbara and Mark Lyons, John Gizzi, John Menna, Pauline Mercado, Bob Sorrentino, Tom Heitz, Patricia Kelly, Tom Meyer, Susan Davis, Phyllis Rogers, Jim Toomey, Bill Haber, Bobby Bragan, and Sister Catherine Long, a Franciscan nun who at age 84 types with the best of them.

Without launching into "This Is Your Life," we shouldn't forget to thank Mom. Utterly bored by the game, she nevertheless in her wisdom saw baseball as a healthy outlet for us kids, and let it develop into a harmless obsession. And of course cheered the book along these past few years.

Thanks also to Vice President Bush for taking time from his schedule to grace these pages with a Foreword and an intelligent ballot. Last but not least, thanks to each and every ballplayer who took part in the survey. Wish we could deliver that personally. And a final note. Four baseball reference books were ever by our side: *The Baseball Encyclopedia*, *Who's Who in Professional Baseball*, *The Sports Encyclopedia of Baseball*, and *The Great All-Time Baseball Record Book*.

INTRODUCTION:
To Boldly Go Where No Scribe
Has Gone Before

How many fans reflect, when the Most Valuable Player and Cy Young awards are handed out, that the winners are picked not by the players' peers, but by baseball writers? How many of us realize that old-timers are immortalized in that most sacred of sports shrines, the Hall of Fame, by a vote, again, of *sportswriters*, not ball players?

This book isn't meant as a giant sneer at sportswriters. Far from it. We just want to repair a gaping hole in baseball literature. No one has ever systematically polled the *real* experts, the players themselves, on their opinions about the game and its greats. As direct-mail advertising specialists and ardent baseball fans, we felt uniquely qualified to do the job.

We mailed a questionnaire to every living ball player, coach, and manager, retired or active, whose address we could find. We mailed over 5,000 surveys; 645 players answered, from every era, post-1900. Some are Hall of Famers, some cup-of-coffee types, and there are all kinds in between. (A sample of our survey appears in the Appendix.)

This is an unscientific survey to be sure. Some players refused to participate on grounds that they couldn't possibly pick one or two guys for a given position who was (were) so clearly better than all the rest. But enough players, including Roy Campanella, the Brooklyn Dodger backstop, wrote us encouraging notes to make this project worthwhile for us and, we trust, for you. And as the box shows, many thought it was about time someone consulted those who know the game best. Space doesn't permit us to reproduce the ballot of every man who took part, but if you want to see the survey of any player, we'll send it along to you via first-class mail for $1 per photocopied ballot. Send us the name or names, along with a check payable to either author, to: Box 255, Harrison, N.Y. 10528. The whole series of surveys, minus of course those players who asked that we *not* quote them, is available for $110. A few players chose to answer only some of the questions. If they answered any, they are listed as participants. Those 645 players are listed at the end of the book.

What Baseball Writer Understood the Game the Best?

HERE'S HOW THE BALL PLAYERS ANSWERED THAT QUESTION:

1.	Red Smith	14.0%	10-13.	Jim Murray	1.5
2.	Dick Young	9.7	10-13.	Sam Greene	1.5
3.	NONE OF THEM	8.5	10-13.	John Carmichael	1.5
4.	Grantland Rice	5.1	10-13.	Dan Daniels	1.5
5.	Peter Gammons	2.3	14-15.	Shirley Povich	1.4
6.	Jerome Holtzman	2.1	14-15.	Roy Stockman	1.4
7-8.	Milt Richman	1.9	16.	John Steadman	1.3
7-8.	Bob Broeg	1.9	17.	Ray Kelley	1.2
9.	Bob Stevens	1.7			

Other votes for: Hal Liebowitz, George Cobbledick, Frank Grayson, Bob Hunter, Bob Considine, Irvine Vaughn, and Joe Falls.

How To Read This Book

Although we've tried to design the book for browsing, certain sections require explanation. In addition to the raw tallies, we developed a rating system to take into account players who split their votes and ballots that were only partially filled out, and for the vagaries of the survey itself (we asked for only *one* all-time defensive team, but two all-time teams, for example). Here, then, is how the rating system works: We use a one-man, one-vote system, but with certain variations. One first-place vote equals four points; one second-place vote equals two points. In cases where a player chooses three or four teams—and some took that option—the scoring is as follows: For three teams, one first-place vote equals three points, one second-place vote equals two points, and a third-place vote equals one point. For four teams, it's first place, two points; second place, two points; third place, one point; and fourth place, one point. This means that if a player was chosen first on every ballot, he would receive 67% of the vote (four points out of every six). Thus the percentage totals for a Babe Ruth or Henry Aaron seem smaller than they are, and this phenomenon is complicated by the fact that they were outfielders, whose percentage totals seem even smaller, because the maximum percentage is 22% (four out of 18).

All the more reason why we decided to *number* the *place* finished by a given player, where appropriate.

On all other questions, two points are credited for each answer. In this way, if a player voted, say, for both John McGraw and Earl Weaver as best manager, each would receive one point.

What follows is a look at the players' responses, question by question, beginning with their first-base picks. We break down the percentages for each choice, and add our own comments where it seems appropriate. We also took the liberty of extrapolating answers. "First basemen on first basemen," for example, means that we took all the ballots of men who played first and tallied them separately. We did that for each position, and the results may stimulate some debates. When done with the ballots of managers and coaches—these men see more players than anybody except Vin Scully—some interesting changes occur. One that leaps out: the managers and coaches think less well of Keith Hernandez's fielding ability than the 645 respondents as a whole do.

Two other sections that our extrapolating generated are the franchise-by-franchise and era-by-era picks. What baseball fan can pass up the chance to compile a few more lists of great teams? Imagine the pleasure of putting these together with the help of guys like Rizzuto, Monte Irvin, Red Schoendienst, George Case and 641 others. Now you have some idea of the fun we had doing this book. Hope you have as much reading it.

PLAYERS' CHOICE:
The All-Time All-Star Teams

Best First Basemen Ever

1.	Lou Gehrig	36.0%	10-12.	Pete Rose	1.7
2.	Stan Musial	7.6	10-12.	Eddie Murray	1.7
3.	Jimmie Foxx	6.1	13-14.	Steve Garvey	1.5
4.	Gil Hodges	5.9	13-14.	Rod Carew	1.5
5.	Willie McCovey	5.6	15.	Mickey Vernon	1.4
6.	George Sisler	5.2	16.	Keith Hernandez	1.2
7.	Bill Terry	5.0	17-19.	Moose Skowron	.8
8.	Hank Greenberg	3.3	17-19.	Harmon Killebrew	.8
9.	Johnny Mize	1.8	17-19.	Jim Bottomley	.8
10-12.	Willie Stargell	1.7	20.	Hal Chase	.7

Best First Basemen: Defense

1.	Gil Hodges	13.3%	10-11.	Charlie Grimm	3.0
2.	Keith Hernandez	8.8	12.	Hal Chase	2.4
3.	Vic Power	7.7	13-15.	Bill White	1.9
4.	Wes Parker	5.9	13-15.	Jim Spencer	1.9
5.	George Sisler	5.4	13-15.	Steve Garvey	1.9
6.	Mickey Vernon	5.2	16-17.	George Scott	1.7
7.	Bill Terry	4.4	16-17.	George McQuinn	1.7
8.	Joe Kuhel	4.2	18.	Frank Chance	1.4
9.	Lou Gehrig	3.6	19-20.	Babe Dahlgren	1.3
10-11.	Ferris Fain	3.0	19-20.	Dolf Camilli	1.3

First Basemen On First Basemen

1.	Lou Gehrig	34.0%	6-7.	Jimmie Foxx	6.3
2.	Stan Musial	9.4	6-7.	Gil Hodges	6.3
3.	Bill Terry	7.6	8.	Mickey Vernon	2.8
4.	Willie McCovey	6.9	9.	Hank Greenberg	2.1
5.	George Sisler	6.6			

First Basemen Rate Each Others' Gloves

1.	Gil Hodges	19.1%	4-5.	Bill Terry	8.5
2-3.	Wes Parker	14.9	6-7.	Ferris Fain	6.4
2-3.	Vic Power	14.9	6-7.	Mickey Vernon	6.4
4-5.	George Sisler	8.5	8.	Keith Hernandez	4.3

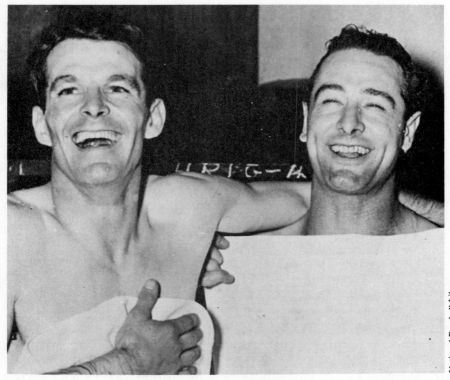

National Baseball Library

Yankee greats George Selkirk (left) and the peerless Lou Gehrig woop it up after the final game of the 1936 World Series. Each belted two homers in the six-game affair.

In the best-ever polling, it's Lou Gehrig by a landslide—the obvious selection. Batting behind Babe Ruth, Lou delivered bushels of RBIs, averaging 153 annually in the 11-year span 1927-1937, during which he led the league five times. In 1930, he accomplished the stupendous feat of driving in 117 runs in 77 *road* games. His defense, maligned by the New Statisticians, was smooth, even graceful once he rounded into form (witness his ninth-place finish as a glove man in our survey). Anyway, we can only think of the player who, asked how another fielded his position, replied, "With his bat."

If all the votes Stan Musial received as an outfielder (he finished seventh) were added to his first-base total, he would still fall far short of first place in the best-ever balloting. Nevertheless, Stan the Man does suffer from the split vote, as do Rod Carew, Jimmie Foxx, Harmon Killebrew, and Pete Rose. In fact, Rose finished in the top 20 at first, second, third *and* the outfield, making him, for lack of a better description, the best tenth man in baseball history.

First base, naturally, has many split-vote (i.e., ex-outfielder) players because the decline of defensive skills is for many of the greats faster than their offensive decline. Even at first base, though, defense obviously counts a great deal in the voting. How else can you explain the strong finish of Gil Hodges, a powerful but very streaky hitter, yet the easy #1 choice among glove men? (Coaches and managers have a very different view of the matter, by the way. Gentleman Gil finished well down in their rating.) Granted, Hodges's leadership qualities have been well documented, but no more so than those of Bill Terry, Willie Stargell, Pete Rose, and Steve Garvey, all of whom finished behind him. Hall of Famers extend down 10 places beneath Hodges; isn't it about time he was admitted?

It's heartening to see the vastly underrated Johnny Mize receive his due in the best-ever voting. It took a long time to get that .562 slugging average (eighth best all-time) into the Hall of Fame. As good a power pinch hitter as there ever was, the Big Cat still holds the St. Louis Cardinals' single season home run record, with 43. He also endeared himself to Yankee and Giant fans during his 15-year career.

The eighth-place finish of Hank Greenberg is something of a mystery. His lifetime slugging average of .605 (fifth all-time) is hard to ignore, though two of the four men ahead of him as sluggers were also first basemen (Gehrig and Foxx). Statistically, there is nothing to indicate that he couldn't field, either: he led the American League in assists twice and once in fielding percentage.

You often hear that a left-handed first baseman has an advantage because (1) more balls are hit to his right than left, (2) it's easier for him to throw to second, and (3) his tag is faster on a pickoff attempt. Only two of the top 12 first basemen are right-handed, but those two (Gil Hodges and Vic Power) rank 1 and 3 on the all-time defensive team.

Recognition by one's peers takes time, and at least three active first basemen stand a good chance to move up in the polling as time goes by. They are Eddie Murray, Don Mattingly, and Keith Hernandez, any one of whom could creep or leap up the ladder if he were to continue in current form. One of the most enduring and fascinating things about being a baseball fan is watching the comparative scales tip as a player's accomplishments mount or diminish. Certainly both Murray and Mattingly, and possibly Hernandez, are on the Cooperstown trail. How high they will go, well, only time will tell.

Notable omissions from the top 20 are Richie Allen, Orlando Cepeda, Boog Powell, Cecil Cooper, Frank Chance, George "Highpockets" Kelly, Tony Perez, Dolf Camilli, and Joe Adcock. (Allen and Perez, of course, began their careers at third base.) Norm Cash, whose 1961 season of .361 with 41 home runs was as good a postwar campaign as anybody's, is also left out of the top 20. Debatable omissions on the all-time defensive balloting: Eddie Murray and Bill Buckner who, despite *twice* setting the single-season record for assists by a first baseman, received only two votes. Interesting for his inclusion on the defensive list is Hal

Chase, who was widely suspected of making errors at crucial moments for nefarious purposes, and was eventually banned from baseball in the wake of the Black Sox scandal in 1919.

Finally, we should point out that the 1.1% difference between Jimmie Foxx in the 3 spot on the best-ever list and Bill Terry at 7 is too small to be statistically significant; any of the five players in that range could have been 3 or 7.

The Best Second Basemen Ever

1.	Charlie Gehringer	17.8%	12.	Pete Rose	3.0
2.	Rogers Hornsby	16.8	13.	Red Schoendienst	2.8
3.	Jackie Robinson	8.8	14.	Billy Herman	2.0
4.	Bill Mazeroski	7.2	15.	Napoleon Lajoie	1.9
5.	Joe Morgan	6.7	16.	Rod Carew	1.7
6.	Joe Gordon	6.1	17.	Tony Lazzeri	1.1
7.	Nellie Fox	5.7	18.	Ryne Sandberg	.8
8-9.	Bobby Richardson	4.0	19.	Bobby Grich	.7
8-9.	Frankie Frisch	4.0	20-22.	Lou Whitaker	.6
10.	Eddie Collins	3.7	20-22.	Manny Trillo	.6
11.	Bobby Doerr	3.2	20-22.	Julian Javier	.6

Courtesy Houston Astros

Joe Morgan

Second Basemen On Second Basemen

1.	Charlie Gehringer	17.8%	7.	Bobby Richardson	5.6
2.	Rogers Hornsby	17.0	8-9.	Joe Morgan	5.1
3.	Jackie Robinson	11.2	8-9.	Nellie Fox	5.1
4-5.	Bill Mazeroski	7.4	10.	Bobby Doerr	4.3
4-5.	Frankie Frisch	7.4	11.	Eddie Collins	3.1
6.	Joe Gordon	6.9			

The Best Second Basemen: Defense

1.	Bill Mazeroski	16.4%	7.	Jackie Robinson	5.7
2.	Bobby Richardson	13.1	8-11.	Hughie Critz	3.3
3-4.	Joe Gordon	11.5	8-11.	Red Schoendienst	3.3
3-4.	Charlie Gehringer	11.5	8-11.	Ken Hubbs	3.3
5-6.	Nellie Fox	8.2	8-11.	Manny Trillo	3.3
5-6.	Bobby Doerr	8.2			

Second Basemen Rate Each Other's Gloves

1.	Bill Mazeroski	20.8%	13.	Frankie Frisch	1.8
2.	Charlie Gehringer	12.6	14.	Frank White	1.6
3.	Joe Gordon	10.5	15.	Rogers Hornsby	1.3
4.	Bobby Richardson	6.8	16.	Ken Hubbs	1.1
5.	Nellie Fox	5.2	17-18.	Bobby Grich	1.0
6.	Joe Morgan	4.0	17-18.	Jerry Coleman	1.0
7.	Red Schoendienst	3.7	19-20.	Julian Javier	.8
8.	Jackie Robinson	3.6	19-20.	Jerry Adair	.8
9.	Bobby Doerr	3.5	11.	Eddie Collins	2.9
10.	Manny Trillo	3.3	12.	Billy Herman	2.4

It's hard to dispute the top eight or nine best-ever second base picks. After these, however, fans of Bobbies Doerr and Grich, Red Schoendienst, and Billy Herman, have some legitimate beefs. Just where Larry Lajoie fits in is hard to say, since so few living players saw him in action and the game was so different then (he came up in 1896). But he did receive 9 1/4 votes.

Unless the players are overrating Yankee Bobby Richardson's offense, his excellent glove has lifted him into some exalted company. In Bobby's best year with the bat, 1962, 209 hits netted him only 99 runs scored—this while leading off for a team that led the league in runs, batting, and slugging. He hit .266 lifetime, without power or many walks, but did have good speed in an era (Mantle, Mays, Maris and Aaron) when speed was undervalued.

Do ball players underrate defense, as has been suggested by Bill James? We would say no, at least not at second base, where their picks show they're fully aware of the double play's value as a defensive weapon. Although none of the top keystone sackers was a bad fielder, two players, Mazeroski and Richardson, made the list essentially for their glove work. Mazeroski turned more double plays than any second baseman in history and was so dominant in this department that he propelled Dick Groat, a good but not great fielder, into fifth place on the all-time list of double plays by shortstops.

A recent survey published by the Society for American Baseball Research (S.A.B.R.) listed the top defensive second basemen from 1900 to 1972 as Collins, Gehringer, Mazeroski, and Lajoie. The players in our survey obviously rate Joe Gordon and Bobby Richardson highly, a position borne out by their defensive statistics. Again, ranking Lajoie is tough, but consider that he led his league in putouts four times, assists twice, double plays five times, and fielding average seven times. (Of course, the top fielding average means much more in a league that fields .940 than in today's leagues, which commonly field about .975.) Also consider the reputation Larry earned from his contemporaries for gracefulness. On the other hand, the majority of players we surveyed who saw both Lajoie and Collins play picked Collins as the superior defensive ball player.

"The Hitter You Found Most Difficult to Get Out" (Asked of Pitchers Only)

		RAW VOTES			
1.	Ted Williams	23	14-17.	Luke Appling	4
2.	Stan Musial	17	14-17.	Lou Gehrig	4
3-4.	Paul Waner	8	14-17.	Al Kaline	4
3-4.	Pete Rose	8	18-27.	George Brett	3
5-7.	Rod Carew	7	18-27.	Jackie Robinson	3
5-7.	Frank Robinson	7	18-27.	Duke Snider	3
5-7.	Roberto Clemente	7	18-27.	Matty Alou	3
8-10.	Willie McCovey	6	18-27.	Ty Cobb	3
8-10.	Hank Aaron	6	18-27.	Charlie Gehringer	3
8-10.	Tony Oliva	6	18-27.	Nellie Fox	3
11-13.	Rogers Hornsby	5	18-27.	Carl Yastrzemski	3
11-13.	Al Oliver	5	18-27.	Willie Stargell	3
11-13.	Yogi Berra	5	18-27.	Billy Williams	3
14-17.	Joe DiMaggio	4			

Another interesting contrast between the S.A.B.R. and our players' surveys is that Eddie Stanky, who the S.A.B.R. folks chose as the top defensive second baseman of the 1940s, finished tied for *20th* place in the players' survey. This is probably due to the shortage of fine fielding second sackers in that decade (most people consider Jackie Robinson and Red Schoendienst primarily 1950s ball players).

Paradox Department: Charlie Gehringer led the American League in errors *and* fielding average in 1936—the first time this happened in baseball history. The only other time it happened was with Frank Malzone at third base in 1957.

Third Base: No Debate?

1.	Brooks Robinson	39.2%	3.	Mike Schmidt	7.1
2.	Pie Traynor	14.8	4.	Eddie Mathews	6.6

5.	George Brett	4.7	14.	Jimmy Collins		.8
6.	George Kell	3.8	15-17.	Billy Cox		.7
7.	Ken Boyer	3.1	15-17.	Al Rosen		.7
8.	Graig Nettles	2.1	15-17.	Harmon Killebrew		.7
9.	Red Rolfe	1.8	18-21.	Joe Dugan		.6
10.	Stan Hack	1.3	18-21.	Ossie Bluege		.6
11.	Pete Rose	1.2	18-21.	Clete Boyer		.6
12.	Ken Keltner	1.1	18-21.	Buddy Bell		.6
13.	Jackie Robinson	.9				

Third Base: No Debate On Defense

1.	Brooks Robinson	79.6%	7.	Ken Keltner	1.8
2.	Clete Boyer	4.0	8.	Stan Hack	1.3
3.	Pie Traynor	3.9	9-11.	Mike Schmidt	1.2
4.	Graig Nettles	3.4	9-11.	Ossie Bluege	1.2
5.	Billy Cox	2.6	9-11.	Floyd Baker	1.2
6.	George Kell	1.9	12.	Buddy Bell	1.0

Third Basemen On Third Basemen

1.	Brooks Robinson	39.7%	6.	George Brett	3.4
2.	Pie Traynor	21.4	7.	Red Rolfe	2.6
3-4.	Eddie Mathews	5.1	8-9.	Ken Boyer	2.1
3-4.	Mike Schmidt	5.1	8-9.	Graig Nettles	2.1
5.	George Kell	3.8	10.	Al Rosen	1.7

Third Basemen Rate Each Other's Gloves

1.	Brooks Robinson	68.9%	5.	Billy Cox	3.4
2-4.	Clete Boyer	4.1	6-7.	Ossie Bluege	2.7
2-4.	Pie Traynor	4.1	6-7.	Willie Kamm	2.7
2-4.	George Kell	4.1			

If the survey were to be repeated in 1995, we believe that the #1 third-base rank-ing would be a nip-and-tuck affair between Mike Schmidt and George Brett. But right now, the results show and even bigger landslide than Lou Gehrig's at first base. Granted, the competition is thinner, certainly the weakest field of all posi-tions. Granted, Brooks garnered and incredible 80% of the vote as the best defens-ive third baseman. Granted, he was a great team leader with steady clutch ability and grace under pressure. And his 25 years of service must be considered. But his best season, 1964, would be an average year for Brett (.317, 28 home runs, 118 RBIs). Both Ken Boyer (ranked seventh) and Graig Nettles (eighth) posted similar stats during the same era in which Brooks played. Conceding Robinson's all-around edge over these two, we come to Eddie Mathews, who hit 244 more home runs than Brooks over his career and managed to bat .004 higher. Is Robinson's big defensive edge worth 244 home runs?

And how about George Kell, an excellent gloveman with a .304 lifetime batting average? Unfortunately, memories of Pie Traynor, the Pirates' superb fielder who hit .320 lifetime in the lively ball era, are beginning to fade. Six times he drove in 103 or more runs with nine or fewer homers, a feat that recently attracted attention when Tommy Herr of St. Louis accomplished it for the first time in 35 years. Surely an argument can be made for Robinson as the all-time best, but 40% of the vote seems a little emphatic.

Conspicuous by their absence from the top 21 on the best-ever list are Ron Santo and Harlond Clift, the power-hitting glovemen for the Chicago Cubs and St. Louis Browns, respectively, who are, incidentally, darlings of the New Statisticians. Four-time batting champion Bill Madlock also received negligible support, perhaps in part because he spent a few years with teams nobody watched. Hall of Famer Joe Sewell, who struck out only 114 times in his *entire career*—in over 7,000 at bats!—is hurt by splitting his time at shortstop. The great dead ball hitter "Home Run" Baker just missed the list. Finally, it is reasonable to assume that Wade Boggs will eventually nestle himself somewhere in the upper echelons.

Ernie Banks: Third-best at short.

The Best Shortstops Ever

1.	Honus Wagner	16.4%	12.	Robin Yount	3.0
2.	Luis Aparicio	13.8	13.	Cal Ripken, Jr.	2.0
3.	Ernie Banks	8.3	14.	Travis Jackson	1.8
4.	Marty Marion	7.3	15.	Maury Wills	1.4
5.	Pee Wee Reese	6.6	16.	Roy McMillan	1.1
6.	Phil Rizzuto	6.5	17.	Mark Belanger	.9
7.	Luke Appling	5.2	18-19.	Glenn Wright	.8
8.	Ozzie Smith	4.9	18-19.	Rabbit Maranville	.8
9.	Joe Cronin	4.7	20-21.	Rogers Hornsby	.7
10.	Lou Boudreau	4.3	20-21.	Larry Bowa	.7
11.	Dave Concepcion	3.2			

The Best Shortstops: Defense

1.	Ozzie Smith	20.0%	9.	Lou Boudreau	2.4
2.	Luis Aparicio	17.9	10.	Larry Bowa	2.3
3.	Marty Marion	15.7	11.	Honus Wagner	2.1
4.	Mark Belanger	9.3	12.	Travis Jackson	1.5
5.	Phil Rizzuto	4.9	13-14.	Rabbit Maranville	1.2
6.	Pee Wee Reese	3.6	13-14.	Eddie Miller	1.2
7.	Dave Concepcion	3.0	15-16.	Robin Yount	1.1
8.	Roy McMillan	2.9	15-16.	Frank Crosetti	1.1

Shortstops on Shortstops

1.	Luis Aparicio	21.4%	8.	Luke Appling	4.6
2.	Honus Wagner	17.3	9.	Phil Rizzuto	4.3
3.	Marty Marion	6.9	10.	Joe Cronin	4.0
4.	Ernie Banks	6.4	11.	Glenn Wright	3.5
5.	Lou Boudreau	6.1	12-13.	Ozzie Smith	1.7
6-7.	Pee Wee Reese	5.2	12-13.	Dave Concepcion	1.7
6-7.	Travis Jackson	5.2			

Shortstops Rate Each Other's Gloves

1.	Ozzie Smith	22.6%	4.	Mark Belanger	6.6
2.	Luis Aparicio	21.7	5.	Roy McMillan	5.7
3.	Marty Marion	18.9	6.	Phil Rizzuto	3.8

Many oldtimers, including John McGraw and Sam Crawford, felt that Honus Wagner was the best player ever, so it's no surprise that he retains the best-ever shortstop title after 70 years. His NL-record eight batting titles has stood since 1911. Interestingly, he played four years at first, second, third, and the outfield before his first game at short in 1901. This was not at all uncommon in those days, when defense was not as specialized as it is today. The Dutchman was also no slouch with the glove (well, whatever it was), leading the league in DPs four times, fielding average three times, and putouts twice.

Year in and year out for 18 seasons, Luis Aparicio set the statistical standards by which Ozzie Smith will be judged. The all-time leader in SS assists and double plays, he also led the AL in stolen bases nine years in a row and in his best year hit .313.

An underrated fielder, Ernie Banks also hit over 40 HRs five times as a shortstop, which is four times more than anyone else. He probably would have received more votes had he not been shifted to first base in 1961.

Marty Marion is not in the Hall of Fame, yet the players rank him above several shortstops who are, every one of whom was a contemporary of "Slats." How is it, then, that during the shortstop-studded era he was known as "Mr. Shortstop"? He was the defensive glue of the best team in baseball in the early-to-middle 40s. He swung a respectable if unspectacular bat (a league-leading 38 doubles in '42), and won an MVP in a year when teammate Stan Musial hit .347 with 51 doubles. The selection was widely applauded at the time. If Phil Rizzuto belongs in Cooperstown (and he does), shouldn't the fourth best shortstop ever be enshrined also?

Marty Marion (center) instructs Jerry Buchek (left), Julio Gotay, and Alex Grammas (right).

The other side of the coin is that managers and coaches drop him down from fourth place to 10th. They also push Luke Appling up to third and Lou Boudreau to seventh. Hall of Famers Pee Wee Reese and Joe Cronin were just off the top 10 in this list, thus reinforcing the case for Marion.

It's unfortunate that injuries have necessitated a shift to the outfield for Robin Yount, because he could have made a real run at Wagner for the top spot; until his injury he was arguably the best all-around player in the game. Both Ozzie Smith and Cal Ripken, Jr. have good chances to move perhaps way up the list.

If you glance at the "Shortstops On Shortstops" list you will note a move upward from 18-19 to 11 for the late Glenn Wright, a lifetime .294 hitter with some power. He also ranked 14 on the "Most Underrated Player" list and held the single-season record for assists for 56 years, broken in 1980 by Ozzie Smith.

Those fans who dislike fielding average as a measure of defensive worth will note that current all-time leader Larry Bowa rates only tenth on the defensive list. We say "current" because (again) Ozzie Smith is hot on his heels. Offense-minded fans might approve of Rogers Hornsby at shortstop on their all-time squad; he did play 356 games there. It's clear, though, that defense reigns supreme at short with the inclusion on the best-ever list of such offensive non-entities as Rabbit Maranville, Mark Belanger, and Roy McMillan. A glance at the era-by-era tallies later in the book confirms this, particularly in the dead-ball days when good defense won many more games than it does today. The top five dead-ball shortstops anchored 15 pennant winners among them. Except for Wagner they had generally low batting averages, yet averaged over 18 years of service, further testifying to their great defensive value.

Amazingly, recent Hall of Fame inductee Arky Vaughan receives only one 2nd-team vote. Others left out by the voters are Vern Stephens, Dick Bartell, Cecil Travis, Dave Bancroft, Dick Groat, and Frank Crosetti, who just missed with the equivalent of 4 3/4 1st-team votes. Cited in the S.A.B.R. defensive survey but absent from the Players' Poll were Bancroft, Leo Durocher, Luke Appling, and Maury Wills.

A Galaxy of Greats:
The Best Outfielders of All Time

1-2.	Joe DiMaggio	12.9%	13-14.	Paul Waner	.9
1-2.	Willie Mays	12.9	15-16.	Al Simmons	.7
3-4.	Babe Ruth	12.2	15-16.	Carl Yastrzemski	.7
3-4.	Ted Williams	12.2	17.	Reggie Jackson	.6
5.	Mickey Mantle	8.0	18.	Pete Rose	.5
6.	Henry Aaron	7.1	19-21.	Mel Ott	.4
7.	Stan Musial	6.2	19-21.	Lou Brock	.4
8.	Ty Cobb	5.8	19-21.	Enos Slaughter	.4
9.	Roberto Clemente	4.7	22-25.	Dale Murphy	.3
10.	Tris Speaker	2.7	22-25.	Roger Maris	.3
11.	Al Kaline	1.3	22-25.	Tommy Henrich	.3
12.	Frank Robinson	1.2	22-25.	Terry Moore	.3
13-14.	Duke Snider	.9			

N.Y. Yankees

"DiMag"

The Top 20 Fielding Outfielders

1.	Willie Mays	24.4%	11.	Jimmy Piersall	1.7
2.	Joe DiMaggio	14.1	12.	Carl Furillo	1.5
3.	Roberto Clemente	13.6	13.	Dwight Evans	1.1
4.	Tris Speaker	4.3	14.	Fred Lynn	.9
5.	Al Kaline	4.1	15-16.	Garry Maddox	.8
6.	Terry Moore	3.6	15-16.	Lloyd Waner	.8
7.	Paul Blair	3.5	17-19.	Richie Ashburn	.5
8.	Dom DiMaggio	3.4	17-19.	Curt Flood	.5
9.	Mickey Mantle	3.3	17-19.	Duke Snider	.5
10.	Carl Yastrzemski	1.9	20.	Enos Slaughter	.4

Outfielders On Outfielders

1.	Ted Williams	13.2%	10.	Tris Speaker	2.5
2.	Willie Mays	13.1	11.	Al Kaline	1.8
3.	Joe DiMaggio	13.0	12.	Frank Robinson	1.7
4.	Babe Ruth	12.1	13-15.	Pete Rose	.8
5.	Mickey Mantle	8.7	13-15.	Paul Waner	.8
6.	Henry Aaron	8.0	13-15.	Duke Snider	.8
7.	Ty Cobb	6.1	16-17.	Al Simmons	.7
8.	Stan Musial	5.4	16-17.	Reggie Jackson	.7
9.	Roberto Clemente	3.9			

Outfielders Rate Each Other's Gloves

1.	Willie Mays	23.5%	8.	Mickey Mantle	3.0
2.	Joe DiMaggio	15.0	9.	Dom DiMaggio	2.5
3.	Roberto Clemente	13.3	10.	Carl Yastrzemski	1.5
4.	Al Kaline	5.7	11-14.	Carl Furillo	1.2
5.	Paul Blair	4.8	11-14.	Henry Aaron	1.2
6.	Tris Speaker	4.3	11-14.	Lloyd Waner	1.2
7.	Terry Moore	3.3	11-14.	Dwight Evans	1.2

The Greatest Outfielders By Position

	LEFT FIELD	CENTER FIELD	RIGHT FIELD
1.	Ted Williams	Joe DiMaggio	Babe Ruth
2.	Stan Musial	Willie Mays	Henry Aaron
3.	Al Simmons	Mickey Mantle	Roberto Clemente
4.	Carl Yastrzemski	Ty Cobb	Al Kaline
5.	Pete Rose	Tris Speaker	Frank Robinson
6.	Lou Brock	Duke Snider	Paul Waner
7.	Joe Medwick	Al Simmons*	Reggie Jackson
8.	Billy Williams	Dale Murphy	Pete Rose+
9.	Chick Hafey	Terry Moore	Mel Ott
10.	Rickey Henderson	Fred Lynn	Enos Slaughter
11.	Charlie Keller	Dom DiMaggio	Roger Maris
12.	Jim Rice	Lloyd Waner	Tommy Henrich

* Placed in both left field and center field
+ Placed in both left field and right field

The Greatest Outfielders By Position: Defense

	LEFT FIELD	CENTER FIELD	RIGHT FIELD
1.	Carl Yastrzemski	Willie Mays	Roberto Clemente
2.	Stan Musial	Joe DiMaggio	Al Kaline
3.	Rickey Henderson	Tris Speaker	Carl Furillo
4.	Joe Rudi	Terry Moore	Dwight Evans
5.	Willie Wilson	Paul Blair	Enos Slaughter
6.	Chick Hafey	Dom DiMaggio	Babe Ruth
7.	Jose Cruz	Mickey Mantle	Rocky Colavito
8.	Ted Williams	Jimmy Piersall	Paul Waner
9.	Vince Coleman	Fred Lynn	Dave Winfield
10.	Jo Jo Moore	Lloyd Waner	
11.		Richie Ashburn	
12.		Curt Flood	
13.		Duke Snider	
14.		Bill Virdon	

Okay, we have the same question: What in the world is Ty Cobb doing in the *eighth* slot on the best-outfielders list? Twelve batting titles, .367 lifetime batting average, 892 stolen bases... and remarkable power, too. Folks compare him with Pete Rose and think of him as a leadoff-type hitter, but the fact is, Cobb batted third in the Tiger lineup, winning eight slugging titles and even leading the majors in homers once. The real measure of power in the dead-ball era is triples, and the Georgia Peach ranks second all-time, behind Wahoo Sam Crawford, with 297, leading the league four times. By reputation he was a good but not great outfielder, with an average arm at best. So why all the way down in the eighth spot?

Our first explanation: Maybe there's a statistical bias in the survey against dead-ball players. It is true that only a small percentage of our respondents ever saw dead-ball era baseball even as boys, and an even smaller percentage actually played back then. Yet at shortstop Honus Wagner is the clear 1 pick, and four of the top ten right-handed pitchers, including the top one, also date back that far. And George Sisler, who straddled the 1920 line as did Ty Cobb and second-sacker Eddie Collins, received a lot of votes at first base.

In filling out their surveys, players were asked to choose from all eras if possible, in other words to evaluate the record with their professional subjective judgment. Some felt they could judge only what they had seen, and for this reason we broke down voting results for each position *by era*, in another section of this book. So yes, there is probably a small bias against players from the early years of the century, and readers can if they wish factor it into the grand totals, but any bias shouldn't change Cobb's ranking by that much. With 50 more votes, Cobb would finish sixth, just behind Mickey Mantle—hardly satisfactory to Cobb partisans.

But now we come to an interesting turn. Tallying the results, we counted 27 ballots that placed Tris "Spoke" Speaker ahead of Ty, thus documenting that many contemporaries believed Speaker—and even Joe Jackson—to be superior all-around ball players. Speaker was unquestionably the better outfielder; he revolutionized center field for the truly swift by playing so shallow he could and did complete many unassisted double plays. He is the all-time leader in both double plays and assists for an outfielder and is second to Willie Mays in putouts.

Many also thought Spoke to be the better "money ball player," at least partly based on his World Series performances. Both played in three series, with Cobb's Detroiters losing all three and Speaker's teams, the Red Sox and Indians, winning all three, the respective team performances hinging in large part on Cobb and Speaker. Spoke hit .306 with four triples (all-time best) in 20 Fall Classic contests, while Cobb hit .262 in 17—not a bust as some say, but a far cry from .367. We think the answer lies in personalities. The phrase "fierce competitor" is tossed about a good deal, and justifiably, in such cases as a Pete Rose or Bob Gibson. But no one ever played the game like Cobb. Casey Stengel said, "I never saw anyone like Cobb. No one even close to him. When he wiggled those wild eyes at a pitcher, you knew you were looking at the bird nobody could beat. It was like he was superhuman." Cobb himself supposedly claimed that he once turned on three muggers who had stabbed him in the back, beating one to death with a pistol butt and chasing the others away; the next day, without so much as a doctor's visit, he went two for three.

This demonic intensity did not endear him even to his teammates, far less to his opponents. Frankly, this has to be the reason a player of Cobb's caliber ranks eighth, and there's *some* merit to making his ability and desire to get along with colleagues one of the factors.

The margin of difference between Joe DiMaggio and Babe Ruth in the survey is statistically insignificant. In fact, the majority of players voted for all of the top four outfielders. If all of Stan Musial's first-base votes were added in here, he would finish fifth, just edging out Mantle, though not threatening the all-time top four.

As for the showing of the man who hit the most HRs in baseball history, Hank Aaron, about all we can say is that while his career statistics are clearly superior to Mantle's, at his peak Mickey hit for a higher average with more power, walks, and speed, and better defense.

Beyond a doubt the finest fielding right fielder ever, Roberto Clemente got as many second-team votes as anyone after Ruth, underscoring the players' high regard for defense. It seemed as though every ballot read, "Mays, Joe D., Clemente" for the defensive team.

Tris Speaker, who with Ruth and Cobb made up the former traditional all-time outfield, dropped to tenth but still pulled the equivalent of 68 1/2 first-team picks. At this point his career total of 793 doubles looks untouchable.

Another apparent mystery is Al Kaline nosing out Frank Robinson for the 11th spot on the best-ever list. While their batting averages are about the same (Kaline .297, Robinson .294), Robby's .537 lifetime slugging average is 57 points higher. Kaline reached the magic 3,000-hit club with seven to spare; Robinson just missed with 2,943. Two-time MVP Robinson finished 11th as the best clutch hitter later in the book; Kaline got only two votes. Robby again ranked 11th as the player who did the most to inspire his team; again, Kaline received just two votes. However, Al is fifth among those voted the most underrated ball players with 21 ballots, and Robinson ranks 39th with six. The high placing of both Kaline and Clemente on the best-ever list must be due to their great defensive abilities. They were selected first and second as the best fielders ever in right. In the managers' picks and again when the outfielders rate themselves, Kaline and Clemente are neck-and-neck in the 11-12 slots. To repeat, the tendency of the players in this survey is to choose the better all-around player when hitting ability is equal or (in some cases) even inferior.

On the best-ever list, Paul Waner gets the nod over his contemporaries Al Simmons and Mel Ott, based presumably on his defense (he just missed that list) and speed. The Society for American Baseball Research fielding survey gave Ott the nod, but here the players chose Waner, seven to three. Big Poison lacked the home run power of Simmons and Ott, but easily outdistanced both in singles, doubles, and triples, tossing in three titles along the way.

Since Pete Rose played more games in the outfield than anywhere else, we might add in his other votes here and move him up to 11th place with 1.9% instead of .5%. As a left fielder, Charley Hustle would then rank third; as a right fielder, fourth. If in ten years' time this survey were repeated, he could rank high among the managers, too.

We hope his 17th-place finish on the best-ever list puts to rest the debate about Reggie Jackson's status as a great ball player. Only Yaz rates a slight edge as the best of the post-1969 outfielders, where admittedly the competition isn't nearly as strong as in any other era in baseball. There seems to be a trend in the game toward great-hitting infielders as opposed to fly-chasers. This is probably due to Astroturf, for now speed is necessary above all else in an outfielder, so the power of the outfielder would tend to decrease while the power of the infielder would have to increase. Of course, another important reason for the dearth of serious competition is that many of today's outfield stars are barely getting started, e.g., Rickey Henderson, Tim Raines, Willie McGee, Daryl Strawberry, and Harold Baines, for just a few. One outfielder who impressed the voters in a very short time was Vince Coleman, who finished seventh on our list of best base stealers and ninth on the defensive tallies as a left fielder.

We have also broken down both the best-ever and defensive teams by the positions generally played by the players. Of course, not many respondents chose left fielders on defense; it's a good deal easier for a player to make that list than it is for his peers in center or right. It should be noted that Willie Wilson and Rickey Henderson are rated as left fielders, and their shift to center undoubtedly decreases their votes in left. While both were outstanding in left, neither has the arm to be considered among the truly great center fielders—at least until they catch a lot more fly balls than they have.

Following Cardinal Hall of Famers Slaughter and Brock on the best-ever list is Dale Murphy, who keeps putting up those good average, great power, and Gold Glove seasons one after another—a grade B Mickey Mantle, if you will (but minus the injuries, a B$^+$). We decided not to include Shoeless Joe Jackson on the Honor Roll; although he tied with Murphy, it just doesn't seem right to put such moral opposites on the same line.

The final three outfielders on the best-ever list might be something of a surprise, but among them they account for 50 picks as the most underrated ballplayers ever. Once more, the players choose players with all-around skills, and in these cases, all three played for great teams—teams that dominated the game in their times. Maris, Henrich, and Terry Moore were also members of some of the greatest outfields of all time. Just for fun, let's see who ball players rank as the top outfield *trios*:

1.	Yankees '41, '42, '46	Joe DiMaggio, Charlie Keller, Tommy Henrich
2.	Cardinals '42, '46	Stan Musial, Terry Moore, Enos Slaughter
3.	Yankees '25-'29	Bob Meusel, Earle Combs, Babe Ruth
4.	Cubs '28-'31	Kiki Cuyler, Hack Wilson, Riggs Stephenson
5.	Tigers '20-'22	Harry Heilmann, Ty Cobb, Bobby Veach
6.	Red Sox '10-'15	Harry Hooper, Tris Speaker, Duffy Lewis
7.	Philadelphia A's '30-'32	Bing Miller, Al Simmons, Mule Haas
8.	Red Sox '75-'80	Jim Rice, Fred Lynn, Dwight Evans

The problem here is that no one considers Yogi Berra as a left fielder, but even as a platoon outfielder near the end of his career he combined with Mantle and Maris to hit 137 home runs in 1961, a good total for a National League *team* today. In fact, though, *any* average outfielder regular tossed into left for the '60-'62 Bronx Bombers would place that outfielder high on such a list. That can be said of several other outfields, too, including the Ted Williams-Dom DiMaggio Red Sox, the Waner brothers in Pittsburgh, and others too numerous to mention. It's a crying shame that World War II broke up that beautiful Cardinal group and put a crimp in Joe D and his boys. Yankee fans still lament Henrich's absence from the 1942 World Series, feeling certain that Old Reliable would have done something clutch to stop the St. Louis Swifties. Military service kept Tommy out, thus preventing a face-off of the two best outfields ever, and the Cards won the series in five games. We placed the Ruth-Combs-Meusel trio third because, although the Babe easily outpolled Stan the Man, three of the Cardinals ranked in the top 25 and Combs and Meusel were far down in the voting for center and left. Keller and Henrich come in at 24th and 32nd, with DiMag of course first, and because (a) their stats are better within the same era and (b) they played together longer, we feel justified in making the Joe D trio Number One.

History seems to have forgotten Bobby Veach, the Detroit Tiger left fielder from 1913-1923. Besides being a good outfielder, he drove in over 100 runs in six seasons, leading the league three times. He also led in doubles twice, and triples and hits once each, compiling a .310 lifetime BA. When Veach joined with Cobb and Heilmann, their dynamite offense held AL pitchers hostage. The same can be said of Hack Wilson, Riggs Stephenson, and Kiki Cuyler of the Cubs. That Red Sox trio of the 1970s is clearly the players' choice among the modern outfields. The one year that Yaz played left field while Rice was the DH, Carl hit .296 with 28 HRs and 102 RBIs, taking nothing away.

Another modern group, Brock-Flood-Maris of the late 1960s Cardinals, presents a problem. Maris's votes are undoubtedly a reflection of his Yankee years, yet when he joined the Redbirds, a mysterious change came over what had been a rather hapless team. They proceeded to ride roughshod over the NL in two straight seasons, notwithstanding the absence of ace Bob Gibson for half of one of them. True, Roger only hit .258 in the magic years of 1967-68, but that was in a pitcher's park (Busch Stadium had grass then) and in a league that hit about .245

over the same span—similar to a .320 in the NL of 1930, where, say, a Riggs Stephenson hit .319. Another factor: Mike Shannon, a Maris teammate and now a Redbird broadcaster, insists he never saw Roger misplay a ball in right field in those two years. This Cardinal outfield, then, probably deserves a spot somewhere near the bottom of the list. Dodger, Giant, and Pirate fans surely have nominations, too, but these are the outfields in which every man received at lease one mention. Speaker, Hooper, and Lewis remain after 70 years the standard by which great fielding outfields are judged, and they could smack that dead ball to boot.

On the best-ever defensive list, the Boston Red Sox dominate, with five of the top 15, including four of the top nine in center field. They used to say in Boston that Ted Williams ought to give half his paycheck to Dom DiMaggio, but the players obviously disagree, because although Dom rates up there, Teddy Ballgame also receives a few nods for defense in left field. The Splendid Splinter acknowledges he was a lousy fielder when he first came up but contends that he worked hard to improve, and the voters agree.

With so many superstar outfielders in the past 30 years, there must be some bias in the survey against some old-time greats who weren't the very best of their day. With that in mind, here is a list of post-1900 Hall of Famers not in the top 25, or even in the era-by-era lists later in the book:

Earl Averill
Kiki Cuyler
Goose Goslin
Joe Kelley
Ralph Kiner
Chuck Klein
Heinie Manush
Sam Rice
Edd Roush
Hack Wilson
Ross Youngs

National Baseball Library Collection

Heinie Manush

By contrast, these nonmembers of the Cooperstown club *did* rate:

Ginger Beaumont
Duffy Lewis
Tommy Henrich
Terry Moore
Roger Maris
Carl Furillo

Here is the average season of all the players in the Hall of Fame group, based on 162 games:

AB	H	2B	3B	HR	R
607	192	33	11	16	108

RBI	BB	SB	AVG	SLG AVG	On Base %
100	66	16	.317	.490	.384

This guy could conceivably find his way into your lineup, no? Now here's the average season of the six non-Hall of Famers:

AB	H	2B	3B	HR	R
589	169	28	7	15	92

RBI	BB	SB	AVG	SLG AVG	On Base %
85	58	10	.286	.431	.350

Still a fine ball player, but inferior in every single offensive category. Ah, but what about defense? All six nonmembers were known as top-drawer outfielders in their time; how do they compare to the first group? One imperfect but useful way to compare the defensive abilities of various players is to add up all the times a player led the league in the positive defense categories: putouts, assists, double plays, chances per game, and fielding average; then count the years he was a regular at the position, multiply by the five categories, and find the percentage of times leading the league. In other words, say Terry Moore led the NL in six categories over eight seasons as a regular. Multiply the eight years times the five categories, divide six into that, and presto: his league-leading percentage is .150. When we do this for all the seasons of each group the results are the following: Hall of Famers .042, non-Hallers .041. No real difference. But seven of the 11 Cooperstown boys led their leagues in errors at least once, compared to only one time for one player in the second group—Roger Maris with nine errors in 1958 (and he was a demonstrably good fielder). Also, two of the four Hall of Famers who didn't lead in errors were Ralph Kiner and Heinie Manush, neither of whom would ever have earned a Gold Glove had the award existed then. Furthermore, according to our defense balloting, the Cooperstown group received an average of one vote, while the non-Hall men, led by Terry Moore and Carl Furillo, averaged 13 1/4. So it's safe to say that the non-Hall of Famers were, according to the surveys, the better glove men. Still, there are not too many fans who'd take a Carl Furillo over a Ralph Kiner.

Speaking of Kiner, if we could nominate the most forgotten great of all time, he would win. How could the guy with one of the best (second, to be exact) home runs-per at-bats ratio in the history of baseball not make the top 25 ranking of his peers? This, we submit, is how: he played on a team for most of his career, the Pittsburgh Pirates (1946-1953), that, save for 1948, did its best to give new meaning to the word *bad*. Pitched around habitually and with a back ailment that forced him to quit after only 10 years, Ralph's HR ratio is all the more amazing.

New York Mets

Yogi Berra

The Best Catchers Ever

1.	Johnny Bench	23.9%	10.	Walker Cooper	.9
2.	Bill Dickey	21.8	11.	Jim Hegan	.7
3.	Yogi Berra	15.2	12-18.	Del Crandall	.6
4.	Mickey Cochrane	11.8	12-18.	Josh Gibson	.6
5.	Roy Campanella	10.2	12-18.	Jimmy Wilson	.6
6.	Gabby Hartnett	6.6	12-18.	Elston Howard	.6
7.	Gary Carter	1.9	12-18.	Al Lopez	.6
8-9.	Thurman Munson	1.3	12-18.	Carlton Fisk	.6
8-9.	Ernie Lombardi	1.3	12-18.	Ray Schalk	.6

The Best Catchers: Defense

1.	Johnny Bench	19.5%	11.	Gary Carter	1.3
2.	Jim Hegan	9.6	12.	Rick Dempsey	1.1
3.	Bill Dickey	7.4	13-19.	Rollie Hemsley	1.0
4.	Roy Campanella	7.0	13-19.	Thurman Munson	1.0
5.	Mickey Cohrane	6.0	13-19.	Tony Pena	1.0
6.	Gabby Hartnett	5.5	13-19.	Wes Westrum	1.0
7.	Al Lopez	3.9	13-19.	Gus Mancuso	1.0
8.	Yogi Berra	3.2	13-19.	Jim Sundberg	1.0
9.	Jerry Grote	2.6	13-19.	Paul Richards	1.0
10.	Del Crandall	2.1			

Catchers On Catchers

1.	Johnny Bench	25.3%	4.	Gabby Hartnett	10.7
2.	Yogi Berra	19.3	5.	Roy Campanella	9.3
3.	Bill Dickey	16.7	6.	Mickey Cochrane	8.7

Catchers Rate Each Other's Gloves

1.	Johnny Bench	29.9%	6.	Gabby Hartnett	6.2
2.	Jim Hegan	16.5	7-9.	Yogi Berra	4.1
3-5.	Bill Dickey	8.2	7-9.	Del Crandall	4.1
3-5.	Mickey Cochrane	8.2	7-9.	Tony Pena	4.1
3-5.	Roy Campanella	8.2			

It is logical that at least one player who came into his prime after 1968 would finish first at some position. The pure physical skill required to play baseball today *must* be greater than in the past, it is often said, because today's people are bigger, stronger, better nourished and conditioned; principles of "improvement of the breed," which apply to all sports, must also apply to baseball. A second school of thought concedes this but contends that the attitude of ballplayers has been corrupted and the fierce competitive drive of yesteryear has been replaced by a selfish softness. They also cite the old pancake gloves, the cratered fields, and the long, uncomfortable train rides as disadvantages not faced by today's "brats." These diehards should remember, though, that the same things have been written before at least as far back as 1880. And is that train ride any more brutal than the afternoon August sun on Astroturf? The poor gloves and fields *were* disadvantages, and therefore served to *stymie* quality competition.

One point made by the old-schoolers that may contain some truth is that today's players generally lack the "baseball smarts" of the old-timers, because they play less baseball from the sandlots through the minor leagues. Fair enough, though bonehead plays did not originate with Lonnie Smith. But this argument hardly applies to a truly great player, which brings us to Johnny Bench, perhaps the best catcher of them all.

As hitters, it's awfully tough to say which of the top six is best. The lifetime slugging averages of five of them are between .489 (Hartnett) and .476 (Bench); Roy Campanella's (.500) tragic accident probably kept his average from falling right into place. Lesser power in one is compensated for by a higher batting average and vice versa. We must look to defense, then, to make some sense of the best-ever standings. A look at the defensive balloting shows that these six are all in the top eight, with defensive specialists Jim Hegan (2) and Al Lopez (7) intervening. The clear #1 choice is Bench, and looking at how the catchers rated themselves we see him jump 10 points to nearly one-third of the vote. On the "Best Throwing Arm" list, later in the book, he ranks 12th, the highest of any non-outfielder. Defense is of course crucial in a backstop, so much so that Jim Hegan, a lifetime .228 hitter, stands in 11th place overall based on a 2nd place defensive finish. Unfortunately, there are no adequate statistics by which to measure a catcher's defensive contribution. But on the most basic level, how many world's champion teams didn't have an outstanding glove man behind the plate?

One stat that fairly leaps off the page about five of the top six (Bench excluded) is their incredibly low strikeout totals, doubly amazing when you consider they drew many walks, and triply so when their power is considered. All five had fewer career strikeouts than walks, and Dickey and Berra (five times each) and Cochrane (twice) had seasons in which they had more home runs than strikeouts. Bill James, in his *Historical Baseball Abstract*, cites the MVP voting of the time as evidence that Cochrane was considered Dickey's superior then, but that time and (it is implied) the media have reversed the opinion. It must be remembered, though, that the Yankees of that era had Ruth, Gehrig, and later DiMaggio while the Tigers had Greenberg and Gehringer—all-time greats certainly, but not the forces the first three were. Cochrane also managed, thus greatly increasing his value to the Tigers. Connie Mack himself, who had every reason to favor Cochrane, could not choose between him and Dickey when he chose his all-time team in 1950.

Josh Gibson, the great Negro League receiver, finished tied for 13th with the equivalent of five first-team votes, an astounding achievement when you consider that few saw him in action and that no records were kept of his accomplishments. There is no doubt that he belongs near the top and would have finished right up there given major-league exposure.

It should be noted that much of this survey was conducted before Carlton Fisk's unprecedented 1985 season cinched his place in Cooperstown; he deserves to move up about even with Carter on the best-ever list, though Carter might answer the challenge yet. At any rate, there is little difference between those who finished numbers 8 through 18—five first-team votes to be precise.

Speaking of the Hall of Fame, recent inductee Rick Ferrell received exactly one 2nd team vote, finishing behind over 20 catchers *not* in, and the reasons aren't hard to find. Let's face it, the guy's brother Wes was a better hitter, slugging .083 higher over his career, but Wes also won 193 games as a pitcher! Defense was Rick's forte, but even here he received just four votes, tied with Bob Boone, Bill Freehan, and Elston Howard. Even on the era-by-era tallies he doesn't rate, though admittedly the competition was stiff between the wars. Ernie Lombardi is rated far ahead of him by both the players and the numbers, and "the Schnozz" has finally, if grudgingly, been admitted to Cooperstown.

Looking at today's catchers, both Carter and Fisk should move up to change the top six into the top eight, and Lance Parrish and Tony Pena both could break into the all-time list.

Notable but not surprising omissions are Joe Torre, Bob O' Farrell, Ted Simmons, Tim McCarver, and Wes Westrum, who once managed to bat .219 with an on-base average of .394!

Right-handed Pitchers: The Top 20

1.	Walter Johnson	17.6%	11.	Robin Roberts	2.7
2.	Bob Feller	16.9	12.	Bob Lemon	2.2
3.	Bob Gibson	13.2	13.	Allie Reynolds	1.9
4.	Tom Seaver	6.3	14.	Nolan Ryan	1.8
5.	Dizzy Dean	4.7	15.	Early Wynn	1.3
6.	Cy Young	4.4	16-17.	Red Ruffing	1.2
7.	Christy Mathewson	3.7	16-17.	Jim Palmer	1.2
8.	Don Drysdale	3.3	18.	Dwight Gooden	1.1
9.	Grover Cleveland Alexander	2.9	19.	Ewell Blackwell	.9
10.	Juan Marichal	2.8	20.	Dazzy Vance	.8

Right-handed Pitchers: The Best Fielders

1.	Bob Gibson	26.6%	9-10.	Robin Roberts	2.6
2.	Freddie Fitzsimmons	8.4	11.	Catfish Hunter	1.7
3.	Bob Lemon	6.6	12.	Walter Johnson	1.4
4.	Jim Palmer	6.0	13.	Dizzy Dean	1.3
5.	Tom Seaver	4.1	14-15.	Wes Ferrell	1.2
6.	Bob Feller	3.9	14-15.	Allie Reynolds	1.2
7.	Phil Niekro	3.6	16-18.	Bruce Sutter	1.0
8.	Don Drysdale	3.3	16-18.	Rick Reuschel	1.0
9-10.	Ted Lyons	2.6	16-18.	Vic Raschi	1.0

Fleishman/St. Louis Cardinals

Bob Gibson

3 Votes Each:

Christy Mathewson
Murry Dickson
Vernon Law

Johnny Sain
Dave Stieb
Andy Messersmith

Early Wynn
Ruben Gomez

Chalk up one for the old-timers, as Walter Johnson noses out Bob Feller for the #1 slot on the all-time list. To compile his stats (W-L: 416-279, 2.17) with only a fastball, well, it must have been some blazer. Relatively, his single-season and career strikeout totals are far more impressive than those of Nolan Ryan, Koufax, Carlton, et al. In 1912, when the Big Train fanned 303, the average major league team struck out 611 times; in 1973, when Ryan set the all-time mark of 383, an average team whiffed 848 times. In the dead-ball era, to strike out was to disgrace oneself, whereas today the "K" is just another out. This point also applies to a lesser extent to Christy Mathewson, Pete Alexander, and Cy Young, among others. National League partisans at the time favored Mathewson or Alexander as the top hurler, but when the chaff is blown away Johnson stands alone.

It's a little surprising to see Bob Gibson receive twice as many votes as Tom Seaver, whose career stats give him a slight edge overall. Perhaps the players feel that at his peak Gibby was more overpowering, particularly in his eye-popping 1968 season, when he had a 1.12 ERA with 13 shutouts. Seaver's excellence has perhaps been a degree less awesome but has been consistent over a greater number of years. The players seem to favor short-term pitching brilliance throughout the survey; hence their high regard for Dizzy Dean (5), Dwight Gooden (18), Ewell Blackwell (19), and among the lefties, for Johnny Vander Meer, Herb Score, and of course Sandy Koufax. To call Dwight Gooden's pitching "short-term brilliance" is only temporary, we strongly suspect, because, barring injury, by 1995 he might easily rate much higher.

As with other pre-1900 players, it is difficult to place Cy Young, but right where he is suits us fine.

Perhaps the biggest surprise of the right-handed pitchers is Don Drysdale (8) over Juan Marichal (10), but although the margin is small (4 1/4 first-team votes), it is a difference that established itself early in the poll and held up. Their lifetime ERAs are about the same, so the only real difference between them is in the won-lost records, 243-142 for Marichal and 209-166 for the Big D. This is probably more a reflection of their offensive support than anything else, for over the course of the 60s the Giants scored over 50 more runs per year than the Dodgers. Two things that can be said for certain: Drysdale was a better fielder (he finished eighth on the defensive list) and a far better hitter. In 1965, when he hit .300 with 7 homers in 130 at bats, Drysdale could quite logically have batted cleanup on that world champ team, and you could look it up. Marichal was never known for swinging the bat. The majority of the greatest pitchers were both good fielders and hitters, factors that undoubtedly contributed several wins (and *years*) to their careers. All the pitchers on the defensive list were at least good pitchers, and it's interesting that two of the very few who weren't great are men of considerable bulk, Rick Reuschel and "Fat Freddie" Fitzsimmons. Through the years baseball experts have said that the most important factor for a good-fielding pitcher is to finish the delivery facing home plate, though Bob Gibson, voted the best fielding right-handed pitcher of all-time, was certainly an exception to this rule.

Pitchers who fall just short of the best-ever list are Satchel Paige (who belongs way up), Catfish Hunter, Jim Bunning, Gaylord Perry, Don Newcombe, George Earnshaw, Waite Hoyt, and Spud Chandler. Dozens of fine righties didn't even get a vote.

"The Toughest Pitcher I Ever Faced"				
	RAW VOTES			
1.	Bob Feller	42	4. Bob Gibson	24
2.	Sandy Koufax	29	5. Nolan Ryan	20
3.	Ewell Blackwell	25	6. Carl Hubbell	17

7.	Lefty Grove	14	18-22.	Tom Seaver	6
8.	J.R. Richard	13	18-22.	Walter Johnson	6
9-10.	Dazzy Vance	12	18-22.	Sal Maglie	6
9-10.	Don Drysdale	12	18-22.	Curt Simmons	6
11.	Allie Reynolds	11	18-22.	Hal Newhouser	6
12-13.	Steve Carlton	10	23-28.	Red Ruffing	5
12-13.	Bob Lemon	10	23-28.	Tommy Bridges	5
14-16.	Sam McDowell	8	23-28.	Juan Marichal	5
14-16.	Whitey Ford	8	23-28.	Spud Chandler	5
14-16.	Herb Score	8	23-28.	Johnny Vander Meer	5
17.	Van Lingle Mungo	7	23-28.	Jim Bunning	5

Southpaws: The Best Ever

1.	Sandy Koufax	31.0%	9.	Herb Score	.8
2.	Lefty Grove	15.8	10.	Herb Pennock	.7
3.	Warren Spahn	15.3	11.	Rube Waddell	.6
4.	Steve Carlton	11.0	12.	Ron Guidry	.5
5.	Carl Hubbell	8.2	13-15.	Billy Pierce	.3
6.	Whitey Ford	6.5	13-15.	Babe Ruth	.3
7.	Lefty Gomez	3.0	13-15.	Eddie Plank	.3
8.	Hal Newhouser	2.5			

Southpaws: The Best Fielders

1.	Jim Kaat	23.5%	9.	Carl Hubbell	3.3
2.	Bobby Shantz	23.0	10.	Ron Guidry	3.2
3.	Warren Spahn	7.2	11.	Lefty Grove	1.6
4.	Harvey Haddix	6.7	12.	Hal Newhouser	.8
5.	Harry Brecheen	6.4	13-15.	Tommy John	.6
6.	Whitey Ford	6.2	13-15.	Larry French	.6
7.	Steve Carlton	3.8	13-15.	Herb Pennock	.6
8.	Sandy Koufax	3.4			

Players' Choice: The Designated Hitter

Pro: 36.1%   Con: 63%   Standardize It: .8%

Players were asked to vote only pro or con, so the five votes to standardize the rule one way or the other—you might call that the Whitey Herzog position—may mean there is more ambivalence out there than meets the eye. Interestingly, pitchers, demonstrating that old playground rule that every boy wants his swings, turned down the DH by 80% to 20%, while nonpitchers opposed it by a mere 54% to 46%. Perhaps pitchers also dislike the DH because it bloats their ERAs.

At his peak (1962-66), Sandy Koufax led the NL in ERA every year with a combined total of 1.95. In the history of the game, one must go back to Rube

Waddell to find a left-hander so unhittable (though pitchers of course had it easier then: Rube's five-year [1904-08] ERA of 1.84 netted him only one league-leading figure). The players also rated Sandy's the best left-handed fastball ever and his curve *the* best ever.

Right-handers Bob Feller and Nolan Ryan of course were among the top 10 pitchers having the best fastballs and curves, but neither of them ever really mastered the strike zone, and hence never reached Sandy's rarefied heights.

Although some claim that Lefty Grove was the best pitcher ever, and a close look at the record does nothing to contradict this view, it should be noted that even among the players who batted against Robert Moses, the most common ballot was filled out: "1. Koufax, 2. Grove." Sandy also received twice as many votes in the "Toughest Pitcher I Ever Faced" category, though this is slightly misleading because more respondents faced Koufax than Grove.

Finishing third on the all-time list is iron man Warren Spahn, who won 20 games (23, actually) for the thirteenth time at the age of 42, throwing seven shutouts to boot. Spahnie also finished third on the best-fielding-pitchers list, was a fine hitter (35 HRs lifetime) and ranked first in our balloting for the "Best Pickoff Move of All-Time." The players also chose his screwball as the fifth all-time best, his change-up ninth, and his curveball 11th. An all-around great, without doubt.

After Spahn, there is a very orderly descent through Carlton, Hubbell, Ford, Gomez, and Newhouser, after whom the bottom falls out. There have been twice as many righties as lefties on the major-league rosters since the beginning, so the list of left-handed greats is correspondingly smaller. Carlton rates over Hubbell because of longevity, we suppose. Whitey Ford, the quintessential crafty southpaw, shows up on the best change-up (seventh), spitball (ninth), and curveball (13th) lists. He also ranks as the sixth-best fielder with the fourth-best pickoff move—all in all, sort of a lower case Warren Spahn. Ford has many things in common with the next man in our spotlight, Lefty Gomez. Both had consistently high winning percentages, both led the AL twice in ERA, and both pitched their best ball with the money on the table. Whitey owns the lion's share of World Series pitching records, and Gomez was 6-0 in seven Series starts. The stylistic difference is that Gomez had an overpowering fastball while Ford relied more on guile. Hal Newhouser had control problems early in his career, but overcame them during World War II and went on to become just about the best pitcher in baseball for the rest of the 40s. A two-time MVP, his change-up rated 10th and his curveball 16th, and his eighth-place finish confirms the high regard for him expressed by revisionist baseball historians.

Rounding out the field are pitchers who flashed brilliance but did not sustain it—Herb Score and Babe Ruth, for very different reasons—and others who pitched very effectively, if not brilliantly, over many years: Herb Pennock, Billy Pierce, and Eddie Plank. Ron Guidry should move up in years to come, and Philadelphia A's left-hander Rube Waddell is undoubtedly hurt by the passage of time, his reputation for instability, and his relatively short career. Just off the list are Johnny Vander Meer, Eddie Lopat, Eppa Rixey, Harry Brecheen, Sam McDowell, Mickey Lolich, and Fernando Valenzuela, who could move way up by, say, 1990.

Receiving virtually no support are Vida Blue, Curt Simmons, Jim Kaat, Johnny Podres, Harvey Haddix, and Rube Marquard. Well, someone has to be left out, but it would have surprised no one to have seen any of these men make the big list. Each played a role in leading his team to at least one pennant.

By the way, of the top eight lefties, only Gomez doesn't rank among the top 12 fielding pitchers.

Firemen of the Century

1.	Goose Gossage	17.1%	12.	Ryne Duren	1.1
2.	Rollie Fingers	15.5	13-15.	Ellis Kinder	1.0
3.	Bruce Sutter	12.9	13-15.	Mike Marshall	1.0
4.	Hoyt Wilhelm	9.6	13-15.	Ron Perranoski	1.0
5.	Elroy Face	7.2	16-17.	Tug McGraw	.9
6.	Joe Page	6.8	16-17.	Stu Miller	.9
7.	Johnny Murphy	4.4	18-19.	Wilcy Moore	.8
8.	Dan Quisenberry	2.4	18-19.	Kent Tekulve	.8
9.	Firpo Marberry	1.9	20-21.	Hugh Casey	.7
10-11.	Dick Radatz	1.7	20-21.	Satchel Paige	.7
10-11.	Jim Konstanty	1.7			

Thinking of Goose Gossage, one is reminded of Sparky Lyle's remark in *The Bronx Zoo*. After Lyle's Cy Young Award season in 1977, the Yanks acquired the Goose as a free agent. There was no doubt in Sparky's mind that he was no longer the bullpen ace: "What would you rather have there with the game on the line, my 80 mph slider or his 95 mph heat?" Sure enough, after 1978 Sparky was dispatched to Texas, going, as Graig Nettles said, "from Cy Young to Sayonara."

The players' choice of Gossage as 1 over the other bullpen greats illustrates the difference between the player's perspective and a fan's. The latter might stack up the career stats of Rollie Fingers or Bruce Sutter against the Goose's. A fan might remember George Brett's upper-deck blast off the Goose in the 1980 playoffs, or Kirk Gibson's shot in the 1984 World Series, or the shellacking Goose got in the 1978 All-Star Game. But what Billy Martin, Dick Williams, Chuck Tanner, and the other managers (see "top managers" list) know that many fans don't, is that *hitters are afraid of this guy*. That sets him apart from all the competition, that psychological element. And when debating all-time greats, that kind of edge for Gossage we think carries the day. You can split hairs over his stats, but the fear factor tips the scales for him, to mix metaphors (allowable for sportswriters).

Flamethrowers and double play-ball pitchers are amply represented, but interestingly, only three of the top 20 are left-handers. Most notably absent is the aforementioned Sparky Lyle, he of the 238 lifetime saves, fourth best all-time. Lyle was no one- or two-season wonder, either, like several pitchers here: Jim Konstanty of the "Whiz Kids" Philadelphia Phillies 1950 team, Ryne Duren of bottle glasses (and whiskey bottles) fame, Yankee left-hander Joe Page, and Wilcy Moore, whose sinkerball finished off many a club during the "five o'clock lightning" year of the 1927 Yanks. A minor league journeyman for several years, Moore was prepared to hang up the glove and head for the farm when the Bronx Bombers bought his contract in 1926. The following year he was 19-7 (13-3 from the bullpen) with a league-leading 2.28 ERA, but he never recaptured that form and retired after 1933.

Moore was not the first relief ace ever, though. Dolf Luque, "the Pride of Havana" and Cincinnati Reds right-hander, was used extensively in relief as early as 1919, and he played a big part in the Reds' pennant drive and tarnished world championship against the infamous Chicago Black Sox. Luque received three first-team votes in the player survey. The first pitcher used *exclusively* in relief was Fred "Firpo" Marberry, players' choice #9, who in 1925 appeared in 55 games without a start. He pitched effective relief for several years, leading the AL in saves (retroactively) five times as a key performer on the fine Washington Senator teams of the mid-1920s. Marberry also picked up three saves in World Series competition.

Although not one reliever finished in the top 25 in the "Toughest Pitcher I Ever Batted Against" category, the lists of the best *pitches* are strewn with the men from the pen. On the "Best Sinker" list, we see Sutter first, Elroy Face's forkball seventh, Wilcy Moore eighth, Frank Linzy ninth, Dan Quisenberry 14th, and Ted Abernathy, Ed Roebuck, and Gerry Staley 16th, 18th, and 19th, respectively.

Mike Marshall (third), Jim Brewer (seventh), Tug McGraw (eighth), Nelson Potter and Jack Baldschun (tied for 11th) all received votes as having the best screwball. And there's more: In the "Best Change-up" category, Stu Miller ranks first, Ellis Kinder 12th, Bill Sherdel 13th, Elroy Face and John Hiller tied for 16th, and Dave Giusti 18th. Rollie Fingers and Sparky Lyle rate fifth and 10th for "Best Slider." And finally, both Ryne Duren (ninth) and Gossage (11th) make the "Best Fastball" list. Striking by contrast is the absence of any relief ace in the curveball or spitball rankings. We have no explanations, but both pitches *are* difficult to control, and managers like a guy who throws strikes in the late innings.

Notice how differently the coaches and managers rate the relievers. Quisenberry, Moore, and Dick Radatz move up, while Joe Page, Johnny Murphy, and Marberry drop down. Mike Marshall, known to have given his managers a problem or two, did not receive a vote, nor did Lyle, again sort of the odd man out.

Satchel Paige's ranking (21st) is an incredible achievement; he did not reach the majors until 1948, at the age of, er, 42. The baseball literature of the time is replete with quotations that he was "better than Dean" or that he "threw harder than Feller with amazing control," and it is a fact that Satch blew away the best big-league hitters in exhibition games long before Branch Rickey broke the color barrier. He even received three votes as "the toughest pitcher I ever faced," and probably not 2% of the respondents ever faced him!

Many fine relievers drew only two or three votes, including poor Lyle, Luis Arroyo, Ted Abernathy, Phil "The Vulture" Regan, Lindy McDaniel, Ace Adams, Dolf Luque, Clint Brown, Don Mossi, and Ray Narleski. John Hiller, who held the major league record in saves for several years before it was smashed to bits by Quisenberry and Sutter, got three second-team votes, undoubtedly suffered in the rankings because he was a great starter, too (he received 16 1/4 first-team votes as the best right-handed pitcher).

CLOSER LOOKS

The Best Fastball of All Time
("Who Is Steve Dalkowski?")

1.	Bob Feller	22.5%	9.	Ryne Duren		1.5
2.	Nolan Ryan	20.4	10.	J.R. Richard		1.4
3.	Sandy Koufax	13.1	11-12.	Goose Gossage		1.3
4.	Walter Johnson	12.1	11-12.	Allie Reynolds		1.3
5.	Lefty Grove	4.2	13.	Van Lingle Mungo		1.1
6.	Herb Score	3.7	14-15.	Dazzy Vance		1.0
7.	Bob Gibson	3.1	14-15.	Dizzy Dean		1.0
8.	Steve Dalkowski	1.6	16.	Tom Seaver		.8

When we asked for the pitcher with the best fastball, we didn't necessarily ask, "Who threw the hardest?" though some players answered that question. Of course, every hurler on this list threw well over 90 mph smoke, but none threw harder than the eighth man on the list, Steve Dalkowski. Claims run as high as *110* mph for his fastball, but since he couldn't be counted on to keep it between the on-deck circles, he never pitched an inning in the major leagues. It must have been a fearful experience to step into the batter's box knowing you could be dead in 4/10 of a second. Perhaps the balance of nature prevents the pitcher with truly awesome stuff from getting it over the plate. Look at the top three fastballers, then check out the curveball results in the next section. You'll see Koufax at the top, Feller fourth, and Ryan ninth. All three undeniably great; all three got the rap for having poor control. It haunted Koufax early, Feller throughout his career, and Ryan to this day. Koufax struggled for the first six years of his career to find the plate, and when he did, he'd probably lost a touch from both fastball and curve, yet it was pitiful to watch the hitters flail at him during his prime. Feller never did have control, yet won 266 games with a 3.25 ERA in a hitter's era. Ryan's best pitching has come with the Astros, well after he turned 30 and cooled his fastball a tad. If these three men could throw to spots at all, there would be no sense in even playing on days when they pitched. Only when they suffered extraordinary bouts of wildness could they be beaten. But that's the beauty of baseball—the Lord giveth, the Lord taketh away.

Walter Johnson, as previously mentioned, compiled his fabulous record without the aid of a crooked pitch, though he did vary the speed of his fastball, saving his hardest stuff for "a pinch," as was customary in the dead-ball days.

Many players who hit against both Lefty Grove and Feller, including Bill Dickey, thought that Grove threw harder. Figure it this way: It takes a 90-mph fastball less than 3/100 of a second longer to reach the plate than a 95-mph pitch. Has there ever been a batting eye discerning enough to note a difference any smaller? It takes longer than that to blink. Therefore, to get a true line on the very best fastball, we must look to the other elements besides velocity, to movement and location. The "Walks" column tells of the latter, but only a hitter can speak knowledgeably about movement. Even television, from a center-field zoom-lens viewpoint, cannot give a true picture because of its two-dimensional image. So while Grove had better control, it seems that Rapid Robert Feller had more "hop" on his heater.

Both Bob Gibson and J. R. Richard could be tossed into the Koufax, Feller, and Ryan group also, though their breaking pitch was the slider. Their careers ran along similar tracks until Richard's injury, with both struggling with control troubles early, then gradually conquering them to rise, teams hooked on for the ride, to the very top of their class. Richard, who was once clocked at 100 mph, took a little longer to emerge, no doubt because of the greater velocity of his fastball. We'll never know how long he could have sustained the peak he reached from the middle of 1979 till the stroke he suffered in 1980, but for that period Richard was every bit as unhittable as Gibby in his prime.

Van Lingle Mungo, in addition to having one of the best names in baseball history, also blazed the ball by NL batters to the tune of 120-115, 3.47 ERA, despite pitching for the horrendous Brooklyn clubs of the 1930s.

The Best Curveball

1.	Sandy Koufax	20.3%	9-10.	Nolan Ryan	1.4
2.	Tommy Bridges	14.5	11-12.	Warren Spahn	1.2
3.	Bert Blyleven	10.6	11-12.	Johnny Sain	1.2
4.	Bob Feller	9.8	13-15.	Mel Harder	1.1
5.	Camilo Pascual	9.0	13-15.	Carl Erskine	1.1
6.	"Toothpick" Sam		13-15.	Whitey Ford	1.1
	Jones	3.9	16-18.	Hal Newhouser	.9
7.	Dazzy Vance	2.4	16-18.	Don Sutton	.9
8.	Sal Maglie	2.0	16-18.	Herb Score	.9
9-10.	Juan Marichal	1.4	19.	Bob Lemon	.8

The only surprise among the curveballers is perhaps the second-place finish of Tommy Bridges, the Detroit Tiger right-hander of the 1930s and early 1940s. He compiled a 194-138 won-lost record and a 3.57 ERA over his career, winning over 20 games three times. That 3.57 ERA might not look too impressive, but nearly every year Bridges allowed a run a game less than the league average, finishing among the leaders several times. He also led the AL in strikeouts twice, and was outstanding in three of his four World Series, posting a 4-1 mark in the Fall Classic.

Journeyman Sam Jones, three-time NL strikeout king, was a better pitcher than the record indicates. Traded by the Indians to the Cubs for Ralph Kiner, Toothpick Sam won 23 games in two years, supported by a woeful Cub attack. For two seasons in St. Louis he was 26-22, but with an ERA of 3.18. Then he was traded to San Francisco for the excellent Bill White and had his best year, going 21-15 with a league-leading 2.83 ERA. Separating Sam Jones from greatness was the same old nemesis of most of the jug-handle artists, the inability to consistently throw strikes.

The Best Slider

1.	Bob Gibson	14.7%	10-11.	Robin Roberts	2.3
2.	Steve Carlton	12.5	12.	Bob Lemon	2.2
3.	Don Drysdale	4.3	13-14.	Ferguson Jenkins	1.8
4.	Ron Guidry	4.1	13-14.	Jim Bunning	1.8
5.	Rollie Fingers	3.8	15-17.	George Blaeholder	1.6
6.	Tom Seaver	3.6	15-17.	Dave Stieb	1.6
7.	Catfish Hunter	3.1	15-17.	Larry Jansen	1.6
8.	Dick Donovan	2.9	18-20.	Sal Maglie	1.3
9.	J.R. Richard	2.8	18-20.	Whitlow Wyatt	1.3
10-11.	Sparky Lyle	2.3	18-20.	Don Newcombe	1.3

The origin of the slider has long been disputed; many credit 15th-place finisher George Blaeholder for using it first. Blaeholder was a solid, finesse hurler for the decidedly below-average St. Louis Browns of the 1930s, once leading the AL in shutouts. Like many other tactical and strategic innovations in baseball, though, the slider probably existed long before Blaeholder's era in less defined form. Cy Young spoke of a pitch in his repertoire that sounds exactly like a slider, to wit: "It was a narrow curve that broke away from the batter and went in just like a fastball."

Considering how hard the slider is on the elbow, the pitchers listed here had long careers, and with a few notable exceptions were relatively free of arm trouble. Excluding Dave Stieb and Ron Guidry, this group lasted an average of over 15 years of major league service, and the aforementioned don't figure to bring that average down. 15 of the 19 were active after their 35th birthday, which is of course testimony to what fine mound artists they were. Too, it would be difficult to blame the slider for the arm miseries of Catfish Hunter and Don Drysdale, because these two worked like dogs for years. For the three years prior to decline in each man's career, Hunter and the Big D averaged 315 innings each. In the context of their times, they worked as often as anyone in history except Mickey Lolich, who averaged 330 innings over four years, and Gaylord Perry, with 321 over a seven-year span.

Burleigh Grimes: Dubious honor.

Red Faber: Sixth-best wet one.

	Guess Who Won "Best Spitball"				
1.	Gaylord Perry	41.2%	8.	Frank Shellenback	1.4
2.	Burleigh Grimes	21.3	9.	Whitey Ford	1.1
3.	Lew Burdette	9.5	10.	Phil Regan	1.0
4.	Preacher Roe	2.6	11.	Ed Walsh	.9
5.	Don Drysdale	2.5	12-13.	Bill Doak	.8
6.	Red Faber	1.9	12-13.	Johnny Allen	.8
7.	Stan Coveleski	1.5			

Here's a list of tough old birds. Their common characteristic: the three-day stubble. Or think of Don Drysdale glaring at a batter, or Whitey Ford turning his back to the plate to laugh at some poor fool in the batter's box.

Naturally, many of those listed respond with wide-eyed innocence to accusations of throwing the spitter. Tim McCarver tells a story about Lew

Burdette. After Lew had retired, he was golfing with Tim and talk turned to the wet pitch. Burdette denied throwing it, and it was McCarver's turn to get wide-eyed. Tim's sputtered reply: "But Lew, I *caught* you. We had a *sign* for it." Burdette wouldn't budge.

International News Photo

Lew Burdette

The spitter is another pitch said to be murder on the arm, but this group averaged 16 seasons in the majors, excluding Frank Shellenback, who was not allowed to pitch in the big leagues after the spitball was banned in 1920. The top three spitballers all pitched into their 40s, and Gaylord Perry and Burleigh Grimes (the last to throw a *legal* spitter) rank fourth and 28th, respectively, among the all-time innings-pitched leaders.

Ty Cobb called White Sox spitballer Ed Walsh "the greatest five-year pitcher I ever saw," and the stats back Tyrus up. Walsh's 1908 numbers are probably the best ever put up for one season: 464 innings pitched (the most ever after 1900), 40 wins (second all-time), 66 games (an AL record for over 50 years), and 42 complete games. Not only that, but he led the league in shutouts with 11 and saves with six, while pitching to a 1.42 ERA. And for icing on the cake, Walsh twice pitched and won both ends of a doubleheader, in one twirling a three-hitter and in the other a four-hitter, allowing one run and striking out 15 in *each* game! By the way, he accomplished all this with a team that hit only three home runs all season. Big Ed also led the "Hitless Wonders" White Sox club to victory in the first "subway series," in 1906, winning two games against a Cub team that had won 116 games. Of Walsh's wet pitch, Sam Crawford said, "I think that ball disintegrated on the way to the plate and the catcher put it back together again. I swear, when it went past the plate it was just the spit went by."

The Best Screwball

1.	Carl Hubbell	42.4%	7.	Jim Brewer	3.0
2.	Fernando Valenzuela	11.5	8-9.	Juan Marichal	2.4
			8-9.	Tug McGraw	2.4
3.	Mike Marshall	7.4	10.	Ruben Gomez	1.9
4.	Luis Arroyo	5.5	11-12.	Nelson Potter	1.1
5.	Warren Spahn	4.0	11-12.	Jack Baldschun	1.1
6.	Mike Cuellar	3.4	13.	Harry Brecheen	.8

It is unfortunate that no respondents faced both Carl Hubbell and Christy Mathewson, because it would be interesting to see just where Mathewson, who invented the screwball, would fit on the list. He did receive two votes, and in this case that means something, because the evaluation of particular pitches is wholly subjective—in other words, the players stuck to what they had actually seen. Considering that not 1 percent of the respondents saw Matty pitch—certainly not in his prime—two votes is not bad at all. Tom Clark, Cincinnati Reds catcher of the teens, was quoted in 1933 as saying that the screwballs of Hubbell and Mathewson were "almost identical." The only difference between them was that Hubbell threw his "nine out of ten pitches" to right-handed hitters, Clark added.

On the subject of Mathewson, the legend goes that when John McGraw came to the Giants in 1902, he found Matty playing first base, and, horrified, handed him the ball and made him a pitcher. The fact is, Mathewson had pitched 336 innings the year before, and furthermore we can find no evidence that he played even one game at first. Perhaps he was taking infield practice there, and he was a good hitter for a pitcher (.215 career BA with seven dead-ball home runs), but that does not a Lou Gehrig make.

It is interesting to note that so many screwballers are relief pitchers, reflecting no doubt most managers' desire to have an unusual pitcher in the pen, *i.e.*, to throw off hitters accustomed to more conventional stuff.

The Best Sinker

1.	Bruce Sutter	13.4%	9-12.	Ewell Blackwell	2.2
2.	Bob Lemon	12.7	9-12.	Carl Hubbell	2.2
3.	Tommy John	5.6	13.	Randy Jones	2.1
4.	Mel Stottlemyre	4.8	14.	Dan Quisenberry	1.9
5.	Lew Burdette	3.2	15.	Whitey Ford	1.7
6.	Don Drysdale	2.9	16-17.	Eldon Auker	1.2
7.	Elroy Face	2.4	16-17.	Ted Abernathy	1.2
8.	Wilcy Moore	2.3	18.	Ed Roebuck	1.1
9-12.	Hal Schumacher	2.2	19.	Gerry Staley	1.0
9-12.	Frank Linzy	2.2	20.	Rick Reuschel	.9

Fastballs, forkballs, scuffballs, submarine balls, and split-fingered fastballs are all given their due here. The mechanics of the sinking fastball are said to be murder on the arm, and at least a third of these pitchers have had arm trouble. As a rule, sinkerballers need to pitch often to stay sharp, and this compounds the strain. Tommy John, Rick Reuschel, and Randy Jones did bounce back from career-threatening injuries, though, and were as good (or in John's case particularly) better than ever.

Of the recent submariners, Dan Quisenberry gets the nod over Ted Abernathy, Kent Tekulve (22nd place) and Jack Aker (one vote). Abernathy, by the way, had one of the best final seasons of any pitcher when at age 39 he appeared in 45 games for Kansas City, pitching to a 1.71 ERA and allowing only 44 hits in 58 innings.

The Best Change-Up

1.	Stu Miller	16.7%	11.	Ted Lyons	2.4
2.	Andy Messersmith	9.5	12.	Ellis Kinder	1.9
3.	Johnny Podres	8.3	13.	Bill Sherdel	1.5
4.	Carl Erskine	7.2	14-15.	Howie Pollet	1.1
5.	Mario Soto	4.8	14-15.	Tom Seaver	1.1
6.	Rip Sewell	4.1	16-17.	Elroy Face	1.0
7.	Whitey Ford	3.3	16-17.	John Hiller	1.0
8.	Eddie Lopat	3.2	18-19.	Dizzy Dean	.9
9.	Warren Spahn	2.9	18-19.	Dave Giusti	.9
10.	Hal Newhouser	2.6			

Managers rarely tout a rookie pitcher's change-up. When scouts beat the bushes they're not looking for crafty 18-year-olds. Maybe it's because the off-speed pitch is somewhat inaccurately thought of as a veteran's pitch, learned when the fastball has begun to cool down. Or maybe it's because the judges of talent believe that a good fireballer will pitch longer and better than his crafty counterpart. Is this true? One way to find out is to analyze the careers of the best fastball pitchers, screwballers, change-up specialists, etc. and see if any patterns emerge. Here, in no particular order, are the average careers of each pitching group voted on by the players:

	WON	LOST	PCT.	ERA
Best Fastballers	197	133	.597	3.13
Best Curveballers	198	141	.583	3.27
Best Screwballers	136	103	.568	3.30
Best Spitballers	203	148	.579	3.15
Best Sliders	171	127	.574	3.29
Best Sinkerballers	136	105	.564	3.26
Best Change-Ups	188	134	.585	3.27

You can see that the flamethrowers finish first easily, even more so when you consider that the records of the spitballers are affected by the fact that five of the 12 pitched before the home run jacked up everybody's ERA and reduced "innings-pitched" and "decisions."

The roster of greatest curveball pitchers certainly *looks* more impressive than that of the off-speed hurlers, but the records are quite similar, with a slight winning percentage to the slowballers. In fact, the change-up artists won more often than any group of pitchers besides the fastballers, demonstrating that winning rave reviews is not so valuable as quietly winning ball games. We think it's fair to say, because these figures back it up, that the sly string-pullers will win an average of one more game per year than another type of pitcher with the same ERA.

The Best Pickoff Move

1.	Warren Spahn	18.1%	7-8.	Phil Niekro	2.0
2.	Steve Carlton	15.3	9-10.	Luis Tiant	1.9
3.	Bill Wight	13.1	9-10.	Bobby Shantz	1.9
4.	Whitey Ford	11.4	11.	Don Drysdale	1.8
5.	Sherrod Smith	2.8	12.	Roger Craig	1.1
6.	Bob McClure	2.3	13-14.	Roy Henshaw	.8
7-8.	Paul Doyle	2.0	13-14.	Ted Lyons	.8

Spahn and Carlton, of course. But left-hander Bill Wight also drew tremendous support, largely from American Leaguers of the 1940s and 50s. Despite the great move to first, Wight was your basic wild lefty, toiling for eight major-league clubs over 12 years and posting a 77-99, 3.95 ERA record lifetime. His stats are a bit misleading because during his three prime years (1948-1950) he pitched well for a White Sox team whose winning percentage was only .378.

Besides being predominantly left-handers (nine of 14), other characteristics of the pickoff masters are that they are more off-speed than power pitching types and that they had longish windups. Both traits of course create the need for a good move to first.

With all the basestealing of the past 25 years, you'd think more moderns would be listed, our reasoning being that supply creates demand (Say's economic law, if you please). One second base star, who unfortunately doesn't want to be quoted (he's a coach and former manager) told us: "Today? There are no good pickoff moves. The umpires won't allow them." In other words, the balk is quickly called today, as Steve Carlton can attest.

The Most Underrated Ball Player

THE NOMINEES		RAW VOTE	HOW PLAYERS RANKED HIM AT HIS POSITION
1.	Enos Slaughter	40	21
2.	Billy Williams	30	32
3.	Roger Maris	27	23
4.	Roberto Clemente	23	9
5-6.	Al Kaline	21	11
5-6.	Rod Carew	21	12
7.	Ernie Lombardi	20	9
8.	Tommy Henrich	18	22
9.	Henry Aaron	17	6
10.	Dom DiMaggio	15	34
11-12.	Marty Marion	14	4
11-12.	Pee Wee Reese	14	6
13.	Nellie Fox	13	7
14.	Glenn Wright	12	18
15-16.	Red Schoendienst	11	13
15-16.	Carl Furillo	11	27
17-19.	Ernie Banks	10	3
17-19.	Tony Oliva	10	36
17-19.	Harmon Killebrew	10	15
20-25.	Mickey Vernon	9	15
20-25.	Hank Bauer	9	unranked
20-25.	Phil Rizzuto	9	5
20-25.	Johnny Mize	9	8
20-25.	Eddie Murray	9	13
20-25.	Al Oliver	9	unranked
26-31.	Luke Appling	8	7
26-31.	Arky Vaughan	8	40
26-31.	Willie McCovey	8	5
26-31.	Tony Perez	8	unranked

26-31.	Luis Aparicio	8	2
26-31.	Charlie Gehringer	8	1
32-38.	Bill Mazeroski	7	6
32-38.	Doc Cramer	7	unranked
32-38.	Lou Gehrig	7	1
32-38.	Vern Stephens	7	32
32-38.	Hack Wilson	7	43
32-38.	Jose Cruz	7	unranked
32-38.	Cecil Travis	7	33

Courtesy Detroit Tigers

Al Kaline: One of the underrateds.

In all of sports, few terms are so nebulous as "underrated." In this survey the word is applied to superstars and minor leaguers and everything in-between. It means so many different things to so many different players that 342 different men received at least one mention out of 1,051 votes cast—an average of only three votes per man. In fact, 170 of the 342 players garnered only one vote. So for a player to get even five votes represents a consensus of sorts.

It seems that every possible definition of underrated is represented on the list, starting with some players whose skills have been recognized but who haven't made the Hall of Fame, like Roger Maris, Billy Williams, and Phil Rizzuto. Some have made the Hall of Fame, but still don't get the respect they deserve, like Enos Slaughter, Johnny Mize, Al Kaline, Pee Wee Reese, Harmon Killebrew, and Luke Appling. Others nominated for the underrated list played magnificently for years before getting their due—Aaron and Clemente are two prime examples. Still others toiled in the shadow of another, greater star, like Tommy Henrich with Joe D., Willie McCovey with Mays, Dom DiMaggio with Ted Williams, and of course Lou Gehrig under the gargantuan (in more ways than one) shadow of the Babe. Dom D. played under his *brother's*, too, making him the victim of both a solar and lunar eclipse, if you will.

Then there are the defensive and "little ball" specialists—Marty Marion, Nellie Fox, Bill Mazeroski (think where he'd be if he *hadn't* hit that World series HR to beat the Yanks), and Luis Aparicio—who tend to be pushed into the background when the discussion turns to the big guns.

Another group made specific and consistent contributions to great teams: Tony Perez, Carl Furillo, and Hank Bauer, for example. Votes for Rod Carew and Al Oliver fly in the face of their exaggerated shortcomings—"he doesn't hit home runs" and "he can't play defense." There is also strong support for a group of middle infielders who could truly do it all: Red Schoendienst, Arky Vaughan, Charlie Gehringer, Vern Stephens, and Glenn Wright, the fine Pirate shortstop of the 1920s who was once termed "flawless" by the *New York Times* sportswriter Arthur Daley.

It is interesting, when dealing with the "underrated," to see where the players themselves rated this group. Put simply, did the players underrate the very guys they nominated? See for yourself on the chart. Bear in mind that 21 of the 38 nominees finished in the top 15 at their positions, though the average rank of the players as a group would be 18th.

Another note is the scarcity of votes for pitchers—only 4 percent of the total. Hal Newhouser and Robin Roberts led the field with three votes each, with Ted Lyons, Larry Jansen, Mel Stottlemeyre, Tommy Bridges, Satchel Paige, Mel Parnell, Van Lingle Mungo, and Ned Garver getting two each.

The Best Pinch Hitter

			CAREER PH AVERAGE	BEST SEASON AVERAGE (PH)
1.	Smoky Burgess	27.4%	.286	.450
2.	Manny Mota	25.4	.297	.400
3.	Johnny Mize	7.6	.283	.429
4.	Dusty Rhodes	5.4	.212	.333
5.	Jerry Lynch	4.9	.260	.404
6.	Rusty Staub	4.2	.282	.375
7.	Dave Philley	3.0	.299	.409
8.	Jose Morales	1.7	.276	.361
9-10.	Johnny Blanchard	1.5	.164	.269
9-10.	Gates Brown	1.5	.258	.462
11.	Ron Northey	1.1	.276	.440
12-13.	Joe Cronin	.8	.288	.429
12-13.	Red Lucas	.8	.261	.364

The pinch hitting batting averages shown have been taken from *The Baseball Encyclopedia*. We used a standard of 20 pinch-hit at bats minimum for the single-season highs.

If a foreigner were to look at a group photo of these men, it would be difficult to convince him that baseball is not a table game. And the photo wouldn't even include Bob "Fatty" Fothergill, the Tiger, White Sox, and Red Sox outfielder, 1922-1933, whose lifetime pinch-hitting average was .300. Of course, the reason these gentlemen were pinch hitters in the first place is because they couldn't run, or couldn't field or throw, or all three. But they could hit. You've heard all the reasons why pinch hitting is so difficult. It's hard to come into a game cold, in a tight spot, with no chance of redemption should you fail, often against a fresh relief specialist. But maybe the physical bulk of these men furnishes a clue to their success. Generally speaking, doesn't it seem reasonable that a ball player who is indifferent to his conditioning might also be indifferent to clutch pressure? After all, pressure is self-imposed. If this were true, their indifference should be reflected by their patience as hitters—in the "Walks" column—and sure enough, with two exceptions, it is. Those two are Manny Mota and Jose Morales, but then Latin hitters rarely walk, and many in fact are first-ball swingers. Exceptions to the Latin "no walk" rule are so rare as to defy a skeptic's challenge.*

The two hitters with both the lowest career and single-season averages were essentially one-year wonders: Johnny Blanchard and Dusty Rhodes. But both were also better than the averages show, because several of their hits were homers. Yankee Blanchard powered seven career pinch-hit homers, including two consecutively in 1961, one of which was a grand slam. Rhodes is well-known for his pinch-hitting heroics in the 1954 World Series, leading the Giants to a four-game sweep. He also hit a pinch-dinger that regular season, his only effective year in the role. Rhodes's fourth-place finish is an example of how legends grow and obscure facts. Jerry Lynch, who finished behind him, was a demonstrably better pinch hitter over a far longer period.

Tiger Gates Brown should have known he was in for a long career as a substitute swatter when he pinch-hit a home run in his first big league at bat in 1963. He went on to hit 16 in his career, tying for second place all-time with Smoky Burgess, Cliff Johnson (who received no votes!), and Willie McCovey. Willie, injured often dur-

• • • • •

*The average major league ball player has walked about once in every ten at bats over the course of the lively ball era. Out of 197 Latin-born major leaguers with over 100 at bats, 159 walked less often (80.3%), ranging from Puerto Ricans (once every 12 at bats) to Dominicans (once every 18 at bats). The complete list, by nation:

Country	At Bats per Walk
Puerto Rico	11.9
Panama	12.7
Mexico	13.0
Cuba	13.0
Venezuela	14.3
Dominican Republic	17.5
Average for all Latins	13.8

No Latin player has ever walked 100 times in a season; the new record, set in 1985, is held by San Diego Padre outfielder Carmello Martinez with 87. Prior to this, the electrifying Minnie Minoso had held the mark since 1956, when he walked 86 times.

ing his career, also came off the bench to hit three pinch grand slams, as did Ron Northey, rated 11th by the players. The all-time leader in pinch-hit home runs is Jerry Lynch, with 18.

In the sixth and seventh slots are Rusty Staub and Dave Philley, who share the remarkable record of nine pinch hits in a row. Philley did that twice, in 1958 and 1959, and Staub tied him in 1984.

Fans love to see a pitcher pinch-hit, and while it is occasionally done today, nobody did it better or more often than Red Lucas, here tied for 12th. It makes sense to use a great-hitting pitcher in this role between starts, and four times Lucas led the NL in pinch hits, in 1929, '30, '31, and '37. He currently stands in fifth place on the all-time list with 114 pinch hits. Two other pitchers got two votes each, Red Ruffing and Wes Ferrell.

The few hackers just missing the list are Terry Crowley, Peanuts Lowrey, and Taft Wright, who had a fine season in the pinch-hitting role for the 1938 Senators. Vic Davalillo, Steve Braun, and Tim McCarver received only one vote each, though in Braun's case he is among the all-time leaders in pinch hits. Ed Kranepool, whose .486 mark in 1974 drove Met fans wild in an otherwise dismal year, got only one vote, though his pinch-hit average is the single-season best ever. Tommy Davis, holder of the best lifetime average (.320), also rated but one vote. Life is hard for pinch hitters.

Phil Rizzuto

SELECTED
PLAYER SURVEYS

If we thought there was a likelihood you'd remember—or *should* remember—any of the men who filled out our survey, or if he has some claim to fame, he is in the following pages. A few of the players are in Cooperstown, and several more belong there. There *were* cases where we let nostalgia get the better of us. George Altman, Phil Linz, and Gary Gentry come to mind. None of these, by the way, was any slouch, and Linz was a first-class comedian. He once delivered this ultimatum to Ralph Houk, longtime Yankee manager: "Play me or keep me."

Not all the participants answered every question we asked them, so you won't find every player's ballot the same in form. Many, for example, chose not to name "two or three players who never lived up to their potential." A few, stars whose opinions you'd dearly love to see, asked that we not quote them at all, so we regret not being able to show you Whitey Ford's answers, or Red Schoendienst's. Phil Rizzuto at first didn't respond at all, but we cleared that up by simply informing him that our maternal grandmother is Italian. Within days, his completed survey arrived in the mail, but he also asked us not to quote his answers.

We briefly introduce each player in the survey and give you his lifetime vitals, as well as his "Best Composite Year." This latter is a composite of stats from several different years; it *doesn't* mean you are looking at the statistics of any player's best season. In the case of pitchers, we *omit* from this line things like hits and walks.

One last thing to keep in mind. In an earlier version of the survey, we didn't ask players to include the year their "greatest team" nominee played. So, for example, many simply said "Yankees," assuming we wanted their pick of the best team *over the years*. Don't blame the player if he leaves out the year in that answer; blame us.

◎ Ethan Allen ◎

1926-1930: Cincinnati Reds; 1930-1932: N.Y. Giants; 1933: St. Louis Cardinals; 1934-1936: Philadelphia Phillies; 1936: Chicago Cubs; 1937-1938: St. Louis Browns

Ethan Allen never played a day of minor-league ball. When he finished his career, he started a new one writing books on baseball techniques and heading up the motion picture department for the National League. He coached the Yale baseball team for over two decades. Though not a home run hitter, Allen was the first player ever to hit a ball over the center field fence at Redland Field (later Crosley Field). The Reds paid him what was one of the biggest bonuses to sign in 1926, the lavish sum of $8,500—the equivalent of $75,000 to $85,000 today. And *very* few prospects get that kind of money today.

Mr. Allen omitted a defensive team, telling us, "I am sure there must be outstanding defensive teams but the Gold Glove business is for the birds. Some players get to balls and receive errors which some Gold Glovers never reach. Zeke Bonura had a high fielding average. One day a ball went by him and later Jimmy Dykes, the White Sox manager, asked Luke Sewell, the Cleveland first-base coach, if Zeke could have gotten the ball. His reply was, 'No, but anyone else could'."

Mr Allen's memory remains razor-sharp, though he is almost 85. We asked him about one of his boys at Yale—George Bush. "Bush was a good ball player—and a *very* good defensive player. He batted about .285 in college, and he worked hard at his hitting," remembers Allen. "We were finalists in two College World Series, and he played in those. Matter of fact, in one of them, we knocked Jackie Jensen [who by 1950, three years later, found himself on the New York Yankees] out of the box.... One day in Raleigh, Bush had a heckuva game, and after the game the scouts all rushed down to see him...."

	AB	H	2B	3B	HR	R
LIFETIME	4418	1325	255	45	47	623
BEST COMPOSITE YEAR	581	192	46	11	10	90

	RBI	BB	SB	BA	SLG.	OB%
LIFETIME	501	223	84	.300	.410	.333
BEST COMPOSITE YEAR	85	43	21	.330	.468	.366

ALL-TIME ALL-STAR TEAM

OUTFIELD: Left: Frank Robinson, Ted Williams, Stan Musial, Hank Aaron **Center:** Ty Cobb, Joe DiMaggio, Willie Mays, Mickey Mantle, Duke Snider **Right:** Babe Ruth, Kiki Cuyler, Roberto Clemente, Reggie Jackson **3B:** Pie Traynor, Eddie Mathews, Brooks Robinson, George Kell **SS:** Honus Wagner,

Arky Vaughan, Luis Aparicio, Luke Appling **2B:** Rogers Hornsby, Charlie Gehringer, Eddie Collins, Nap Lajoie **1B:** Lou Gehrig, Bill Terry, Johnny Mize, Hank Greenberg **RH PITCHER:** Walter Johnson, Bob Feller, Dizzy Dean, Bob Gibson **LH PITCHER:** Carl Hubbell, Whitey Ford, Warren Spahn, Lefty Grove **CATCHER:** Bill Dickey, Gabby Hartnett, Mickey Cochrane, Johnny Bench **RELIEF PITCHER:** Rollie Fingers, Bruce Sutter, Rich Gossage

HONORABLE MENTION: Tris Speaker, Mel Ott, Jim Bottomley

BEST CLUTCH HITTER EVER: Rube Bressler—great 2-strike man
GAME 7 WORLD SERIES PITCHER: Sandy Koufax
BEST MANAGER OF ALL TIME: John McGraw—because he got on every
  player for mistakes, whether you were a rookie or a veteran
BEST TEAM: 1927 Yankees
BEST FASTBALL: Walter Johnson/Lefty Gomez
BEST CURVE: Dazzy Vance
BEST SCREWBALL: Carl Hubbell
BEST SPITBALL: Burleigh Grimes
BEST PICKOFF MOVE: Sherrod Smith/Clarence Mitchell
BEST SINKER/DROP: Carl Mays
BEST CHANGE-UP: Willie Sherdel
BEST BASE STEALER OF ALL TIME: Ty Cobb
BEST BUNTER: Max Bishop
MOST KNOWLEDGEABLE BASEBALL BROADCASTERS: Red Barber,
  Lou Boudreau
BEST UMPIRE YOU EVER SAW: Bill Klem
BALL PLAYER WHO DID THE MOST TO INSPIRE HIS TEAM: Pepper
  Martin
**THE BASEBALL WRITER WHO UNDERSTOOD THE GAME
  BEST:** Frank Graham, Sr.

⚾Matty Alou⚾

1960-1965: San Francisco Giants; 1966-1970: Pittsburgh Pirates; 1971-1972: St. Louis Cardinals; 1972: Oakland Athletics; 1973: N.Y. Yankees-St. Louis Cardinals; 1974: San Diego Padres

All three Alou boys, Matty, Jesus, and Felipe, were fine ball players. Matty was the best of the three, and it isn't an exaggeration to call him a star, or at least a batting star. His lifetime average: .307. Let's just list some of his career highlights:

1. Batting title (.342) in 1966 with the Pirates.
2. Part of all-.300-hitting outfield that year (with Clemente and Stargell).
3. Led NL in doubles, hits and at bats in 1969, with 41, 231, and 698, respectively.

4. Batted over .300 eight times in his 15-year career, and just missed that mark three times with BAs in the .290s.
5. Finished first, third, second and fourth in the NL in batting in 1966, '67, '68 and '69.

The Pirates figured something was wrong when Matty's average dropped to .297 in 1970 and they dealt him to St. Louis, where he rebounded to .315, knocking in 74 runs to boot. He credits Harry the Hat Walker and Roberto Clemente with changing his batting style and making him a consistent hitter.

Notable Alou picks—smart ones, if we may say so—are Bo Belinsky ("never lived up to his potential") and, yes, *himself* as best bunter ever. Alou left the "underrated" space on the survey blank. We have a hunch he felt like picking himself. And again, we think it would have been appropriate.

	AB	H	2B	3B	HR	R
LIFETIME	5789	1777	236	50	31	780
BEST COMPOSITE YEAR	698	231	41	9	7	105

	RBI	BB	SB	BA	SLG.	OB%
LIFETIME	427	311	156	.307	.381	.342
BEST COMPOSITE YEAR	74	42	23	.342	.455	.370

ALL-TIME ALL-STAR TEAM 1

OUTFIELD: Willie Mays, Mickey Mantle, Roberto Clemente **3B:** Brooks Robinson **SS:** Ozzie Smith **2B:** Bill Mazeroski **1B:** Willie McCovey **RH PITCHER:** Juan Marichal **LH PITCHER:** Sandy Koufax **CATCHER:** Johnny Bench **RELIEF PITCHER:** Roy Face

ALL-TIME ALL-STAR TEAM 2

OUTFIELD: Ted Williams, Stan Musial, Frank Robinson **3B:** Ron Santo **SS:** Dave Concepcion **2B:** Rod Carew **1B:** Keith Hernandez **RH PITCHER:** Bob Gibson **LH PITCHER:** Whitey Ford **CATCHER:** Gary Carter **RELIEF PITCHER:** Willie Hernandez

ALL-TIME DEFENSIVE TEAM

OUTFIELD: Willie Mays, Willie Davis, Roberto Clemente **1B:** Keith Hernandez **2B:** Julian Javier **3B:** Brooks Robinson **SS:** Ozzie Smith **RH PITCHER:** Al McBean **LH PITCHER:** Bobby Shantz **CATCHER:** Johnny Bench

BEST CLUTCH HITTER EVER: Willie Mays
BEST PINCH HITTER: Jerry Lynch
BEST SS-2B DOUBLE-PLAY COMBINATION EVER: Gene Alley-Bill Mazeroski
GAME 7 WORLD SERIES PITCHER: Juan Marichal
BEST MANAGER OF ALL TIME: Billy Martin
THE BEST TEAM: 1962 Yankees
FAVORITE STADIUM TO PLAY IN: Forbes Field
CITY WITH THE BEST FANS: San Francisco
DESIGNATED HITTER: Favor
BEST FASTBALL: Sandy Koufax
BEST CURVE: Bert Blyleven
BEST SCREWBALL: Sal Maglie
BEST SPITBALL: Gaylord Perry
BEST PICKOFF MOVE: Whitey Ford
BEST SINKER/DROP: Bob Purkey
BEST CHANGE-UP: Stu Miller
BEST SLIDER: J.R. Richard
BEST BASE STEALER OF ALL TIME: Lou Brock
BEST BUNTER: Matty Alou
BEST HIT-AND-RUN MAN: Danny O'Connell
BEST THROWING ARM OF ALL TIME: Roberto Clemente
MOST KNOWLEDGEABLE BASEBALL BROADCASTERS: Phil Rizzuto, Joe Garagiola
BEST UMPIRE YOU EVER SAW: Jocko Conlan
BALL PLAYERS WHO NEVER PLAYED UP TO THEIR POTENTIAL: Richie Allen, George Hendrick, Bo Belinsky
TOUGHEST PITCHER YOU EVER BATTED AGAINST: Sandy Koufax
BALL PLAYER WHO DID THE MOST TO INSPIRE HIS TEAM: Willie Mays
BEST TEAM OWNER YOU'VE KNOWN: Dan Galbreath
THE BASEBALL WRITER WHO UNDERSTOOD THE GAME BEST: Dick Young

✺ George Altman ✺

1959-1962: Chicago Cubs; 1963: St. Louis Cardinals; 1964: N.Y. Mets; 1965-1967: Chicago Cubs

Make no mistake, Altman was a good ball player. There's a tendency for Met fans to chuckle because they associate him with the bad old days at Shea. This outfielder-with-power (27 HRs in 1961) also hit for average: .303, .318, .274, in his best and fullest seasons. He led the NL in triples in 1961 and collected 96 RBIs that year. George is one of the few men who hit a home run in his first All-Star appearance, and even with the pathetic Mets of '64, he knocked in 47 runs in just 422 at bats, attesting to his value as an RBI man.

Having played during the Koufax-era, it isn't surprising to see Sandy's name repeated on his ballot. And having spent most of his time with the Cubs, a prime Koufax target, it is less surprising still that Altman nominates the greatest of Dodger southpaws for five awards: best lefty ever, World Series Game 7 pitcher, best fastball, best sinker/drop, and toughest pitcher to hit.

	AB	H	2B	3B	HR	R
LIFETIME	3091	832	132	34	101	409
BEST COMPOSITE YEAR	534	170	28	12	27	77

	RBI	BB	SB	BA	SLG.	OB%
LIFETIME	403	268	52	.269	.432	.327
BEST COMPOSITE YEAR	96	62	19	.318	.511	.389

ALL-TIME ALL-STAR TEAM 1

OUTFIELD: Willie Mays, Hank Aaron, Babe Ruth **3B:** Richie Allen **SS:** Ernie Banks **2B:** Rogers Hornsby **1B:** Frank Robinson **RH PITCHER:** Christy Mathewson **LH PITCHER:** Sandy Koufax **CATCHER:** Josh Gibson **RELIEF PITCHER:** Satchel Paige

ALL-TIME ALL-STAR TEAM 2

OUTFIELD: Mickey Mantle, Roberto Clemente, Ted Williams **3B:** Eddie Mathews **SS:** Dick Groat **2B:** Rod Carew **1B:** Stan Musial **RH PITCHER:** Bob Gibson **LH PITCHER:** Warren Spahn **CATCHER:** Johnny Bench **RELIEF PITCHER:** Bruce Sutter

ALL-TIME DEFENSIVE TEAM

OUTFIELD: Willie Mays, Roberto Clemente, Carl Yastrzemski **1B:** Vic Power **2B:** Bill Mazeroski **3B:** Brooks Robinson **SS:** Luis Aparicio **RH PITCHER:** Bob Gibson **LH PITCHER:** Harvey Haddix **CATCHER:** Johnny Bench

MOST UNDERRATED BALL PLAYER OF ALL TIME: Billy Williams
BEST CLUTCH HITTER EVER: Ernie Banks
BEST PINCH HITTER: Smoky Burgess
GAME 7 WORLD SERIES PITCHER: Sandy Koufax

BEST MANAGER OF ALL TIME: John McGraw
THE BEST TEAM: 1927 Yankees
FAVORITE STADIUM TO PLAY IN: Wrigley Field
CITY WITH THE BEST FANS: Chicago
DESIGNATED HITTER: Favor
BEST FASTBALL: Sandy Koufax
BEST CURVE: Sam Jones
BEST SCREWBALL: Juan Marichal
BEST SPITBALL: Lew Burdette
BEST PICKOFF MOVE: Warren Spahn
BEST SINKER/DROP: Sandy Koufax (drop)
BEST CHANGE-UP: Stu Miller
BEST SLIDER: Joey Jay
BEST BASE STEALER OF ALL TIME: Lou Brock
BEST BUNTER: Rod Carew
BEST THROWING ARM OF ALL TIME: Roberto Clemente
BEST UMPIRE YOU EVER SAW: Al Barlick
**BALL PLAYERS WHO NEVER PLAYED UP TO THEIR POTEN-
TIAL:** George Altman, Adolfo Phillips
TOUGHEST PITCHER YOU EVER BATTED AGAINST: Sandy Koufax

⚾ Wally Berger ⚾

1930-1937: Boston Braves; 1937-1938: N.Y. Giants; 1938-1940: Cincinnati Reds;
1940: Philadelphia Phillies

After over 55 years, Wally Berger still shares the record (with Frank Robinson) for the most home runs by a rookie, 38. That same year, 1930, he also set the National League mark for RBIs by a freshman, 119. Lest you be tempted to think that this was just another fluke of that year, remember that Wally started in center field for the Nationals in the first three All-Star games. A five-time .300 hitter, Berger also has seven grand slams to his credit.

In his selections, note Charlie Root as the second right-handed pitcher. Root was quite a pitcher for 17 years, but is only remembered today for giving up the alleged "called shot" Babe Ruth home run in the 1932 World Series. A hard-nosed starter-reliever, he won 201 games with a fine (for the time) ERA of 3.58. Root's career high in victories: 26 in 1927.

	AB	H	2B	3B	HR	R
LIFETIME	5163	1550	299	59	242	806
BEST COMPOSITE YEAR	617	199	44	14	38	98

	RBI	BB	SB	BA	SLG.	OB%
LIFETIME	898	435	36	.300	.522	.355
BEST COMPOSITE YEAR	130	55	13	.323	.614	.379

Wally Berger with the Babe, 1935.

ALL-TIME ALL-STAR TEAM 1

OUTFIELD: Babe Ruth, Ty Cobb, Tris Speaker **3B:** Pie Traynor **SS:** Honus Wagner **2B:** Eddie Collins **1B:** Bill Terry **RH PITCHER:** Dazzy Vance **LH PITCHER:** Lefty GRove **CATCHER:** Gabby Hartnett **RELIEF PITCHER:** Firpo Marberry

ALL-TIME ALL-STAR TEAM 2

OUTFIELD: Terry Moore, Lloyd Waner, Paul Waner **3B:** Fred Lindstrom **SS:** Travis Jackson **2B:** Billy Herman **1B:** Lou Gehrig **RH PITCHER:** Charlie Root **LH PITCHER:** Lefty Gomez **CATCHER:** Mickey Cochrane **RELIEF PITCHER:** Dolf Luque

ALL-TIME DEFENSIVE TEAM

OUTFIELD: Lloyd Waner, Terry Moore, Kiki Cuyler **1B:** Dolf Camilli **2B:** Charlie Gehringer **3B:** Willie Kamm **SS:** Honus Wagner **RH PITCHER:** Fred Fitzsimmons **LH PITCHER:** Ed Lopat **CATCHER:** Mickey Cochrane

MOST UNDERRATED BALL PLAYER OF ALL TIME: Ernie Lombardi, Leo Durocher
BEST CLUTCH HITTER EVER: Riggs Stephenson
BEST PINCH HITTER: Dixie Walker
BEST SS-2B DOUBLE-PLAY COMBINATION EVER: Woody English-Billy Herman
GAME 7 WORLD SERIES PITCHER: My first starter
BEST MANAGER OF ALL TIME: John McGraw
THE BEST TEAM: 1927 Yankees
FAVORITE STADIUM TO PLAY IN: Forbes Field, Pittsburgh
CITY WITH THE BEST FANS: Chicago (Cubs)
DESIGNATED HITTER: Oppose
BEST FASTBALL: Dazzy Vance
BEST CURVE: Tommy Bridges
BEST SCREWBALL: Carl Hubbell
BEST SPITBALL: Burleigh Grimes
BEST PICKOFF MOVE: Ray Kremer
BEST SINKER/DROP: Bucky Walters
BEST CHANGE-UP: Red Lucas
BEST SLIDER: Ray Benge
BEST BASE STEALER OF ALL TIME: Lou Brock
BEST BUNTER: Lloyd Waner
BEST THROWING ARM OF ALL TIME: Bob Meusel
MOST KNOWLEDGEABLE BASEBALL BROADCASTERS: Vin Scully, Mel Allen

BEST UMPIRE YOU EVER SAW: Bill Klem
TOUGHEST PITCHER YOU EVER BATTED AGAINST: Carl Hubbell
BALL PLAYER WHO DID THE MOST TO INSPIRE HIS TEAM: Rabbit
  Maranville
BEST TEAM OWNER YOU'VE KNOWN: Col. Jake Ruppert
BASEBALL WRITER WHO UNDERSTOOD THE GAME BEST: Joe
  Cashman

⊘Paul Blair ⊙

1964-1976: Baltimore Orioles; 1977-1979: N.Y. Yankees; 1979: Cincinnati Reds;
1980: N.Y. Yankees

The players' choice as one of the truly great defensive outfielders (seventh place), this Orioles' center fielder dominated the Gold Glove Award voting in the late sixties and early seventies, and indeed picks himself, along with a pair of Red Sox, as the best fielding outfielder ever.

Blair could also hit, and with some power. He belted three career grand slams, and in 1969 he hit 26 home runs. Early the following season, he hit three homers in one game, though he stopped his fine hitting after a severe beaning limited him to facing only left-handed pitchers.

Blair's picks are predominantly of players of the recent past, in part because, as he told us, these guys are better in general. "They are bigger, conditions are better, equipment better," and, he adds, their ability is better overall.

	AB	H	2B	3B	HR	R
LIFETIME	6042	1513	282	55	134	776
BEST COMPOSITE YEAR	625	178	32	12	26	102

	RBI	BB	SB	BA	SLG.	OB%
LIFETIME	620	449	171	.250	.382	.302
BEST COMPOSITE YEAR	76	56	27	.293	.477	.352

ALL-TIME ALL-STAR TEAM 1

OUTFIELD: Frank Robinson, Willie Mays, Hank Aaron **3B:** Brooks Robinson **SS:** Luis Aparicio **2B:** Joe Morgan **1B:** Willie McCovey **RH PITCHER:** Bob Gibson **LH PITCHER:** Sandy Koufax **CATCHER:** Johnny Bench **RELIEF PITCHER:** Stu Miller

ALL-TIME ALL-STAR TEAM 2

OUTFIELD: Carl Yastrzemski, Tony Oliva, Billy Williams **3B:** Mike Schmidt **SS:** Dave Concepcion **2B:** Rod Carew **1B:** Pete Rose **RH PITCHER:** Jim Palmer **LH PITCHER:** Sam McDowell **CATCHER:** Thurman Munson **RELIEF PITCHER:** Rich Gossage

ALL-TIME DEFENSIVE TEAM

OUTFIELD: Paul Blair, Dwight Evans, Carl Yastrzemski **1B:** George Scott **2B:** Dave Johnson **3B:** Brooks Robinson **SS:** Mark Belanger **RH PITCHER:** Jim Palmer **LH PITCHER:** Jim Kaat **CATCHER:** Johnny Bench

BEST CLUTCH HITTER EVER: Frank Robinson
BEST PINCH HITTER: Manny Mota
BEST SS-2B DOUBLE-PLAY COMBINATION EVER: Mark Belanger-
   Dave Johnson
GAME 7 WORLD SERIES PITCHER: Sandy Koufax/Bob Gibson
BEST MANAGER OF ALL TIME: Earl Weaver/Billy Martin
THE BEST TEAM: 1969 Baltimore Orioles
FAVORITE STADIUM TO PLAY IN: Fenway Park
CITY WITH THE BEST FANS: New York
BEST FASTBALL: Vida Blue
BEST CURVE: Sandy Koufax
BEST SCREWBALL: Mike Cuellar
BEST SPITBALL: Gaylord Perry
BEST SINKER/DROP: Jack Aker
BEST CHANGE-UP: Stu Miller
BEST BASE STEALER OF ALL TIME: Lou Brock
BEST THROWING ARM OF ALL TIME: Reggie Smith
MOST KNOWLEDGEABLE BASEBALL BROADCASTERS: Vin Scully
BEST UMPIRE YOU EVER SAW: Nestor Chylak
TOUGHEST PITCHER YOU EVER BATTED AGAINST: Bob Gibson
BALL PLAYER WHO DID THE MOST TO INSPIRE HIS TEAM: Frank
   Robinson

⊘Bobby Bragan⊘

1940-1942: Philadelphia Phillies; 1943-1948: Brooklyn Dodgers

Bobby Bragan was the only 20th-century player we could find who played over 100 games at both catcher and shortstop, a bizarre combination but somehow right in character for the innovative Bragan.

Texas Rangers

Bobby Bragan

Recently the president of the Texas League, Bragan's professional baseball career spans nearly 50 years. Never much of a hitter, his one claim to batting fame was a pinch-RBI-double for the Dodgers during the winning rally of the sixth game of the 1947 World Series.

It is as a fiesty, creative manager that Bragan should be remembered. He was an outspoken advocate of big-inning baseball, shunning both the sacrifice bunt and the hit and run, which he thought severly handicapped the hitter. But he was no Earl Weaver, waiting for the three-run homer; Bragan liked to use the third-base steal and the suicide squeeze. His most daring strategy was rearranging his batting order so that the traditional cleanup man would bat leadoff, the #3 hitter second, the #5 man third, and so on in declining order of ability. His reasoning was that the extra at bats (about 18 per year for each slot in the order) would more than compensate for any lack of runners on base. Furthermore, Bragan realized that since more runs are scored off pitchers in the first inning that in any other, his best hitters could take the most advantage of a hurler's early shakiness. He claimed that this lineup won two extra games for the Pirates over one-third of the 1956 season—which is like the Old Perfessor and the 1962 Mets touting a strategy because it brought them one game closer to first place. Bragan's innovation did not catch on. As with all the new wrinkles in baseball, if a team wins everyone imitates it, but if a team loses the strategy is dropped faster than you can say "Fabian." We're skeptical, but we'd like to see a manager try this type of lineup with a good ball club. How the arguments would rage.

Bragan's ballot is a characteristically well-thought-out affair, with selections drawn from the entire 20th century. Note his high regard for Dave Concepcion, doubly notable coming from a fellow shortstop who has seen, if not all of them, then most of 'em.... You can also see in Bragan yet another right-handed batter who *still* bails out when he sees Ewell Blackwell.

	AB	H	2B	3B	HR	R
LIFETIME	1900	456	62	12	15	136
BEST COMPOSITE YEAR	557	140	19	4	7	37

	RBI	BB	SB	BA	SLG.	OB%
LIFETIME	172	110	12	.240	.309	.282
BEST COMPOSITE YEAR	69	28	7	.267	.341	.311

MANAGER
(7 years)

	W-L	PCT.
Pirates	102-155	.391
Indians	31-36	.463
Braves	310-287	.518
Total:	443-478	.481

ALL-TIME ALL-STAR TEAM 1

OUTFIELD: Babe Ruth, Ty Cobb, Joe DiMaggio **3B:** Brooks Robinson **SS:** Honus Wagner **2B:** Rogers Hornsby **1B:** George Sisler **RH PITCHER:** Walter Johnson **LH PITCHER:** Lefty Grove **CATCHER:** Yogi Berra **RELIEF PITCHER:** Bruce Sutter

ALL-TIME ALL-STAR TEAM 2

OUTFIELD: Hank Aaron, Willie Mays, Tris Speaker **3B:** Pie Traynor **SS:** Dave Concepcion **2B:** Eddie Collins **1B:** Jimmie Foxx **RH PITCHER:** Cy Young **LH PITCHER:** Babe Ruth **CATCHER:** Roy Campanella **RELIEF PITCHER:** Dan Quisenberry

ALL-TIME DEFENSIVE TEAM

OUTFIELD: Roberto Clemente, Willie Mays, Tris Speaker **1B:** Hal Chase **2B:** Bill Mazeroski **3B:** Brooks Robinson **SS:** Mark Belanger **RH PITCHER:** Ruben Gomez **LH PITCHER:** Jim Kaat **CATCHER:** Jim Hegan

MOST UNDERRATED BALL PLAYERS OF ALL TIME: Arky Vaughan, Clete Boyer
BEST CLUTCH HITTER EVER: Paul Waner
BEST PINCH HITTER: Smoky Burgess/Manny Mota
BEST SS-2B DOUBLE-PLAY COMBINATION EVER: Reese-Robinson
GAME 7 WORLD SERIES PITCHER: Walter Johnson
BEST MANAGER OF ALL TIME: John McGraw
THE BEST TEAM: 1927 Yankees
FAVORITE STADIUM TO PLAY IN: Dodger Stadium
CITY WITH THE BEST FANS: Chicago or L.A.
DESIGNATED HITTER: Favor
BEST FASTBALL: Walter Johnson
BEST CURVE: Sandy Koufax
BEST SCREWBALL: Carl Hubbell
BEST SPITBALL: Burleigh Grimes
BEST PICKOFF MOVE: Warren Spahn
BEST SINKER/DROP: Alpha Brazle
BEST CHANGE-UP: Carl Erskine
BEST SLIDER: Whitlow Wyatt
BEST BASE STEALER OF ALL TIME: Maury Wills
BEST THROWING ARM OF ALL TIME: Roberto Clemente
MOST KNOWLEDGEABLE BASEBALL BROADCASTERS: Vin Scully, Jack Buck
BEST UMPIRE YOU EVER SAW: Bill Klem

BALL PLAYERS WHO NEVER PLAYED UP TO THEIR POTEN-TIAL: Jim Gentile, Willie Davis, Jeff Burroughs
TOUGHEST PITCHER YOU EVER BATTED AGAINST: Ewell Blackwell
BALL PLAYER WHO DID THE MOST TO INSPIRE HIS TEAM: Joe DiMaggio
BEST TEAM OWNER YOU'VE EVER KNOWN: Gene Autry
BASEBALL WRITER WHO UNDERSTOOD THE GAME THE BEST: Red Smith/Dick Young

---

Bobby Bragan on batting the cleanup hitter first in the order:

"Lou Boudrea was doing it in Kansas City at the same time I was doing it in Pittsburgh... If Roger Maris had been leading off in 1961, the home run record would not have been 61. It would have been 63 or 64. He'd have gone to bat more times—17 or 18 more. If Babe Ruth had led off, he'd hit 62 or 63 instead of 60. Same reason. He'd have gotten 17 or 18 more at bats during the season, and hit one out every 11 at bats... If George Brett was leading off, he wouldn't be intentionally walked as much—there'd be 162 times when he'd be *sure* he'd be pitched to... As (Branch) Rickey once told me, you couldn't be criticized for putting your best hitters first, second third, and so on down the order. If a hitter is going to get up five times, I'd rather have Frank Howard hitting than Maury Wills. I'd rather have Moose Skowron, or Mantle, or Berra than Bobby Richardson or Scooter Rizzuto. There's nothing wrong with leading off the ball game with a home run."

⊘Ernie Broglio⊘

1959-1964: St. Louis Cardinals; 1964-1966: Chicago Cubs

You remember Ernie Broglio—the guy the Cubs traded Lou Brock for in '64. It was by no means clear at the time that the Cards got the better of the deal. Ernie went 18-8, 2.99 ERA, the year before the trade, and in 1960, he led the NL in victories (21-9), appearing in 52 games. 23% of his career wins were shutouts. Ernie has choosen some unorthodox selections, but we get a kick out of seeing Tim McCarver choosen as the best-ever catcher. He was excellent, and clearly he and Ernie were a battery. And McCarver ia a superb baseball analyst. We get him in the New York area telecasting Mets games on WOR, and he and Ralph Kiner, Hall of Famer and probaly a descendent of Demosthenes, talk intelligently on the intricacies of this great game, teaching us all (without being patronizing) what *really* happens on the diamond. On a couple of occasions, Timmy has "gone national"—*e.g.*, the 1985 World Series—and often he is smothered by those unseen directors and producers, or by colleagues who talk too much, and he comes off—we've heard people say—as nothing special. But it is a commentary on what big-time TV "specialists" do to a sporting event that the premier baseball color man can't be made to feel comfortable enough *to say what he wants to say*. What this has to do with Ernie Broglio is a good question.

	W-L	PCT.	ERA	G
LIFETIME	77-74	.510	3.74	259
BEST COMPOSITE YEAR	21-12	.700	2.74	52

	IP	H	BB	SO	SHO.
LIFETIME	1337.1	1216	587	849	18
BEST COMPOSITE YEAR	250			188	5

ALL-TIME ALL-STAR TEAM 1

OUTFIELD: Hank Aaron, Willie Mays, Roberto Clemente **3B:** Ken Boyer **SS:** Roy McMillan **2B:** Ron Hunt **1B:** Willie McCovey **RH PITCHER:** Bob Gibson **LH PITCHER:** Sandy Koufax **CATCHER:** Tim McCarver **RELIEF PITCHER:** Lindy McDaniel

ALL-TIME ALL-STAR TEAM 2

OUTFIELD: Stan Musial, Frank Robinson, Eddie Mathews **3B:** Jimmy Davenport **SS:** Maury Wills **2B:** Pete Rose **1B:** Gil Hodges **RH PITCHER:** Don Drysdale **LH PITCHER:** Warren Spahn **CATCHER:** Del Crandall **RELIEF PITCHER:** Elroy Face

ALL-TIME DEFENSIVE TEAM

OUTFIELD: Roberto Clemente, Willie Mays, Curt Flood **1B:** Willie Stargell **2B:** Bill Mazeroski **3B:** Jim Davenport **SS:** Roy McMillan **RH PITCHER:** Bob Gibson **LH PITCHER:** Warren Spahn **CATCHER:** Del Crandall

MOST UNDERRATED BALL PLAYERS OF ALL TIME: Del Crandall, Dick Groat, Richie Allen
BEST CLUTCH HITTER EVER: Roberto Clemente
BEST PINCH HITTER: Jerry Lynch

BEST SS-2B DOUBLE-PLAY COMBINATION EVER: Dick Groat-Bill
  Mazeroski
GAME 7 WORLD SERIES PITCHER: Sandy Koufax
BEST MANAGER OF ALL TIME: Walter Alston
FAVORITE STADIUM TO PLAY IN: Forbes Field (Pittsburgh)
CITY WITH THE BEST FANS: St. Louis
DESIGNATED HITTER: Oppose
BEST FASTBALL: Bob Gibson/Sandy Koufax
BEST CURVE: Sam Jones
BEST SPITBALL: Lew Burdette
BEST PICKOFF MOVE: John Antonelli
BEST SINKER/DROP: Larry Jackson
BEST CHANGE-UP: Johnny Podres
BEST SLIDER: Bob Buhl
BEST BASE STEALER OF ALL TIME: Maury Wills
BEST BUNTER: Jim Gilliam
BEST THROWING ARM OF ALL TIME: Gino Cimoli
MOST KNOWLEDGEABLE BASEBALL BROADCASTERS: Bob Prince,
  Vin Scully
BEST UMPIRE YOU EVER SAW: Al Barlick/Jocko Conlan
**BALL PLAYERS WHO NEVER PLAYED UP TO THEIR POTEN-
TIAL:** Vada Pinson, Joe Adcock
HITTER YOU FOUND THE HARDEST TO GET OUT: Harvey Kuenn
BEST TEAM OWNER YOU'VE KNOWN: Augie Busch
**BASEBALL WRITER WHO UNDERSTOOD THE GAME THE
BEST:** None

⊘ Jim Brosnan ⊗

1954-1958: Chicago Cubs; 1958-1959: St. Louis Cardinals; 1959-1963:
Cincinnati Reds; 1963: Chicago White Sox

Jim Brosnan wrote the original inside-the-clubhouse jock journal, *The Long
Season*, in 1960. It was good, like Brosnan's pitching was in most years.
"Professor" Brosnan, as he was called, sent his survey back neatly typed. He
spelled Carl Yastrzemski's name correctly, and we took notice. Arresting choices
of Jim's: El Tappe, a Chicago Cub catcher who saw very little duty in his six-year
career (he managed the Cubs in 1961 and '62, by the way, for part of each year),
and perhaps Ozzie Smith as *the* greatest shortstop ever. Brosnan, mostly a relief
pitcher himself, offers no surprises in his picks there.

	W-L	PCT.	ERA	G
LIFETIME	55-47	.539	3.54	385
BEST COMPOSITE YEAR	11-9	1.000	2.36	57

	IP	H	BB	SO	SHO.
LIFETIME	831.1	790	312	507	2
BEST COMPOSITE YEAR	166.2			89	1

ALL-TIME ALL-STAR TEAM 1
OUTFIELD: Babe Ruth, Joe DiMaggio, Ted Williams   **3B:** Mike Schmidt **SS:** Ozzie Smith **2B:** Rogers Hornsby **1B:** Stan Musial **RH PITCHER:** Walter Johnson **LH PITCHER:** Sandy Koufax **CATCHER:** Johnny Bench **RELIEF PITCHER:** Bruce Sutter

ALL-TIME ALL-STAR TEAM 2

OUTFIELD: Hank Aaron, Willie Mays, Roberto Clemente **3B:** Brooks Robinson **SS:** Honus Wagner **2B:** Jackie Robinson **1B:** George Sisler **RH PITCHER:** Bob Gibson **LH PITCHER:** Lefty Grove **CATCHER:** Yogi Berra **RELIEF PITCHER:** Hoyt Wilhelm

ALL-TIME DEFENSIVE TEAM

OUTFIELD: Carl Yastrzemski, Omar Moreno, Roberto Clemente **1B:** Mickey Vernon **2B:** Bill Mazeroski **3B:** Graig Nettles **SS:** Ozzie Smith **RH PITCHER:** Phil Niekro **LH PITCHER:** Jim Kaat **CATCHER:** Elvin Tappe

MOST UNDERRATED BALL PLAYERS OF ALL TIME: Josh Gibson, Luis Aparicio
BEST CLUTCH HITTER EVER: Yogi Berra
BEST PINCH HITTER: Manny Mota
BEST SS-2B DOUBLE-PLAY COMBINATION EVER: Luis Aparicio and Nellie Fox
GAME 7 WORLD SERIES PITCHER: Bob Gibson
BEST MANAGER OF ALL TIME: Earl Weaver
THE BEST TEAM: 1961 Yankees
FAVORITE STADIUM TO PLAY IN: Milwaukee County Stadium
CITY WITH THE BEST FANS: Chicago
DESIGNATED HITTER: Oppose

BEST FASTBALL: Walter Johnson
BEST CURVE: Sandy Koufax
BEST SCREWBALL: Carl Hubbell
BEST SPITBALL: Lew Burdette
BEST PICKOFF MOVE: Bill Wight
BEST SINKER/DROP: Grover Cleveland Alexander
BEST CHANGE-UP: Carl Erskine
BEST SLIDER: Bob Gibson
BEST BASE STEALER OF ALL TIME: Lou Brock
BEST BUNTER: Ty Cobb
BEST THROWING ARM OF ALL TIME: Roberto Clemente
MOST KNOWLEDGEABLE BASEBALL BROADCASTERS: Red Barber, Vin Scully
BEST UMPIRE YOU EVER SAW: Doug Harvey
TOUGHEST PITCHER YOU EVER BATTED AGAINST: Sandy Koufax
HITTER YOU FOUND HARDEST TO GET OUT: Frank Thomas
BALL PLAYER WHO DID THE MOST TO INSPIRE HIS TEAM: Frank Robinson
BEST TEAM OWNER YOU'VE EVER KNOWN: P.K. Wrigley
BASEBALL WRITER WHO UNDERSTOOD THE GAME BEST: Jim Brosnan

⊘ Guy Bush ⊗

1923-1934: Chicago Cubs; 1935-1936: Pittsburgh Pirates; 1936-1937: Boston Braves; 1938: St. Louis Cardinals; 1945: Cincinnati Reds

The late Guy Bush was a workhorse starter-reliever through the height of the lively ball era. The Mississippi Mudcat was often among the league leaders in winning percentage and twice led the National League in saves. A perfect microcosm of the rabbit baseball of 1930 is contained in the record of Guy's ERAs. In the three years before 1930 his earned run average was 3.53. In the three years after, it was 3.37. So how come in 1930 it was 6.20? And despite this astronomical ERA, Bush's record was 15-10 with three saves. His right-handed screwball helped the Cubbies win two pennants, in 1929 and 1932; he was excellent in his first World Series (1-0, 0.82) and had the misfortune of facing the 1932 Yankees in his second (0-1, 14.29).

	W-L	PCT.	ERA	G
LIFETIME	176-136	.564	3.85	542
BEST COMPOSITE YEAR	20-15	.720	2.75	50

	IP	H	BB	SO	SHO.
LIFETIME	2726	2950	859	850	16
BEST COMPOSITE YEAR	271			84	4

BEST CLUTCH HITTER EVER: Rogers Hornsby
BEST SS-2B DOUBLE-PLAY COMBINATION EVER: Travis Jackson-Billy Herman
GAME 7 WORLD SERIES PITCHER: Steve Carlton
BEST MANAGER OF ALL TIME: Joe McCarthy
THE BEST TEAM: 1932 Yankees
FAVORITE STADIUM TO PLAY IN: Wrigley Field
CITY WITH THE BEST FANS: Chicago
BEST FASTBALL: Nolan Ryan
BEST CURVE: Steve Carlton
BEST SCREWBALL: Guy Bush
BEST SPITBALL: Burleigh Grimes
MOST KNOWLEDGEABLE BASEBALL BROADCASTERS: Bob Elson, Joe Garagiola
BEST UMPIRE YOU EVER SAW: Bill Klem
TOUGHEST PITCHER YOU EVER BATTED AGAINST: Dazzy Vance
HITTER YOU FOUND THE HARDEST TO GET OUT: Rogers Hornsby
BASEBALL WRITER WHO UNDERSTOOD THE GAME THE BEST: Irvine Vaughn

⚾ Dave Campbell ⚾

1967-1969: Detroit Tigers; 1970-1973: San Diego Padres; 1973: St. Louis Cardinals; 1973-1974: Houston Astros

San Diego Padres broadcaster Dave Campbell is a likable former infielder who, save for the 1970 season when he played second base every day, served as a utility man.

	AB	H	2B	3B	HR	R
LIFETIME	1252	267	54	4	20	128
BEST COMPOSITE YEAR	581	127	28	2	12	71

	RBI	BB	SB	BA	SLG.	OB%
LIFETIME	89	102	29	.213	.311	.273
BEST COMPOSITE YEAR	40	40	18	.240	.336	.315

ALL-TIME ALL-STAR TEAM 1

OUTFIELD: Babe Ruth, Joe DiMaggio, Willie Mays **3B:** Brooks Robinson **SS:** Honus Wagner **2B:** Charlie Gehringer **1B:** Lou Gehrig **RH PITCHER:** Walter Johnson **LH PITCHER:** Steve Carlton **CATCHER:** Johnny Bench **RELIEF PITCHER:** Rollie Fingers

ALL-TIME ALL-STAR TEAM 2

OUTFIELD: Stan Musial, Mickey Mantle, Hank Aaron **3B:** Pie Traynor **SS:** Luis Aparicio **2B:** Rogers Hornsby **1B:** Willie McCovey **RH PITCHER:** Grover Alexander **LH PITCHER:** Warren Spahn **CATCHER:** Yogi Berra **RELIEF PITCHER:** Bruce Sutter

ALL-TIME DEFENSIVE TEAM

OUTFIELD: Willie Mays, Ken Berry, Al Kaline **1B:** Vic Power/Ferris Fain **2B:** Bobby Richardson **3B:** Brooks Robinson **SS:** Ozzie Smith **RH PITCHER:** Phil Niekro **LH PITCHER:** Jim Kaat **CATCHER:** Johnny Bench

MOST UNDERRATED BALL PLAYERS OF ALL TIME: Luis Aparicio, Al Oliver
BEST CLUTCH HITTER EVER: Lou Gehrig
BEST PINCH HITTER: Smoky Burgess, Manny Mota
BEST SS-2B DOUBLE-PLAY COMBINATION EVER: Phil Rizzuto-Jerry Coleman
GAME 7 WORLD SERIES PITCHER: Sandy Koufax
BEST MANAGER OF ALL TIME: John McGraw
THE BEST TEAM: 1976 Cincinnati Reds
FAVORITE STADIUM TO PLAY IN: Wrigley Field
CITY WITH THE BEST FANS: Most interested: New York; Best behaved: Montreal
DESIGNATED HITTER: Opposed
BEST FASTBALL: Nolan Ryan
BEST CURVE: Sandy Koufax
BEST SCREWBALL: Carl Hubbell
BEST SPITBALL: Gaylord Perry
BEST PICKOFF MOVE: Steve Carlton
BEST SINKER/DROP: Bruce Sutter
BEST CHANGE-UP: John Hiller/Johnny Podres
BEST SLIDER: J.R. Richard
BEST BASE STEALER OF ALL TIME: Lou Brock
BEST BUNTER: Phil Rizzuto
BEST THROWING ARM OF ALL TIME: Roberto Clemente

MOST KNOWLEDGEABLE BASEBALL BROADCASTERS: Dick Enberg, Dave Campbell
BEST UMPIRE YOU EVER SAW: Doug Harvey
BALLPLAYERS WHO NEVER PLAYED UP TO THEIR POTENTIAL: Dave Parker, Joe Pepitone, Ellis Valentine
TOUGHEST PITCHER YOU EVER BATTED AGAINST: Bob Gibson
BALL PLAYER WHO DID THE MOST TO INSPIRE HIS TEAM: Pete Rose
BEST TEAM OWNER YOU'VE KNOWN: Most successful: Walter O'Malley; Nicest: Bob Laurie
BASEBALL WRITER WHO UNDERSTOOD THE GAME THE BEST: Tom Boswell

Don Cardwell

1957-1960: Philadelphia Phillies; 1960-1962: Chicago Cubs; 1963-1966: Pittsburgh Pirates; 1967-1970: N.Y. Mets; 1970: Atlanta Braves

There were a couple of highlights to Don Cardwell's long career. He pitched a no-hitter against a tough opponent, the St. Louis Cardinals, in 1960. And he chipped in eight wins and a 3.01 ERA to the Miracle Mets pennant in 1961. He was a workhorse starter, and as a matter of fact, led the NL in starts in 1961. He also clouted 15 career home runs, five in one fun season, 1960.

Cardwell limits his choices strictly to the men he played with or against, and it is a bit odd to see him pick John Roseboro over Johnny Bench, the runaway winner for best defensive catcher (whereas Roseboro didn't even rank in our survey). It's hard to quibble with his other picks, however, and note that he agrees with Matty Alou—that Matty Alou was the best bunter around.

	W-L	PCT.	ERA	G
LIFETIME	102-138	.425	3.92	410
BEST COMPOSITE YEAR	15-16	.565	2.79	41

	IP	H	BB	SO	SHO.
LIFETIME	2123	2009	671	1211	17
BEST COMPOSITE YEAR	259.1			156	3

ALL-TIME ALL-STAR TEAM 1

OUTFIELD: Willie Mays, Hank Aaron, Frank Robinson **3B:** Ken Boyer **SS:** Gene Alley **2B:** Bill Mazeroski **1B:** Gil Hodges **RH PITCHER:** Bob Gibson **LH PITCHER:** Sandy Koufax **CATCHER:** Del Crandall **RELIEF PITCHER:** Elroy Face

ALL-TIME ALL-STAR TEAM 2

OUTFIELD: Willie Stargell, Curt Flood, Vada Pinson **3B:** Eddie Mathews **SS:** Bud Harrelson **2B:** Julian Javier **1B:** Wes Parker **RH PITCHER:** Tom Seaver **LH PITCHER:** Waren Spahn **CATCHER:** John Roseboro **RELIEF PITCHER:** Mike Marshall

ALL-TIME DEFENSIVE TEAM

OUTFIELD: Willie Mays, Hank Aaron, Bill Virdon **1B:** Wes Parker **2B:** Bill Mazeroski **3B:** Ken Boyer **SS:** Gene Alley **RH PITCHER:** Elroy Face **LH PITCHER:** Ron Perranoski **CATCHER:** John Roseboro

MOST UNDERRATED BALL PLAYERS OF ALL TIME: Hank Aaron, Bill Virdon, Bill Mazeroski
BEST CLUTCH HITTER EVER: Smoky Burgess
BEST PINCH HITTER: Smoky Burgess
BEST SS-2B DOUBLE-PLAY COMBINATION EVER: Gene Alley-Bill Mazeroski
GAME 7 WORLD SERIES PITCHER: Sandy Koufax/Bob Gibson
BEST MANAGER OF ALL TIME: Manny Murtaugh
THE BEST TEAM: 1957 Milwaukee Braves
FAVORITE STADIUM TO PLAY IN: Forbes Field Pittsburgh
CITY WITH THE BEST FANS: New York
BEST FASTBALL: Sandy Koufax
BEST CURVE: Nolan Ryan
BEST SCREWBALL: Tug McGraw
BEST SPITBALL: Don Drysdale/Gaylord Perry
BEST PICKOFF MOVE: Warren Spahn
BEST SINKER/DROP: Frank Linzy
BEST CHANGE-UP: Johnny Podres
BEST BASE STEALER OF ALL TIME: Lou Brock
BEST BUNTER: Matty Alou
BEST THROWING ARM OF ALL TIME: Roberto Clemente
MOST KNOWLEDGEABLE BASEBALL BROADCASTERS: Vin Scully Bob Prince
BEST UMPIRE YOU EVER SAW: Al Barlick

BALL PLAYERS WHO NEVER PLAYED UP TO THEIR POTEN-TIAL: Ed Bouchee, Seth Morehead, Harry Anderson
HITTER YOU FOUND HARDEST TO GET OUT: Frank Bolling
BEST TEAM OWNER YOU'VE KNOWN: Joe Brown (general manager, Pirates)

⚾ George Washington Case ⚾

1937-1945: Washington Senators; 1946: Cleveland Indians; 1947: Washington Senators

One of the better lead-off men in American League history, George Case led the junior circuit in stolen bases six times and scored over 100 runs four times. He played all three outfield positions well enough to draw three players' votes on their all-time defensive teams. Case shares (with three others) the major-league record for most hits in a doubleheader, with nine.

Three distinguished Senators (left to right): Mickey Vernon, Clyde Wilson, and George Case

Case chose his all-star teams exclusively from American Leaguers of the 1930s and '40s, hence the votes for Buddy Lewis, Stan Spence, et al. Gordon Maltzberger, Case's second choice for best reliever, twice led the AL in saves and went 19-9 for the White Sox during the three best years of a career abbreviated by an arm injury, military service, and a late arrival (age 30) in the big leagues.... SABRmetricians will be delighted by the nod to Harland Clift at third base; the reasons for their devotion are Clift's solid batting averages with good power and a fine eye for walks, coupled with consistently brilliant defense.... Case votes for himself as the best bunter, an opinion shared by four others among his peers.

George was generally regarded as the fastest man in the majors in his time, and he often raced other players to prove it. He would like to see such an annual affair today, as he mentioned in his chapter of *Baseball Between the Lines*. He suggests that each year at the All-Star game the three fastest runners from each league sprint for a purse, dismissing the threat of injury by noting that running is the livelihood of these guys, just as pitchers make a living throwing.

Fans are always arguing about who is the fastest. We'd like to see a field of Vince Coleman, Willie McGee, and Tim Raines matched against Willie Wilson, Rickey Henderson, and Kirk Gibson, but the contestants could be nominated via the All-Star ballots currently used. Incidentally, George finds that ball players of the 1930s, '40s, and '50s were "better hitters" than today's counterparts, but he gives the nod to the modern ball player in fielding.

	AB	H	2B	3B	HR	R
LIFETIME	5017	1415	233	43	21	785
BEST COMPOSITE YEAR	656	192	36	8	5	109

	RBI	BB	SB	BA	SLG.	OB%
LIFETIME	377	425	349	.282	.358	.338
BEST COMPOSITE YEAR	56	56	61	.320	.407	.373

ALL-TIME ALL-STAR TEAM 1

OUTFIELD: Ted Williams, Joe DiMaggio, Tommy Henrich **3B:** Ken Keltner **SS:** Luke Appling/Lou Boudreau **2B:** Joe Gordon **1B:** Hank Greenberg **RH PITCHER:** Bob Feller **LH PITCHER:** Hal Newhouser **CATCHER:** Bill Dickey **RELIEF PITCHER:** Joe Page

ALL-TIME ALL-STAR TEAM 2

OUTFIELD: Charlie Keller, Stan Spence, Buddy Lewis **3B:** Harlond Clift **SS:** Phil Rizzuto/Cecil Travis **2B:** Bobby Doerr **1B:** Mickey Vernon **RH PITCHER:** Dizzy Trout **LH PITCHER:** Eddie Lopat **CATCHER:** Rollie Hemsley **RELIEF PITCHER:** Gordon Maltzberger

ALL-TIME DEFENSIVE TEAM

OUTFIELD: Willie Mays, Joe DiMaggio, Tommy Henrich **1B:** George McQuinn **2B:** Joe Gordon **3B:** Ken Keltner **SS:** Phil Rizzuto **RH PITCHER:** Dutch Leonard **LH PITCHER:** Bobby Shantz **CATCHER:** Bill Dickey

MOST UNDERRATED BALL PLAYERS OF ALL TIME: Cecil Travis, Tommy Bridges, Rudy York
BEST CLUTCH HITTER EVER: Ted Williams
BEST PINCH HITTER: Smoky Burgess
BEST SS-2B DOUBLE-PLAY COMBINATION EVER: Phil Rizzuto-Joe Gordon
BEST MANAGER OF ALL TIME: Bucky Harris
THE BEST TEAM: 1937-40 Yankees
FAVORITE STADIUM TO PLAY IN: Comiskey Park
CITY WITH THE BEST FANS: Chicago
BEST FASTBALL: Bob Feller
BEST CURVE: Bob Feller/Tommy Bridges
BEST SCREWBALL: Nelson Potter
BEST SPITBALL: Johnny Allen
BEST PICKOFF MOVE: Bill Wight
BEST CHANGE-UP: Hal Newhouser
BEST BASE STEALER OF ALL TIME: Ty Cobb
BEST BUNTER: George Case
BEST THROWING ARM OF ALL TIME: Roberto Clemente
MOST KNOWLEDGEABLE BASEBALL BROADCASTERS: Red Barber, Mel Allen
BEST UMPIRE YOU EVER SAW: Bill McGowan
BALL PLAYERS WHO NEVER PLAYED UP TO THEIR POTENTIAL: Roy Weatherly, Dick Wakefield
TOUGHEST PITCHER YOU EVER BATTED AGAINST: Bob Feller
BALL PLAYER WHO DID THE MOST TO INSPIRE HIS TEAM: Tommy Henrich
BEST TEAM OWNER YOU'VE KNOWN: Clark Griffith
BASEBALL WRITER WHO UNDERSTOOD THE GAME THE BEST: Fred Lieb

⊘ George Culver ⊘

1966-1967: Cleveland Indians; 1968-1969: Cincinnati Reds; 1970: St. Louis Cardinals; 1970-1972: Houston Astros; 1973-1974: Los Angeles Dodgers-Philadelphia Phillies

George Culver's principal claim to fame: he threw a no-hitter against the Philadelphia Phillies in 1968, though most of his nine years was spent in bullpens. He is currently a minor-league pitching coach.

	W-L	PCT.	ERA	G	
LIFETIME	48-49	.495	3.62	335	
BEST COMPOSITE YEAR	11-16	1.000	2.65	59	

	IP	H	BB	SO	SHO.
LIFETIME	788.1	793	352	451	2
BEST COMPOSITE YEAR	226			114	2

ALL-TIME ALL-STAR TEAM 1

OUTFIELD: Carl Yastrzemski, Roberto Clemente, Hank Aaron **3B:** Mike Schmidt **SS:** Cal Ripken **2B:** Joe Morgan **1B:** Willie McCovey **RH PITCHER:** Bob Gibson **LH PITCHER:** Sandy Koufax **CATCHER:** Johnny Bench **RELIEF PITCHER:** Bruce Sutter

ALL-TIME ALL-STAR TEAM 2

OUTFIELD: Mickey Mantle, Willie Mays, Frank Robinson **3B:** Brooks Robinson **SS:** Maury Wills **2B:** Pete Rose **1B:** Eddie Murray **RH PITCHER:** Don Drysdale **LH PITCHER:** Steve Carlton **CATCHER:** Yogi Berra **RELIEF PITCHER:** Goose Gossage

ALL-TIME DEFENSIVE TEAM

OUTFIELD: Roberto Clemente, Paul Blair, Carl Yastrzemski **1B:** Wes Parker **2B:** Frank White **3B:** Brooks Robinson **SS:** Larry Bowa **RH PITCHER:** Bob Gibson **LH PITCHER:** Jim Kaat **CATCHER:** Johnny Bench

MOST UNDERRATED BALL PLAYER OF ALL TIME: Joe Rudi, Tony
Perez, Lee May
BEST CLUTCH HITTER EVER: Carl Yastrzemski
BEST PINCH HITTER: Manny Mota
BEST *PURE* HITTER: Al Kaline
BEST SS-2B DOUBLE-PLAY COMBINATION EVER: Dave Concepcion-
Joe Morgan
GAME 7 WORLD SERIES PITCHER: Sandy Koufax
BEST MANAGER OF ALL TIME: Sparky Anderson
THE BEST TEAM: 1975 Cincinnati Reds
FAVORITE STADIUM TO PLAY IN: Wrigley Field
CITY WITH THE BEST FANS: Chicago (Wrigley Field)
DESIGNATED HITTER: Oppose
BEST FASTBALL: Sandy Koufax
BEST CURVE: Sandy Koufax
BEST SCREWBALL: Jim Brewer
BEST SPITBALL: Gaylord Perry/Don Drysdale
BEST PICKOFF MOVE: Luis Tiant
BEST SINKER/DROP: Frank Linzy
BEST CHANGE-UP: Dave Giusti
BEST SLIDER: Bob Gibson
BEST BASE STEALER OF ALL TIME: Lou Brock
BEST BUNTER: Maury Wills
BEST HIT-AND-RUN MAN: Tommy Helms
BEST THROWING ARM OF ALL TIME: Roberto Clemente
MOST KNOWLEDGEABLE BASEBALL BROADCASTERS: Vin Scully,
Al Michaels
BEST UMPIRE YOU EVER SAW: Bob Engel
**BALL PLAYERS WHO NEVER PLAYED UP TO THEIR POTEN-
TIAL:** Sam McDowell, Wayne Simpson, Cesar Cedeno
TOUGHEST PITCHER YOU EVER BATTED AGAINST: Don Drysdale
HITTER YOU FOUND HARDEST TO GET OUT: Willie McCovey/Carl
Yastrzemski
BALL PLAYER WHO DID THE MOST TO INSPIRE HIS TEAM: Carl
Yastrzemski/Pete Rose
BEST TEAM OWNER YOU'VE KNOWN: Ruly Carpenter
**THE BASEBALL WRITER WHO UNDERSTOOD THE GAME
BEST:** Earl Lawson/Tom Boswell

⚾ Virgil "Spud" Davis ⚾

1928: St. Louis Cardinals; 1928-1933: Philadelphia Phillies; 1934-1936: St. Louis
Cardinals; 1937-1938: Cincinnati Reds; 1938-1939: Philadelphia Phillies; 1940-
1945: Pittsburgh Pirates

A lifetime .308 hitter, the late Spud Davis was the regular catcher on the Gashouse Gang Cardinals of the mid-1930s, and he also managed briefly. 10 times he topped .300, with a modicum of power and more walks than strikeouts. He also delivered when the chips were down, going two-for-two with an RBI in the 1934 World Series vs. the Detroit Tigers. Davis also bore the dubious distinction of catching perhaps the worst pitching staff of all time, the 1930 Philadelphia Phillies. Now the baseball was juiced up in 1930 (the NL combined batting average was .303), and Baker Bowl was a notorious hitter's park, but the Phillies *staff* ERA was 6.71, a full 1.47 behind the seventh-place Pirates. We don't blame Spud, though. He just caught what they threw.

	AB	H	2B	3B	HR	R
LIFETIME	4255	1312	244	22	77	388
BEST COMPOSITE YEAR	495	173	32	5	14	51

	RBI	BB	SB	BA	SLG.	OB%
LIFETIME	647	386	6	.308	.430	.366
BEST COMPOSITE YEAR	70	402	.349	.522	.396	

ALL-TIME ALL-STAR TEAM 1

OUTFIELD: Babe Ruth, Earle Combs, Riggs Stephenson **3B:** Pie Traynor **SS:** Marty Marion **2B:** Frank Frisch **1B:** Lou Gehrig **RH PITCHER:** Grover Cleveland Alexander **LH PITCHER:** Carl Hubbell **CATCHER:** Bill Dickey **RELIEF PITCHER:** Wilcy Moore

ALL-TIME ALL-STAR TEAM 2

OUTFIELD: Chick Hafey, Chuck Klein, Al Simmons **3B:** Brooks Robinson **SS:** Honus Wagner **2B:** Eddie Collins **1B:** Jim Bottomley **RH PITCHER:** George Earnshaw **LH PITCHER:** Lefty Grove **CATCHER:** Gabby Hartnett **RELIEF PITCHER:** Mace Brown

ALL-TIME DEFENSIVE TEAM

OUTFIELD: Terry Moore, Taylor Douthit, Duke Snider **1B:** Charlie Grimm **2B:** Charlie Gehringer **3B:** Pinky Whitney **SS:** Leo Durocher **RH PITCHER:** Freddie Fitzsimmons **LH PITCHER:** Bill Sherdel **CATCHER:** Micky Cochrane

MOST UNDERRATED BALL PLAYERS OF ALL TIME: Eddie Stanky, Tommy Thevenow
BEST CLUTCH HITTER EVER: Rogers Hornsby
BEST PINCH HITTER: Smoky Burgess
BEST SS-2B DOUBLE-PLAY COMBINATION EVER: Billy Jurges-Billy Herman
GAME 7 WORLD SERIES PITCHER: Grover Cleveland Alexander
BEST MANAGER OF ALL TIME: Connie Mack
THE BEST TEAM: 1927 Yankees
FAVORITE STADIUM TO PLAY IN: Wrigley Field
CITY WITH THE BEST FANS: St. Louis
DESIGNATED HITTER: Oppose
BEST FASTBALL: Bob Feller
BEST CURVE: Bill Hallahan
BEST SCREWBALL: Herb Pruitt
BEST SPITBALL: Burleigh Grimes
BEST PICKOFF MOVE: Willard Schmidt
BEST SINKER/DROP: Carl Hubbell
BEST CHANGE-UP: Pete Donahue
BEST SLIDER: Ray Benge
BEST BASE STEALER OF ALL TIME: Ty Cobb
BEST BUNTER: Frank Frisch
BEST THROWING ARM OF ALL TIME: Chick Hafey
MOST KNOWLEDGEABLE BASEBALL BROADCASTERS: Franz Laux, Red Barber
BEST UMPIRE YOU EVER SAW: Bill Klem
TOUGHEST PITCHER YOU EVER BATTED AGAINST: Pat Malone
HITTER YOU FOUND THE HARDEST TO GET OUT: Paul Waner
BALL PLAYER WHO DID THE MOST TO INSPIRE HIS TEAM: Al Lopez
BEST TEAM OWNER YOU'VE EVER KNOWN: Phil Wrigley
BASEBALL WRITER WHO UNDERSTOOD THE GAME THE BEST: Roy Stockman

⚾ Bob Dillinger ⚾

1946-1949: St. Louis Browns; 1950: Philadelphia Athletics; 1950-1951: Pittsburgh Pirates; 1951: Chicago White Sox

Bob was a promising minor leaguer when World War II interrupted his career, but when he finally reached the majors he led the AL in stolen bases three times and in hits once. In a six-year career span, he never batted under .280 and played a fine third base. Dillinger hit safely in 27 straight games during his best season, 1948. Look at his stats. This man was underrated!

	AB	H	2B	3B	HR	R
LIFETIME	2904	888	123	47	10	401
BEST COMPOSITE YEAR	644	207	34	13	4	110

	RBI	BB	SB	BA	SLG.	OB%
LIFETIME	213	249	104	.306	.391	.361
BEST COMPOSITE YEAR	51	65	34	.324	.417	.384

ALL-TIME ALL-STAR TEAM 1

OUTFIELD: Joe DiMaggio, Ted Williams, Willie Mays **3B:** George Brett **SS:** Pee Wee Reese **2B:** Joe Gordon **1B:** Stan Musial **RH PITCHER:** Bob Lemon **LH PITCHER:** Hal Newhouser **CATCHER:** Johnny Bench **RELIEF PITCHER:** Goose Gossage

ALL-TIME ALL-STAR TEAM 2

OUTFIELD: Hank Aaron, Mickey Mantle, Roger Maris **3B:** Brooks Robinson **SS:** Vern Stephens **2B:** Nellie Fox **1B:** Mickey Vernon **RH PITCHER:** Don Drysdale **LH PITCHER:** Sandy Koufax **CATCHER:** Yogi Berra **RELIEF PITCHER:** None

BEST CLUTCH HITTER EVER: Stan Musial
BEST SS-2B DOUBLE-PLAY COMBINATION EVER: Joe Gordon-Lou Boudreau
GAME 7 WORLD SERIES PITCHER: Sandy Koufax
BEST MANAGER OF ALL TIME: Walter Alston
THE BEST TEAM: Yankees
FAVORITE STADIUM TO PLAY IN: Detroit or St. Louis
CITY WITH THE BEST FANS: Boston
DESIGNATED HITTER: Favor
BEST FASTBALL: Virgil Trucks
BEST CURVE: Hal Newhouser
BEST SPITBALL: Gaylord Perry
BEST BASE STEALER OF ALL TIME: Bob Dillinger
BEST BUNTER: Barney McCosky
MOST KNOWLEDGEABLE BASEBALL BROADCASTERS: Vin Scully, Red Barber
BEST UMPIRE YOU EVER SAW: Dusty Burgess

TOUGHEST PITCHER YOU EVER BATTED AGAINST: Virgil Trucks
BALL PLAYER WHO DID THE MOST TO INSPIRE HIS TEAM: Joe
   DiMaggio
BEST TEAM OWNER YOU'VE KNOWN: Tom Yawkey
**BASEBALL WRITER WHO UNDERSTOOD THE GAME THE
   BEST:** Kane (Sacramento)

⊘ Bobby Doerr ◎

1937-1944, 1946-1951: Boston Red Sox

A nine-time All-Star, Hall of Famer Bobby Doerr was excellent around second base, particularly on the double-play pivot, leading the American League five times despite competition from Joe Gordon in that department. Doerr was better than reliable with the glove, setting an AL record that stood for 30 years when he handled 414 consecutive chances without an error in 1948. He was good enough to bat fifth in a powerful Red Sox lineup that included Ted Williams, Vern Stephens, Dom DiMaggio, and Billy Goodman. Unfortunately for his future fame, those fine Bosox clubs won only one pennant, but in his only World Series, 1946, Doerr hit .409 in a losing cause. Bobby saw a lot as a player, and afterward he worked as a scout, coach, and minor-league instructor for the Red Sox. He is currently employed by the Toronto Blue Jays.

Doerr's selection of Ted Williams as the best clutch hitter is a bit of a pie in the face for the old Boston writers, who mercilessly maligned the Kid's performance when games were on the line. Also note Frank Shellenback as the best spitball artist; Doerr saw him in the Pacific Coast League on his way up.

	AB	H	2B	3B	HR	R
LIFETIME	7093	2042	381	89	223	1094
BEST COMPOSITE YEAR	604	173	37	11	27	103

	RBI	BB	SB	BA	SLG.	OB%
LIFETIME	1247	809	54	.288	.461	.361
BEST COMPOSITE YEAR	120	83	10	.325	.528	.399

ALL-TIME ALL-STAR TEAM 1

OUTFIELD: Ted Williams, Joe DiMaggio, Babe Ruth **3B:** Brooks Robinson **SS:** Joe Cronin **2B:** Charlie Gehringer **1B:** Lou Gehrig **RH PITCHER:** Bob Feller **LH PITCHER:** Lefty Grove **CATCHER:** Bill Dickey **RELIEF PITCHER:** Bruce Sutter

ALL-TIME ALL-STAR TEAM 2

OUTFIELD: Al Simmons, Stan Musial, Willie Mays **3B:** Pie Traynor **SS:** Honus Wagner **2B:** Rogers Hornsby **1B:** Jimmie Fox **RH PITCHER:** Dizzy Dean **LH PITCHER:** Sandy Koufax **CATCHER:** Mickey Cochrane **RELIEF PITCHER:** Goose Gossage

ALL-TIME DEFENSIVE TEAM

OUTFIELD: Joe DiMaggio, Willie Mays, Roberto Clemente **1B:** Ferris Fain **2B:** Charlie Gehringer **3B:** Brooks Robinson **SS:** Mark Balanger **RH PITCHER:** Robin Roberts **LH PITCHER:** Bobby Shantz **CATCHER:** Mickey Cochrane

BEST CLUTCH HITTER EVER: Ted Williams
BEST PINCH HITTER: Joe Cronin
BEST SS-2B DOUBLE-PLAY COMBINATION EVER: Lou Boudreau-Joe Gordon
GAME 7 WORLD SERIES PITCHER: Lefty Grove
BEST MANAGER OF ALL TIME: Joe McCarthy
THE BEST TEAM: Yankees
FAVORITE STADIUM TO PLAY IN: Fenway Park
CITY WITH THE BEST FANS: Boston
DESIGNATED HITTER: Favor
BEST FASTBALL: Lefty Grove
BEST CURVE: Cy Blanton
BEST SCREWBALL: Carl Hubbell
BEST SPITBALL: Frank Shellenback
BEST PICKOFF MOVE: Bill Wight
BEST SINKER/DROP: Mel Harder
BEST CHANGE-UP: Eddie Lopat
BEST SLIDER: Ron Guidry
BEST BASE STEALER OF ALL TIME: Rickey Henderson
BEST BUNTER: Phil Rizzuto
BEST THROWING ARM OF ALL TIME: Joe DiMaggio
MOST KNOWLEDGEABLE BASEBALL BROADCASTERS: Curt Gowdy, Vin Scully
BEST UMPIRE YOU EVER SAW: Bill McGowan
TOUGHEST PITCHER YOU EVER BATTED AGAINST: Bob Feller
BALL PLAYER WHO DID THE MOST TO INSPIRE HIS TEAM: Joe DiMaggio
BEST TEAM OWNER YOU'VE KNOWN: Tom Yawkey
BASEBALL WRITER WHO UNDERSTOOD THE GAME THE BEST: Grantland Rice

Pete Donohue

1921-1930: Cincinnati Reds; 1930-1931: N.Y. Giants; 1931: Cleveland Indians; 1932: Boston Red Sox

Pete Donohue is hardly remembered at all today, but during the twenties he was one of the premier pitchers in the National League, winning 20 or more games three times. Throwing a fine change-up, the big right-hander pitched mostly for some good Cincinnati clubs, but they were never quite good enough to win, probably the reason Pete's name doesn't come up much anymore. Twice he led the NL in games started and innings pitched, once each in shutouts, victories, and winning percentage, and his ERAs were usually among the league's best, as was his control. Notable among his selections is his second-team catcher, teammate Bubbles Hargrave, who hit over .300 six years in a row for the Reds, including a batting title in 1926 for his .353 mark.

National Baseball Library

Pete Donohue

	W-L	PCT.	ERA	G
LIFETIME	134-118	.532	3.87	344
BEST COMPOSITE YEAR	21-16	.667	3.08	47

	IP	H	BB	SO	SHO.
LIFETIME	2112	2439	422	571	16
BEST COMPOSITE YEAR	301			84	5

ALL-TIME ALL-STAR TEAM 1

OUTFIELD: Roberto Clemente, Willie Mays, Paul Waner **3B:** Brooks Robinson **SS:** Dave Concepcion **2B:** Eddie Collins **1B:** Bill Terry **RH PITCHER:** Walter Johnson **LH PITCHER:** Lefty Gomez **CATCHER:** Yogi Berra **RELIEF PITCHER:** Rich Gossage

ALL-TIME ALL-STAR TEAM 2

OUTFIELD: Al Simmons, Eddie Roush, Joe DiMaggio **3B:** Pie Traynor **SS:** Travis Jackson **2B:** Frankie Frisch **1B:** Jim Bottomley **RH PITCHER:** Don Drysdale **LH PITCHER:** Sandy Koufax **CATCHER:** Bubbles Hargrave **RELIEF PITCHER:** Grover Cleveland Alexander

ALL-TIME DEFENSIVE TEAM

OUTFIELD: JoJo Moore, Sam Rice, Ross Youngs **1B:** Jake Daubert **2B:** Frankie Frisch **3B:** Brooks Robinson **SS:** Charlie Hollocher **RH PITCHER:** Fred Fitzsimmons **LH PITCHER:** Eppa Rixey **CATCHER:** Ivey Wingo

MOST UNDERRATED BALL PLAYERS OF ALL TIME: Eddie Roush, Zack Wheat, Glenn Wright
BEST CLUTCH HITTER EVER: Paul Waner
BEST PINCH HITTER: Johnny Mize
BEST SS-2B DOUBLE-PLAY COMBINATION EVER: Dave Concepcion-Joe Morgan
GAME 7 WORLD SERIES PITCHER: Carl Hubbell
BEST MANAGER OF ALL TIME: John McGraw
THE BEST TEAM: The old Yankees
FAVORITE STADIUM TO PLAY IN: Redland Field, Cincinnati
CITY WITH THE BEST FANS: Cincinnati
DESIGNATED HITTER: Oppose
BEST FASTBALL: Walter Johnson

BEST CURVE: Dolf Luque
BEST SCREWBALL: Carl Hubbell
BEST SPITBALL: Bill Doak
BEST PICKOFF MOVE: Clarence Mitchell
BEST SINKER/DROP: Dolf Luque
BEST CHANGE-UP: Pete Donohue
BEST SLIDER: We didn't have one when I pitched
BEST BASE STEALER OF ALL TIME: Lou Brock
BEST BUNTER: Jake Daubert
BEST THROWING ARM OF ALL TIME: Bob Meusel
MOST KNOWLEDGEABLE BASEBALL BROADCASTERS: Waite Hoyt,
   Joe Garagiola
BEST UMPIRE YOU EVER SAW: Bill Klem
TOUGHEST PITCHER YOU EVER BATTED AGAINST: Carl Hubbell
HITTER YOU FOUND HARDEST TO GET OUT: Charlie Hollocher
BALL PLAYER WHO DID THE MOST TO INSPIRE HIS TEAM: Pete
   Donohue

⚾ Al Downing ⚾

1961-1969: N.Y. Yankees; 1970: Oakland Athletics-Milwaukee Brewers; 1971-1977: Los Angeles Dodgers

Al was a highly touted Yankee rookie who was accused of never living up to his potential. Yet he not only lasted 17 years in the big leagues, he shined in several campaigns. And let it not be forgotten that he played for some of the lousiest—no, *the* lousiest—Yankee teams in memory, carding ERAs in those years of 3.40, 3.56, 2.63, 3.52, and 3.38. In his best year, he went 20-9 with the L.A. Dodgers, less than two years after the Yanks let him go. As a rookie at New York, he garnered 171 strikeouts, seventh best in AL history for first-year men, and he wasn't called up till June.

Downing told us, "I feel it only fair to select players I have played with or against," so read his ballot with that in mind. It's very interesting, isn't it, to see someone rank Ken Boyer ahead of Mike Schmidt? Downing must have handled Mike pretty easily—or was it that Kenny hit a grand slam off Al in game four of the 1964 World Series, wiping out the Yanks' 3-0 lead in the fifth inning of a game that turned the tide in the Cards' favor? That kind of hitting a pitcher doesn't forget. And Downing was cruising along in that game, too. Note Downing's three nominees for "never living up to their potential": three Yankees from the dismal mid -and late sixties.

	W-L	PCT.	ERA	G
LIFETIME	123-07	.535	3.22	405
BEST COMPOSITE YEAR	20-14	.722	2.56	37

	IP	H	BB	SO	SHO.
LIFETIME	2268	1946	933	1639	24
BEST COMPOSITE YEAR	262			217	5

ALL-TIME ALL-STAR TEAM 1

OUTFIELD: Hank Aaron, Willie Mays, Roberto Clemente **3B:** Ken Boyer **SS:** Maury Wills **2B:** Joe Morgan **1B:** Willie McCovey **RH PITCHER:** Juan Marichal **LH PITCHER:** Sandy Koufax **CATCHER:** Elston Howard **RELIEF PITCHER:** Rollie Fingers

ALL-TIME ALL-STAR TEAM 2

OUTFIELD: Frank Robinson, Al Kaline, Mickey Mantle **3B:** Mike Schmidt **SS:** Luis Aparicio **2B:** Bill Mazeroski **1B:** Harmon Killebrew **RH PITCHER:** Bob Gibson **LH PITCHER:** Whitey Ford **CATCHER:** John Roseboro **RELIEF PITCHER:** Tug McGraw

ALL-TIME DEFENSIVE TEAM

OUTFIELD: Willie Mays, Roberto Clemente, Al Kaline **1B:** Keith Hernandez **2B:** Manny Trillo **3B:** Clete Boyer **SS:** Luis Aparicio **RH PITCHER:** Bob Gibson **LH PITCHER:** Jim Kaat **CATCHER:** Elston Howard

MOST UNDERRATED BALL PLAYERS OF ALL TIME: Elston Howard, Roberto Clemente, Jim Gilliam
BEST CLUTCH HITTER EVER: Hank Aaron
BEST PINCH HITTER: Manny Mota
BEST SS-2B DOUBLE-PLAY COMBINATION EVER: Dave Concepcion-Joe Morgan
GAME 7 WORLD SERIES PITCHER: Sandy Koufax/Bob Gibson
BEST MANAGER OF ALL TIME: Casey Stengel
THE BEST TEAM: 1961 Yankees
FAVORITE STADIUM TO PLAY IN: Yankee Stadium
CITY WITH THE BEST FANS: Los Angeles/New York
DESIGNATED HITTER: Oppose
BEST FASTBALL: Sandy Koufax
BEST CURVE: Sandy Koufax
BEST SCREWBALL: Luis Arroyo/Jim Brewer
BEST PICKOFF MOVE: Whitey Ford
BEST SINKER/DROP: Mel Stottlemyre
BEST CHANGE-UP: Al Downing/Andy Messersmith
BEST SLIDER: Bob Gibson

BEST BASE STEALER OF ALL TIME: Maury Wills
BEST BUNTER: Rod Carew
BEST THROWING ARM OF ALL TIME: Ollie Brown
MOST KNOWLEDGEABLE BASEBALL BROADCASTERS: Red Barber,
   Vin Scully
BEST UMPIRE YOU EVER SAW: Doug Harvey
BALL PLAYERS WHO NEVER PLAYED UP TO THEIR POTENTIAL:
   Joe Pepitone, Tom Tresh, Bill Stafford
HITTER YOU FOUND HARDEST TO GET OUT: Roberto Clemente
BALL PLAYER WHO DID THE MOST TO INSPIRE HIS TEAM: Maury
   Wills
BEST TEAM OWNER YOU'VE KNOWN: Dan Topping/Walter O'Malley
BASEBALL WRITER WHO UNDERSTOOD THE GAME THE BEST:
   Arthur Daley

⚾ Johnny Edwards ⚾

1961-1967: Cincinnati Reds; 1968: St. Louis Cardinals; 1969-1974: Houston
Astros

   This durable backstop holds the major-league record for most consecutive error-
less games by a catcher, 138. He is 22nd on the all-time list for most games caught,
and was behind the plate for two no-hitters, one by fastballer Jim Maloney of the
Reds and the other, the second of a back-to-back affair in 1968, by Ray Washburn
of the Cardinals, which followed Gaylord Perry's of the day before. Johnny was on
the NL All-Star team in 1963, '64, and '65, and led the Reds in hitting in their
World Series loss to the Yankees in 1961. Interesting, isn't it, that although
Edwards spent only one season in St. Louis before being traded to Houston, he
picks Augie Busch, the still-somewhat-active (as we write in spring 1986) owner
of the Redbirds, as the best owner he's encountered? As for his choice of Wrigley
Field to play in, could it be that has something to do with a very short backstop?

	AB	H	2B	3B	HR	R
LIFETIME	4577	1106	202	32	81	430
BEST COMPOSITE YEAR	496	128	28	6	17	52

	RBI	BB	SB	BA	SLG.	OB%
LIFETIME	524	465	15	.242	.353	.312
BEST COMPOSITE YEAR	67	53	2	.281	.474	.335

ALL-TIME ALL-STAR TEAM 1

OUTFIELD: Ted Williams, Henry Aaron, Babe Ruth **3B:** Eddie Mathews **SS:** Ernie Baaks **2B:** Pete Rose **1B:** Willie McCovey **RH PITCHER:** Bob Gibson **LH PITCHER:** Sandy Koufax **CATCHER:** Johnny Bench **RELIEF PITCHER:** Goose Gossage

ALL-TIME ALL-STAR TEAM 2

OUTFIELD: Roberto Clemente, Al Kaline, Mickey Mantle **3B:** Brooks Robinson **SS:** Pee Wee Reese **2B:** Nellie Fox **1B:** Eddie Murray **RH PITCHER:** Juan Marichal **LH PITCHER:** Whitey Ford **CATCHER:** Yogi Berra **RELIEF PITCHER:** Rollie Fingers

ALL-TIME DEFENSIVE TEAM

OUTFIELD: Willie Mays, Bill Virdon, Roberto Clemente **1B:** Keith Hernandez **2B:** Bill Mazeroski **3B:** Brooks Robinson **SS:** Ozzie Smith **RH PITCHER:** Bob Gibson **LH PITCHER:** Bobby Shantz **CATCHER:** Roy Campanella

MOST UNDERRATED BALL PLAYERS OF ALL TIME: Billy Williams, Willie McCovey
BEST CLUTCH HITTER EVER: Willie McCovey
BEST PINCH HITTER: Jerry Lynch
BEST *PURE* HITTER: Billy Williams
BEST SS-2B DOUBLE-PLAY COMBINATION EVER: Kessinger / Beckert
GAME 7 WORLD SERIES PITCHER: Bob Gibson
BEST MANAGER OF ALL TIME: Fred Hutchinson
THE BEST TEAM: 1961 Yankees
FAVORITE STADIUM TO PLAY IN: Wrigley Field
CITY WITH THE BEST FANS: Chicago
DESIGNATED HITTER: Oppose
BEST FASTBALL: Sandy Koufax
BEST CURVE: Sandy Koufax
BEST SCREWBALL: Elroy Face
BEST SPITBALL: Gaylord Perry
BEST PICKOFF MOVE: Roger Craig
BEST SINKER/DROP: Bruce Sutter
BEST CHANGE-UP: Stu Miller
BEST SLIDER: Bob Gibson
BEST BASE STEALER OF ALL TIME: Lou Brock
BEST BUNTER: Richie (Whitey) Ashburn
BEST HIT-AND-RUN MAN: Dick Groat
BEST THROWING ARM OF ALL TIME: Dave Parker
MOST KNOWLEDGEABLE BASEBALL BROADCASTERS: Harry Kalas
BEST UMPIRE YOU EVER SAW: Al Barlick
TOUGHEST PITCHER YOU EVER BATTED AGAINST: Juan Marichal

BALL PLAYER WHO DID THE MOST TO INSPIRE HIS TEAM: Frank
  Robinson
BEST TEAM OWNER YOU'VE KNOWN: Augie Busch
BASEBALL WRITER WHO UNDERSTOOD THE GAME THE BEST:
  Ritter Collett

⊘Carl Erskine⊘

1948-1959: Brooklyn (Los Angeles) Dodgers

In his 10 years in Brooklyn, Oisk never had a losing record, though he pitched
his whole career with a sore arm, which caused his retirement at the age of 32.
Erskine's ERAs look high through modern eyes, but they represent almost exactly
the league ERAs of his era. Furthermore, the Dodgers of those days led the NL in
runs scored annually, giving him the luxury of pitching with many big leads. And
last but not least, Ebbets Field was no pitchers' paradise.

Oisk finished 14 on the best curveball list, receiving six votes. Besides twirling
two no-hitters, his most memorable performance was the third game of the 1953
World Series, when he struck out 14 of the hated Yankees in a 3-2 victory, breaking
the Series strikeout record set in 1929 by Howard Ehmke. Later, of course, both
Sandy Koufax and Bob Gibson surpassed his mark.

Erskine confesses that in some cases he doesn't "have the strongest feelings
about my picks . . . there were just *so* many good players to choose from. The
hardest position was shortstop. I almost picked Dave Conception." We spoke to
Carl while he was at the Mayo Clinic "having an old hip injury checked out." The
conversation drifted. We asked him who'd be the next Babe Ruth. "No one." he
shot back. "Ruth's career hasn't *ever* been matched. Mantle was awesome, and
might have, except for injuries."

	W-L	PCT.	ERA	G
LIFETIME	122-78	.610	4.00	335
BEST COMPOSITE YEAR	20-15	.769	2.70	46

	IP	H	BB	SO	SHO
LIFETIME	1719	1637	646	981	14
BEST COMPOSITE YEAR	260			187	4

ALL-TIME ALL-STAR TEAM 1

OUTFIELD: Babe Ruth, Hank Aaron, Joe DiMaggio **3B:** Brooks Robinson **SS:**

Honus Wagner **2B:** Jackie Robinson **1B:** Lou Gehrig **RH PITCHER:** Cy Young **LH PITCHER:** Warren Spahn **CATCHER:** Roy Campanella **RELIEF PITCHER:** Hoyt Wilhelm

ALL-TIME ALL-STAR TEAM 2

OUTFIELD: Willie Mays, Mickey Mantle, Duke Snider **3B:** Eddie Mathews **SS:** Pee Wee Reese **2B:** Charlie Gehringer **1B:** Gil Hodges **RH PITCHER:** Walter Johnson **LH PITCHER:** Whitey Ford **CATCHER:** Yogi Berra **RELIEF PITCHER:** Ron Perranoski

ALL-TIME DEFENSIVE TEAM:

OUTFIELD: Tris Speaker, Ty Cobb, Willie Mays **1B:** Mickey Vernon **2B:** Nellie Fox **3B:** Brooks Robinson **SS:** Lou Boudreau **RH PITCHER:** Grover Alexander **LH PITCHER:** Warren Spahn **CATCHER:** Roy Campanella

MOST UNDERRATED BALL PLAYERS OF ALL TIME: Carl Furillo, Babe Herman
BEST PINCH HITTER: Babe Ruth
BEST *PURE* HITTER: Ted Williams
GAME 7 WORLD SERIES PITCHER: Lefty Gomez
THE BEST TEAM: 1927 Yankees
FAVORITE STADIUM TO PLAY IN: Ebbets Field
CITY WITH THE BEST FANS: Currently, Los Angeles
DESIGNATED HITTER: Oppose
BEST FASTBALL: Sandy Koufax
BEST CURVE: Sal Maglie
BEST SCREWBALL: Carl Hubbell
BEST SPITBALL: Preacher Roe
BEST SINKER/DROP: Clem Labine
BEST CHANGE-UP: Howie Pollet
BEST SLIDER: Robin Roberts
BEST BASE STEALER OF ALL TIME: Lou Brock
BEST BUNTER: Pee Wee Reese
BEST HIT-AND-RUN MAN: Alvin Dark
BEST THROWING ARM OF ALL TIME: Roberto Clemente
MOST KNOWLEDGEABLE BASEBALL BROADCASTERS: Ernie Harwell, Red Barber
BEST UMPIRE YOU EVER SAW: Al Barlick
TOUGHEST PITCHER YOU EVER BATTED AGAINST: Robin Roberts
HITTER YOU FOUND HARDEST TO GET OUT: Stan Musial
BALL PLAYER WHO DID THE MOST TO INSPIRE HIS TEAM: Jackie Robinson
BEST TEAM OWNER YOU'VE KNOWN: Walter O'Malley
BASEBALL WRITER WHO UNDERSTOOD THE GAME THE BEST: Dick Young

⊘ Tito Fuentes ⊗

1965-1974 San Francisco Giants; 1975-1976: San Diego Padres; 1977: Detroit Tigers; 1978: Oakland Athletics

After being brushed back once, the fine Cuban second baseman was heard to say angrily, "They shouldn't throw at me. I'm the father of five or six kids." An original hot dog, Fuentes had something to show off, and left baseball in a blaze of glory, with a .309 BA in his last full season (Tigers, 1977).

Tito's is a Hispanic-laden ballot, and worth a good look. Remember his nominee for best shortstop ever, Zoilo Versalles? We'll refresh your memory on him. Zoilo was the AL MVP in 1965, and in his career broke up *four* no-hitters. Good fielder, dangerous stick, surely underrated—as is Jose Cardenal, whom Tito names, along with Joe Rudi and himself, as the most underrated of all time. In an 18-year career, Cardenal collected 1,913 hits and a .275 BA.

	AB	H	2B	3B	HR	R
LIFETIME	5566	1491	211	46	45	610
BEST COMPOSITE YEAR	656	190	33	10	9	83

	RBI	BB	SB	BA	SLG.	OB%
LIFETIME	438	298	80	.268	.347	.305
BEST COMPOSITE YEAR	63	45	16	.309	.397	.349

ALL-TIME ALL-STAR TEAM 1

OUTFIELD: Roberto Clemente, Willie Mays, Mickey Mantle **3B:** Aurelio Rodriguez **SS:** Zoilo Versalles **2B:** Jackie Robinson **1B:** Orlando Cepeda **RH PITCHER:** Juan Marichal **LH PITCHER:** Sandy Koufax **CATCHER:** Roy Campanella **RELIEF PITCHER:** Mike Marshall

ALL-TIME ALL-STAR TEAM 2

OUTFIELD: Curt Flood, Paul Blair, Fred Lynn **3B:** Brooks Robinson **SS:** Luis Aparicio **2B:** Bill Mazeroski **1B:** Vic Power **RH PITCHER:** Bob Gibson **LH PITCHER:** Warren Spahn **CATCHER:** Steve Yeager **RELIEF PITCHER:** Jerry Johnson

ALL-TIME DEFENSIVE TEAM

OUTFIELD: Roberto Clemente, Paul Blair, Curt Flood **1B:** Vic Power **2B:** Jackie Robinson **3B:** Aurelio Rodriguez **SS:** Zoilo Versalles **RH PITCHER:** Bob Gibson **LH PITCHER:** Mike McCormick **CATCHER:** Roy Campanella

MOST UNDERRATED BALL PLAYERS OF ALL TIME: Jose Cardenal, Joe Rudi, Tito Fuentes
BEST CLUTCH HITTER EVER: Joe Rudi
BEST PINCH HITTER: Manny Mota
BEST SS-2B DOUBLE-PLAY COMBINATION EVER: Chris Speier-Tito Fuentes
GAME 7 WORLD SERIES PITCHER: Juan Marichal
BEST MANAGER OF ALL TIME: John McNamara
THE BEST TEAM: Brooklyn Dodgers
FAVORITE STADIUM TO PLAY IN: Chavez Ravine (Dodgers)
CITY WITH THE BEST FANS: Los Angeles (Dodgers)
DESIGNATED HITTER: Oppose
BEST FASTBALL: Nolan Ryan
BEST CURVE: Sandy Koufax
BEST SCREWBALL: Mike Cuellar
BEST SPITBALL: Gaylord Perry
BEST PICKOFF MOVE: Luis Tiant
BEST SINKER/DROP: Al McBean
BEST CHANGE-UP: Andy Messersmith
BEST SLIDER: Fergie Jenkins
BEST BASE STEALER OF ALL TIME: Lou Brock
BEST BUNTER: Rod Carew/Tito Fuentes
BEST THROWING ARM OF ALL TIME: Roberto Clemente
MOST KNOWLEDGEABLE BASEBALL BROADCASTERS: Vin Scully
BEST UMPIRE YOU EVER SAW: Doug Harvey
BALL PLAYERS WHO NEVER PLAYED UP TO THEIR POTENTIAL: Ken Henderson, Chris Speier
TOUGHEST PITCHER YOU EVER BATTED AGAINST: Dock Ellis/Andy Messersmith
BALL PLAYER WHO DID THE MOST TO INSPIRE HIS TEAM: Maury Wills
BEST TEAM OWNER YOU'VE KNOWN: Horace Stoneham
BASEBALL WRITER WHO UNDERSTOOD THE GAME THE BEST: None

Charlie Gehringer

1924-1942: Detroit Tigers

Detroit Tigers

Charlie Gehringer

The players' choice as the #1 second baseman of all-time, Charlie was called "the Mechanical Man" because he did everything that can be done on a ball field with no apparent effort—sort of the Joe DiMaggio of second-sackers. His accomplishments? Just for starters, at various times he led the AL in hits, doubles, triples, batting average, runs scored, stolen bases, pinch hits, putouts, assists, double plays, and fielding average.

The only active (or anywhere near active) player to make Gehringer's list is Wade Boggs as the best clutch hitter. More important, Charlie's authoritative voice puts Rogers Hornsby over Eddie Collins at the keystone sack.

	AB	H	2B	3B	HR	R
LIFETIME	8860	2839	574	146	184	1774
BEST COMPOSITE YEAR	641	227	60	19	20	144

	RBI	BB	SB	BA	SLG.	OB%
LIFETIME	1427	1185	182	.320	.480	.401
BEST COMPOSITE YEAR	127	112	28	.371	.555	.457

ALL-TIME ALL-STAR TEAM 1

OUTFIELD: Ty Cobb, Tris Speaker, Harry Heilmann or Babe Ruth **3B:** Pie Traynor **SS:** Lou Boudreau **2B:** Rogers Hornsby **1B:** Lou Gehrig **RH PITCHER:** Bob Feller **LH PITCHER:** Lefty Grove **CATCHER:** Mickey Cochrane

ALL-TIME ALL-STAR TEAM 2

OUTFIELD: Ted Williams, Joe DiMaggio, Babe Ruth or Harry Heilmann **3B:** Jimmie Foxx **SS:** Pee Wee Reese **2B:** Eddie Collins **1B:** Hank Greenberg **RH PITCHER:** Walter Johnson **LH PITCHER:** Lefty Gomez **CATCHER:** Bill Dickey

ALL-TIME DEFENSIVE TEAM:

OUTFIELD: Joe DiMaggio **1B:** Joe Judge **2B:** Nellie Fox **SS:** Pee Wee Reese

MOST UNDERRATED BALL PLAYERS OF ALL TIME: Too many to count
BEST CLUTCH HITTER EVER: Wade Boggs
BEST *PURE* HITTER: Ted Williams
GAME 7 WORLD SERIES PITCHER: Lefty Grove
BEST MANAGER OF ALL TIME: Connie Mack
THE BEST TEAM: Yankees (late 1920s)
FAVORITE STADIUM TO PLAY IN: Yankee Stadium

CITY WITH THE BEST FANS: Boston
DESIGNATED HITTER: Favor
BEST FASTBALL: Lefty Grove
BEST CURVE: Tommy Bridges
BEST SCREWBALL: Didn't hit at many
BEST SPITBALL: Red Faber
BEST PICKOFF MOVE: Bill Wight
BEST SINKER/DROP: Johnny Allen
BEST CHANGE-UP: Several
BEST SLIDER: Did not use in my day
BEST BASE STEALER OF ALL TIME: So many nowadays
MOST KNOWLEDGEABLE BASEBALL BROADCASTERS: Ernie
   Harwell, Mel Allen
**BALL PLAYERS WHO NEVER PLAYED UP TO THEIR POTEN-
TIAL:** No way to tell
TOUGHEST PITCHER YOU EVER BATTED AGAINST: Already
   mentioned
BALL PLAYER WHO DID THE MOST TO INSPIRE HIS TEAM: Usually
   every team had one or two

⊘ Gary Gentry ⊗

1969-1972: N.Y. Mets; 1973-1975: Atlanta Braves

One of the "Miracle Mets" of 1969, Gentry was one of the most highly touted college pitchers ever, and another in a slew of superb young pitching prospects the Mets produced. He never lived up to his potential—he mentions this in his survey—but still played a key role in the Mets' stunning performance in '69, pitching them to the divisional title-clinching game, and throwing a masterful game in the World Series against the bewildered Baltimore Orioles. Study his lifetime record below.

What hitter did Gentry find toughest to get out? "None," he says. The guy was talented, brash—like the Mets of '69.

	W-L	PCT.	ERA	G
LIFETIME	46-49	.484	3.56	157
BEST COMPOSITE YEAR	13-12	.520	1.29	35

	IP	H	BB	SO	SHO.
LIFETIME	902.2	770	369	615	8
BEST COMPOSITE YEAR	233.2			155	3

ALL-TIME ALL-STAR TEAM 1

OUTFIELD: Babe Ruth, Willie Mays, Ted Williams **3B:** Mike Schmidt **SS:** Ozzie Smith **2B:** Joe Morgan **1B:** Willie McCovey **RH PITCHER:** Bob Gibson **LH PITCHER:** Sandy Koufax **CATCHER:** Johnny Bench **RELIEF PITCHER:** Joe Page

ALL-TIME ALL-STAR TEAM 2

OUTFIELD: Joe DiMaggio, Hank Aaron, Roberto Clemente/Mickey Mantle **3B:** Brooks Robinson **SS:** Robin Yount **2B:** Lou Boudreau **1B:** Lou Gehrig **RH PITCHER:** Bob Feller **LH PITCHER:** Steve Carlton **CATCHER:** Yogi Berra/ Roy Campanella

ALL-TIME DEFENSIVE TEAM:

OUTFIELD: Roberto Clemente, Gary Maddox, Willie Mays **1B:** Mike Jorgensen **2B:** Willie Randolph **3B:** Brooks Robinson **SS:** Ozzie Smith **RH PITCHER:** Bob Gibson **LH PITCHER:** Ron Guidry **CATCHER:** Jerry Grote

MOST UNDERRATED BALL PLAYERS OF ALL TIME: Tony Perez
BEST CLUTCH HITTER EVER: Pete Rose
BEST PINCH HITTER: Manny Mota/Smoky Burgess
BEST SS-2B DOUBLE-PLAY COMBINATION EVER: Marty Marion-Red Schoendienst
GAME 7 WORLD SERIES PITCHER: Bob Gibson
BEST MANAGER OF ALL TIME: John McGraw
THE BEST TEAM: 1950s Yankees
FAVORITE STADIUM TO PLAY IN: Any of the older parks
CITY WITH THE BEST FANS: New York
DESIGNATED HITTER: Oppose
BEST FASTBALL: Nolan Ryan
BEST CURVE: Sandy Koufax
BEST SCREWBALL: Juan Marichal
BEST SPITBALL: Gaylord Perry
BEST PICKOFF MOVE: Tippy Martinez
BEST CHANGE-UP: Stu Miller
BEST SLIDER: Bob Gibson
BEST BASE STEALER OF ALL TIME: Lou Brock
BEST BUNTER: Mickey Mantle
BEST THROWING ARM OF ALL TIME: Roberto Clemente
MOST KNOWLEDGEABLE BASEBALL BROADCASTERS: Vin Scully, Red Barber
BEST UMPIRE YOU EVER SAW: Augie Donatelli/Jocko Conlan

**BALL PLAYERS WHO NEVER PLAYED UP TO THEIR POTEN-
TIAL:** Dave Kingman, Cleon Jones, myself
TOUGHEST PITCHER YOU EVER BATTED AGAINST: Bob Gibson
HITTER YOU FOUND HARDEST TO GET OUT: None
BALL PLAYER WHO DID THE MOST TO INSPIRE HIS TEAM: Willie
Stargell
BEST TEAM OWNER YOU'VE KNOWN: Joan Payson
**BASEBALL WRITER WHO UNDERSTOOD THE GAME THE
BEST:** Milt Richman

Mike Hargrove

1974-1978: Texas Rangers; 1979: San Diego Padres; 1979-present: Cleveland Indians

If nothing else, Mike Hargrove will go down in baseball history as the kid who broke into the bigs the same year George Brett did—and beat Brett out for AL Rookie of the Year. Through 1984, this world-class time-waster at the plate (some call him "the human rain delay") had a lifetime BA of .290, though he's dipped the past few years, perhaps because he plays in the game's dreariest city and stadium. That's bound to depress a fellow. Four times, incidentally, Mike has collected over 100 walks. And he's no power hitter, either. He walks every 6.7 times he comes to the plate, and if the Indian first baseman keeps up that pace, he'll be in the record books. He also has a shot at 2,000 hits: that batting eye should keep him in the game for a time as a DH.

	AB	H	2B	3B	HR	R
LIFETIME	5564	1614	266	28	80	783
BEST COMPOSITE YEAR	589	179	30	6	18	98

	RBI	BB	SB	BA	SLG.	OB%
LIFETIME	686	965	24	.290	.391	.396
BEST COMPOSITE YEAR	85	111	5	.323	.476	.424

ALL-TIME ALL-STAR TEAM 1

OUTFIELD: Ted Williams, Willie Mays, Babe Ruth **3B:** Brooks Robinson **SS:** Luis Aparicio **2B:** Bobby Richardson **1B:** Lou Gehrig **RH PITCHER:** Bob Feller **LH PITCHER:** Sandy Koufax **RELIEF PITCHER:** Rollie Fingers

ALL-TIME ALL-STAR TEAM 2

OUTFIELD: Joe DiMaggio, Mickey Mantle, Frank Robinson **3B:** Eddie Mathews **SS:** Lou Boudreau **2B:** Bill Mazeroski **1B:** Gil McDougald **RH PITCHER:** Gaylord Perry **LH PITCHER:** Whitey Ford **CATCHER:** Yogi Berra **RELIEF PITCHER:** Sparky Lyle

ALL-TIME DEFENSIVE TEAM:

OUTFIELD: Willie Mays, Joe DiMaggio, Dwight Evans **1B:** Wes Parker **2B:** Bobby Richardson **3B:** Brooks Robinson **SS:** Lou Boudreau **RH PITCHER:** Fergie Jenkins **LH PITCHER:** Jim Kaat **CATCHER:** Roy Campanella

MOST UNDERRATED BALL PLAYERS OF ALL TIME: Joe Rudi, Toby Harrah, Eddie Murray
BEST CLUTCH HITTER EVER: Thurman Munson
BEST PINCH HITTER: Gates Brown
BEST SS-2B DOUBLE-PLAY COMBINATION EVER: Tony Kubek-Bobby Richardson
GAME 7 WORLD SERIES PITCHER: Don Drysdale
BEST MANAGER OF ALL TIME: Earl Weaver
THE BEST TEAM: Yankees
FAVORITE STADIUM TO PLAY IN: Anaheim Stadium, L.A.
CITY WITH THE BEST FANS: Boston
BEST FASTBALL: Nolan Ryan
BEST CURVE: Bert Blyleven
BEST SCREWBALL: Mike Marshall
BEST SPITBALL: Gaylord Perry
BEST PICKOFF MOVE: Bob McClure
BEST SINKER/DROP: Bruce Sutter
BEST CHANGE-UP: Andy Messersmith
BEST BASE STEALER OF ALL TIME: Rickey Henderson
BEST BUNTER: Rod Carew
BEST THROWING ARM OF ALL TIME: Rocky Colavito
MOST KNOWLEDGEABLE BASEBALL BROADCASTERS: Lindsay Nelson, Jack Buck
BEST UMPIRE YOU EVER SAY: Nestor Chylak
TOUGHEST PITCHER YOU EVER BATTED AGAINST: Ron Guidry
BEST TEAM OWNER YOU'VE KNOWN: Brad Corbett

⚾ Babe Herman ⚾

1926-1931: Brooklyn Dodgers; 1932: Cincinnati Reds; 1933-1934: Chicago Cubs; 1935: Pittsburgh Pirates; 1935-1936: Cincinnati Reds; 1937: Detroit Tigers; 1945: Brooklyn Dodgers

You can say what you want about Babe's fielding and baserunning antics, but he sure could belt out extra-base hits. Including a short-lived return to Flatbush in 1945, he slugged .532 lifetime, 23rd best in baseball history. He hit for the cycle three times in one year, 1931, and no other National Leaguer has *ever* done that.

In his selections note that Babe, the original DH, rejects that newfangled gimmick. His choice of Johnny Frederick as underrated highlights the fact that Frederick holds the all-time rookie record of 52 doubles. Herman also chooses Frederick as the best pinch hitter; Johnny hit .306 lifetime in that capacity.

	AB	H	2B	3B	HR	R
LIFETIME	5603	1818	399	110	181	882
BEST COMPOSITE YEAR	614	241	48	19	35	143

	RBI	BB	SB	BA	SLG.	OB%
LIFETIME	997	520	94	.324	.532	.382
BEST COMPOSITE YEAR	130	66	21	.393	.678	.451

ALL-TIME ALL-STAR TEAM 1

OUTFIELD: Ty Cobb, Babe Ruth, Ted Williams **3B:** Pie Traynor **SS:** Travis Jackson **2B:** Rogers Hornsby **1B:** Lou Gehrig **RH PITCHER:** Grover Cleveland Alexander **LH PITCHER:** Carl Hubbell **CATCHER:** Gabby Hartnett **RELIEF PITCHER:** Carl Hubbell

ALL-TIME ALL-STAR TEAM 2

OUTFIELD: Joe DiMaggio, Mickey Mantle, Willie Mays **3B:** Brooks Robinson **SS:** Pee Wee Reese **2B:** Charlie Gehringer **1B:** Bill Terry **RH PITCHER:** Walter Johnson **LH PITCHER:** Lefty Grove/Sandy Koufax **CATCHER:** Bill Dickey **RELIEF PITCHER:** Firpo Marberry

ALL-TIME DEFENSIVE TEAM

OUTFIELD: Joe DiMaggio, Mickey Mantle, Willie Mays **1B:** Bill Terry **2B:** Charlie Gehringer **3B:** Pie Traynor **SS:** Billy Jurges **RH PITCHER:** Fred Fitzsimmons **CATCHER:** Al Lopez

MOST UNDERRATED BALL PLAYERS OF ALL TIME: Johnny Frederick
BEST PINCH HITTER: Johnny Frederick
BEST SS-2B DOUBLE-PLAY COMBINATION EVER: Gordon-Rizzuto
GAME 7 WORLD SERIES PITCHER: Carl Hubbell

BEST MANAGER OF ALL TIME: Joe McCarthy
THE BEST TEAM: Yankees
FAVORITE STADIUM TO PLAY IN: Brooklyn
CITY WITH THE BEST FANS: Brooklyn/Detroit
DESIGNATED HITTER: Oppose
BEST FASTBALL: Walter Johnson
BEST CURVE: Dolf Luque
BEST SCREWBALL: Carl Hubbell
BEST SPITBALL: Burleigh Grimes/Red Faber
BEST PICKOFF MOVE: Roy Joiner
BEST SINKER/DROP: Hal Schumacher
BEST CHANGE-UP: Dizzy Dean
BEST BASE STEALER OF ALL TIME: Max Carey/Ty Cobb
BEST BUNTER: Travis Jackson
BEST THROWING ARM OF ALL TIME: Bob Meusel
MOST KNOWLEDGEABLE BASEBALL BROADCASTERS: Vin Scully
BEST UMPIRE YOU EVER SAW: Bill Klem
BALL PLAYERS WHO NEVER PLAYED UP TO THEIR POTEN-TIAL: Harvey Hendrick
TOUGHEST PITCHER YOU EVER BATTED AGAINST: Wild Bill Hallahan
BALL PLAYER WHO DID THE MOST TO INSPIRE HIS TEAM: Mickey Cochrane
BEST TEAM OWNER YOU'VE KNOWN: Sid Weil/now, Walter O'Malley
BASEBALL WRITER WHO UNDERSTOOD THE GAME THE BEST: Grantland Rice

⚾ Monte Irvin ⚾

1949-1955: N.Y. Giants; 1956: Chicago Cubs

This is one of the most interesting ballots, coming from a true expert on the Negro Leagues and indeed, on the National and American as well. It has often been contended, and it makes sense, that many of the superstars before Jackie Robinson would not have been quite so statistically impressive had black men been playing. After all, if the 25 worst white players were replaced by the 25 best black players, the level of competition would rise dramatically. This doesn't mean that Babe Ruth wouldn't have been the greatest slugger ever if he had to face Satchel Paige, Smokey Joe Williams, and Slim Jones. But it does mean he would have struck out several more times.

Note that Monte gives the nod to his old skipper Leo Durocher, and also that the chooses Roy Campanella over the legendary Josh Gibson.

	AB	H	2B	3B	HR	R
LIFETIME	2499	731	97	31	99	366
BEST COMPOSITE YEAR	558	174	21	11	24	94

	RBI	BB	SB	BA	SLG.	OB%
LIFETIME	443	351	28	.293	.475	.380
BEST COMPOSITE YEAR	121	89	12	.329	.541	.406

National Baseball Library

New York Giant Monte Irvin touches home after a three-run blast against the Pittsburgh Pirates during the stretch run in 1952. Welcoming committee: Whitey Lockman (25), Alvin Dark (19), and Bobby Thomson (23).

ALL-TIME ALL-STAR TEAM 1

OUTFIELD: Babe Ruth, Willie Mays, Joe DiMaggio **3B:** Brooks Robinson **SS:** Honus Wagner **2B:** Charlie Gehringer **1B:** Lou Gehrig **RH PITCHER:** Bob Feller **LH PITCHER:** Sandy Koufax **CATCHER:** Roy Campanella **RELIEF PITCHER:** Joe Page

ALL-TIME ALL-STAR TEAM 2

OUTFIELD: Cool Papa Bell, Martin Dihigo, Clint Thomas **3B:** Ray Dandridge **SS:** Willie Wells **2B:** Sammy T. Hughes **1B:** Buck Leonard **RH PITCHER:** Smokey Joe Williams **LH PITCHER:** Slim Jones **CATCHER:** Josh Gibson **RELIEF PITCHER:** Hilton Smith

ALL-TIME DEFENSIVE TEAM

OUTFIELD: Willie Mays, Joe DiMaggio, Hank Aaron **1B:** Gil Hodges **2B:** Jackie Robinson **3B:** Brooks Robinson **SS:** Marty Marion **RH PITCHER:** Gary Nolan **LH PITCHER:** Bobby Shantz **CATCHER:** Roy Campanella

MOST UNDERRATED BALL PLAYERS OF ALL TIME: Gene Woodling, Cecil Travis, Ned Garver
BEST CLUTCH HITTER EVER: Stan Musial
BEST PINCH HITTER: Manny Mota
BEST SS-2B DOUBLE-PLAY COMBINATION EVER: Pee Wee Reese-Jackie Robinson
GAME 7 WORLD SERIES PITCHER: Bob Gibson
BEST MANAGER OF ALL TIME: Leo Durocher
THE BEST TEAM: 1931 Philadelphia Athletics
FAVORITE STADIUM TO PLAY IN: Wrigley Field (Chicago)
CITY WITH THE BEST FANS: Los Angeles
BEST FASTBALL: Satchel Paige
BEST CURVE: Camilo Pascual
BEST SCREWBALL: Carl Hubbell
BEST SPITBALL: Burleigh Grimes
BEST PICKOFF MOVE: Billy Pierce
BEST SINKER/DROP: Bruce Sutter
BEST CHANGE-UP: Carl Erskine
BEST BASE STEALER OF ALL TIME: Rickey Henderson
BEST BUNTER: Phil Rizzuto
BEST THROWING ARM OF ALL TIME: Roberto Clemente
MOST KNOWLEDGEABLE BASEBALL BROADCASTERS: Red Barber, Vin Scully

BEST UMPIRE YOU EVER SAW: Bill Klem
**BALL PLAYERS WHO NEVER PLAYED UP TO THEIR POTEN-
TIAL:** Clint Hartung, Dave Nicholson, Earl Williams
TOUGHEST PITCHER YOU EVER BATTED AGAINST: Ewell Blackwell
BALL PLAYER WHO DID THE MOST TO INSPIRE HIS TEAM: Jackie
Robinson
BEST TEAM OWNER YOU'VE KNOWN: Tom Yawkey and Horace
Stoneham
**BASEBALL WRITER WHO UNDERSTOOD THE GAME THE
BEST:** Fred Lieb

⚾ Larry Jansen ⚾

1947-1954: N.Y. Giants; 1956: Cincinnati Reds

As a 27-year-old rookie in 1947, Larry Jansen went 21-5 for the Giants, establishing himself as the ace of the staff, which he was for five years. He received seven votes (including his own) for throwing the best slider ever, and was also known for his pinpoint control. Jansen led the major leagues with five shutouts in 1950 and won 23 games for the pennant-winning Giants of 1951, once again topping all pitchers that year.

	W-L	PCT.	ERA	G
LIFETIME	122-89	.578	3.58	291
BEST COMPOSITE YEAR	23-16	.808	3.01	42

	IP	H	BB	SO	SHO.
LIFETIME	1767	1751	410	842	17
BEST COMPOSITE YEAR	278			161	5

ALL-TIME ALL-STAR TEAM 1

OUTFIELD: Hank Aaron, Willie Mays, Bob Thomson/Ted Williams **3B:** George Brett **SS:** Phil Rizzuto **2B:** Jackie Robinson **1B:** Gil Hodges **RH PITCHER:** Larry Jansen/Bob Gibson **LH PITCHER:** Sandy Koufax **CATCHER:** Roy Campanella **RELIEF PITCHER:** Hoyt Wilhelm

ALL-TIME ALL-STAR TEAM 2

OUTFIELD: Roberto Clemente, Joe DiMaggio, Dale Murphy **SS:** Pee Wee Reese **2B:** Pete Rose/Red Schoendienst **1B:** Stan Musial **RH PITCHER:** Juan Marichal **LH PITCHER:** Warren Spahn **CATCHER:** Bill Dickey **RELIEF PITCHER:** Rollie Fingers

ALL-TIME DEFENSIVE TEAM

OUTFIELD: Roberto Clemente, Willie Mays, Joe DiMaggio **1B:** Frank McCormick **2B:** Jackie Robinson **3B:** Brooks Robinson **SS:** Phil Rizzuto **RH PITCHER:** Larry Jansen/Bob Gibson **LH PITCHER:** Bobby Shantz **CATCHER:** Wes Westrum/Ray Mueller

MOST UNDERRATED BALL PLAYERS OF ALL TIME: Larry Jansen
BEST CLUTCH HITTER EVER: Joe DiMaggio/Stan Musial
BEST PINCH HITTER: Smoky Burgess
BEST SS-2B DOUBLE-PLAY COMBINATION EVER: Pee Wee Reese-
  Jackie Robinson
GAME 7 WORLD SERIES PITCHER: Sandy Koufax
BEST MANAGER OF ALL TIME: Leo Durocher
THE BEST TEAM: 1951 Giants
FAVORITE STADIUM TO PLAY IN: Dodger Stadium
CITY WITH THE BEST FANS: Los Angeles
DESIGNATED HITTER: Oppose
BEST FASTBALL: Nolan Ryan/Jim Maloney
BEST CURVE: Tommy Bridges
BEST SCREWBALL: Carl Hubbell
BEST SPITBALL: Gaylord Perry
BEST SINKER/DROP: Frank Linzy
BEST CHANGE-UP: Johnny Podres
BEST SLIDER: Larry Jansen
BEST BASE STEALER OF ALL TIME: Lou Brock
BEST BUNTER: Eddie Stanky
BEST THROWING ARM OF ALL TIME: Willie Mays
MOST KNOWLEDGEABLE BASEBALL BROADCASTERS: Howard
  Cosell, Ernie Harwell
BEST UMPIRE YOU EVER SAW: Doug Harvey
TOUGHEST PITCHER YOU EVER BATTED AGAINST: Ewell Blackwell
HITTER YOU FOUND HARDEST TO GET OUT: Hank Greenberg
BALL PLAYER WHO DID THE MOST TO INSPIRE HIS TEAM: Alvin
  Dark
BEST TEAM OWNER YOU'VE KNOWN: Phil Wrigley
**BASEBALL WRITER WHO UNDERSTOOD THE GAME THE
  BEST:** Dick Young

⬤ Buck Jordan ⬤

1927, 1929: N.Y. Giants; 1931: Washington Senators; 1932-1937: Boston Braves; 1937-1938: Cincinnati Reds-Philadelphia Phillies

Buck Jordan wants his opinion known: "I think artificial turf is the worst thing ever brought into baseball and all of it should be torn out." We don't know, Buck, is it worse than Fredbird?

Besides good batting averages and fine glove work, Jordan holds a claim to fame for twice hammering out eight hits in a doubleheader.

Jordan's choice of Dave Harris as the best pinch hitter deserves special attention. Harris, a right-handed-hitting outfielder for the Braves and Senators in the 1930s, posted a lifetime average of .310 coming off the bench in 129 at bats. Despite this and also leading the American League in pinch hits in 1935, only one other player chose him.

	AB	H	2B	3B	HR	R
LIFETIME	2980	890	153	35	17	396
BEST COMPOSITE YEAR	588	179	29	9	5	81

	RBI	BB	SB	BA	SLG.	OB%
LIFETIME	281	182	20	.299	.391	.339
BEST COMPOSITE YEAR	66	45	6	.323	.432	.373

ALL-TIME ALL-STAR TEAM 1

OUTFIELD: Babe Ruth, Ty Cobb, Tris Speaker **3B:** Pie Traynor **SS:** Joe Cronin **2B:** Rogers Hornsby **1B:** Lou Gehrig **RH PITCHER:** Walter Johnson **LH PITCHER:** Carl Hubbell **CATCHER:** Mickey Cochrane **RELIEF PITCHER:** Fred Marberry

ALL-TIME ALL-STAR TEAM 2

OUTFIELD: Willie Mays, Joe DiMaggio, Stan Musial **3B:** Ossie Bluege **SS:** Leo Durocher **2B:** Frankie Frisch **1B:** Bill Terry **RH PITCHER:** Dizzy Dean **LH PITCHER:** Lefty Grove **CATCHER:** Gabby Hartnett **RELIEF PITCHER:** Goose Gossage

ALL-TIME DEFENSIVE TEAM:

OUTFIELD: Willie Mays, Joe DiMaggio, Lloyd Waner **1B:** Bill Terry **2B:** Billy Herman **3B:** Ossie Bluege **SS:** Leo Durocher **RH PITCHER:** Fred Fitzsimmons **LH PITCHER:** Carl Hubbell **CATCHER:** Al Lopez

MOST UNDERRATED BALL PLAYERS OF ALL TIME: Ernie Lombardi, Pinkey Whitney, Baxter Jordan
BEST CLUTCH HITTER EVER: Lou Gehrig

BEST PINCH HITTER: Dave Harris

BEST SS-2B DOUBLE-PLAY COMBINATION EVER: Frankie Frisch-Leo Durocher

GAME 7 WORLD SERIES PITCHER: Walter Johnson

BEST MANAGER OF ALL TIME: John McGraw

THE BEST TEAM: 1929 Yankees

FAVORITE STADIUM TO PLAY IN: Sportsman's Park (St. Louis)

CITY WITH THE BEST FANS: Boston

DESIGNATED HITTER: Oppose

BEST FASTBALL: Walter Johnson

BEST CURVE: Dazzy Vance

BEST SCREWBALL: Carl Hubbell

BEST SPITBALL: Burleigh Grimes

BEST PICKOFF MOVE: Ed Brandt

BEST SINKER/DROP: Hal Schumacher

BEST CHANGE-UP: Dizzy Dean

BEST SLIDER: Van Mungo

BEST BASE STEALER OF ALL TIME: Ty Cobb

BEST BUNTER: Travis Jackson

BEST THROWING ARM OF ALL TIME: Gabby Hartnett

MOST KNOWLEDGEABLE BASEBALL BROADCASTERS: Red Barber, Dizzy Dean

BEST UMPIRE YOU EVER SAW: Bill Klem

BALL PLAYERS THAT NEVER PLAYED UP TO THEIR POTEN-TIAL: Baxter Jordan, Lou Riggs

TOUGHEST PITCHER YOU EVER BATTED AGAINST: Van Mungo

BALL PLAYER WHO DID THE MOST TO INSPIRE HIS TEAM: Mickey Cochrane

BEST TEAM OWNER YOU'VE KNOWN: Felix Hyman (Charlotte, N.C.)

BASEBALL WRITER WHO UNDERSTOOD THE GAME THE BEST: Paul Shannon

⚾ George Kelly ⚾

1915-1926: N.Y. Giants (1917: Pittsburgh Pirates, eight games); 1927-1930: Cincinnati Reds; 1930-1931: Chicago Cubs; 1932: Brooklyn Dodgers

Recently deceased Hall of Famer "Highpockets" Kelly played his first game for the New York Giants in 1915 and remained active as a player and coach until 1948. He was one of the few survey respondents who could rightly claim to have "seen 'em all," and he viewed the game from the vantage point of one of the top sluggers of his time.

National Baseball Library

George "Highpockets" Kelly

Feared in the clutch, Kelly was the top RBI man in the NL twice and hit nine grand slams during his career, which is tremendous (and *real* clutch hitting) for a man with only 148 homers (he was a dead-ball era slugger in the beginning, remember). Five times he drove in over 100 runs, seven times he hit over .300, and once he led the league in home runs. Kelly was also known for his rifle arm, unusual for a first sacker, though he did play second base and the outfield as well. A *very* unusual aspect of his record on defense is that he was shifted from first, briefly, to second base, in the middle of his career, instead of the other way around as is more typical.

Kelly takes an old-timer's view of the greats, with Warren Spahn the most recent player on his ballot, which was filled out in 1983. It is interesting that he considered Spahn superior to Carl Hubbell, whose name would look more natural on this team, but King Carl did get the nod from Highpockets as the best screwballer. Another interesting choice here is Ernie Lombardi at catcher; Kelly saw him play every day when he coached for the Reds in 1935-37.

By the way, when we asked George what city had the best fans, he had this unromantic reply: "A winner."

	AB	H	2B	3B	HR	R
LIFETIME	5993	1778	337	76	148	819
BEST COMPOSITE YEAR	592	194	45	11	23	96

	RBI	BB	SB	BA	SLG.	OB%
LIFETIME	1020	65	65	.297	.451	.339
BEST COMPOSITE YEAR	136	47	14	.328	.531	.366

ALL-TIME ALL-STAR TEAM 1

OUTFIELD: Ty Cobb, Babe Ruth, Tris Speaker **3B:** Pie Traynor **SS:** Honus Wagner **2B:** Frank Frisch **1B:** George Sisler **RH PITCHER:** Walter Johnson **LH PITCHER:** Lefty Grove **CATCHER:** Ernie Lombardi

ALL-TIME ALL-STAR TEAM 2

RH PITCHER: Grover Cleveland Alexander **LH PITCHER:** Warren Spahn

MOST UNDERRATED BALL PLAYERS OF ALL TIME: Glenn Wright
BEST CLUTCH HITTER EVER: John Mize
BEST PINCH HITTER: Red Lucas
GAME 7 WORLD SERIES PITCHER: Grover Cleveland Alexander
BEST MANAGER OF ALL TIME: John J. McGraw
THE BEST TEAM: New York Giants
FAVORITE STADIUM TO PLAY IN: Polo Grounds
DESIGNATED HITTER: Oppose
BEST FASTBALL: Walter Johnson
BEST CURVE: Dazzy Vance
BEST SCREWBALL: Carl Hubbell
BEST SPITBALL: Burleigh Grimes
BEST PICKOFF MOVE: Sherry Smith
BEST CHANGE-UP: Bill Sherdel
BEST BASE STEALER OF ALL TIME: Ty Cobb
BEST BUNTER: Travis Jackson
BEST THROWING ARM OF ALL TIME: Chick Hafey
MOST KNOWLEDGEABLE BASEBALL BROADCASTERS: Dizzy Dean, Red Barber
BEST UMPIRE YOU EVER SAW: Bill Klem
TOUGHEST PITCHER YOU EVER BATTED AGAINST: Christy Mathewson, Walter Johnson, Grover Alexander, etc.
BALL PLAYER WHO DID THE MOST TO INSPIRE HIS TEAM: All 25

BASEBALL WRITER WHO UNDERSTOOD THE GAME THE BEST: Sam Crane

⚾ Ken Keltner ⚾

1937-1949: Cleveland Indians; 1950: Boston Red Sox

Ken Keltner finished in 12th place on the players' survey and seventh best with the glove at the hot corner. The seven-time AL All-Star is best remembered for the two great plays that stopped Joe DiMaggio's 56-game hitting streak in 1941. Before a throng of over 67,000, at that time the largest night baseball crowd ever, Kenny twice made sensational stops of hot smashes and twice rose to nip DiMag at first. He ranks ninth lifetime with a .965 fielding average and 14th in double plays with 307, quite an achievement considering he played only a little more than 10 seasons and lost a year and a half to World War II. Keltner also swung a big stick, usually batting fifth for some good Cleveland clubs, including the world champions of 1948.

	AB	H	2B	3B	HR	R
LIFETIME	5683	1570	308	69	163	737
BEST COMPOSITE YEAR	624	191	41	13	31	91

	RBI	BB	SB	BA	SLG.	OB%
LIFETIME	852	514	39	.276	.441	.336
BEST COMPOSITE YEAR	119	89	10	.325	.522	.394

ALL-TIME ALL-STAR TEAM 1

OUTFIELD: Joe DiMaggio, Tommy Henrich, Ted Williams **3B:** Harlond Clift **SS:** Joe Cronin **2B:** Charlie Gehringer **1B:** Jimmie Foxx **RH PITCHER:** Ted Lyons **LH PITCHER:** Hal Newhouser **CATCHER:** Bill Dickey **RELIEF PITCHER:** Johnny Murphy

ALL-TIME ALL-STAR TEAM 2

OUTFIELD: Dom DiMaggio, Bob Kennedy, Bob Johnson **3B:** Red Rolfe **SS:** Lou Boudreau **2B:** Joe Gordon **1B:** Hank Greenberg **RH PITCHER:** Bob Feller **LH PITCHER:** Lefty Grove **CATCHER:** Jim Hegan **RELIEF PITCHER:** Dave (Boo) Ferris

ALL TIME DEFENSIVE TEAM

OUTFIELD: Joe DiMaggio, Tommy Henrich, Ted Williams **1B:** Ferris Fain **2B:** Charlie Gehringer **3B:** Bill Werber **SS:** Phil Rizzuto **RH PITCHER:** Ted Lyons **LH PITCHER:** Mel Parnell **CATCHER:** Jim Hegan

MOST UNDERRATED BALL PLAYERS OF ALL TIME: Cecil Travis, Jim Hegan, Barney McCosky
BEST CLUTCH HITTER EVER: Joe Cronin
BEST PINCH HITTER: Mickey Vernon
BEST *PURE* HITTER: Ted Williams
BEST SS-2B DOUBLE-PLAY COMBINATION EVER: Lou Boudreau-Ray Mack
GAME 7 WORLD SERIES PITCHER: Bob Feller
BEST MANAGER OF ALL TIME: Joe McCarthy
THE BEST TEAM: Yankees
FAVORITE STADIUM TO PLAY IN: Fenway Park
CITY WITH THE BEST FANS: Cleveland
DESIGNATED HITTER: Oppose
BEST FASTBALL: Bob Feller
BEST CURVE: Tommy Bridges
BEST SCREWBALL: Ed Lopat
BEST SPITBALL: Johnny Allen
BEST PICKOFF MOVE: Joe Page
BEST SINKER/DROP: Nelson Potter
BEST CHANGE-UP: Ed Lopat
BEST SLIDER: George Blaeholder
BEST BASE STEALER OF ALL TIME: George Case
BEST BUNTER: Phil Rizzuto
BEST HIT-AND-RUN MAN: Luke Appling
BEST THROWING ARM OF ALL TIME: Bob Kennedy
MOST KNOWLEDGEABLE BASEBALL BROADCASTERS: Jack Crane, Mel Allen
BEST UMPIRE YOU EVER SAW: Jocko Conlan
BALL PLAYERS THAT NEVER PLAYED UP TO THEIR POTENTIAL: Mickey Rocco, Benny McCoy, Eddie Robinson
TOUGHEST PITCHER YOU EVER BATTED AGAINST: Al Benton
BALL PLAYER WHO DID THE MOST TO INSPIRE HIS TEAM: Joe Gordon
BEST TEAM OWNER YOU'VE KNOWN: Tom Yawkey
BASEBALL WRITER WHO UNDERSTOOD THE GAME THE BEST: None

⚾ Bob Kennedy ⚾

1939-1948: Chicago White Sox; 1949-1954: Cleveland Indians; 1954-1955: Baltimore Orioles; 1955-1956: Chicago White Sox; 1956: Detroit Tigers; 1957: Chicago White Sox and Brooklyn Dodgers

The title of a show about Bob Kennedy's playing career could be "Have Gun, Will Travel." As a third baseman-outfielder from 1939-1957, as a manager and coach, and in various executive and scouting capacities, he has certainly seen it all. His throwing arm was good enough to land him tenth place in that category on the players' survey. No doubt his son Terry, the fine receiver for the Baltimore Orioles, wishes he had not inherited the throwing ability of his mother. Although Bob has seen the entire current generation of ball players, the only active player on his ballot is Goose Gossage, and with Bob's breadth of knowledge and experience you've got to respect his preference for past stars.

	AB	H	2B	3B	HR	R
LIFETIME	4624	1176	196	41	63	514
BEST COMPOSITE YEAR	606	157	27	5	9	79

	RBI	BB	SB	BA	SLG.	OB%
LIFETIME	514	364	45	.254	.355	.309
BEST COMPOSITE YEAR	57	53	11	.291	.417	.354

ALL-TIME ALL-STAR TEAM 1

OUTFIELD: Babe Ruth, Ty Cobb, Willie Mays **3B:** Pie Traynor **SS:** Honus Wagner **2B:** Charlie Gehringer **1B:** Lou Gehrig **RH PITCHER:** Bob Gibson **LH PITCHER:** Warren Spahn **CATCHER:** Mickey Cochrane **RELIEF PITCHER:** Rich Gossage

ALL-TIME ALL-STAR TEAM 2

OUTFIELD: Hank Aaron, Ted Williams, Stan Musial **3B:** Ed Mathews **SS:** Phil Rizzuto **2B:** Rogers Hornsby **1B:** Jimmie Foxx **RH PITCHER:** Walter Johnson **LH PITCHER:** Lefty Grove **CATCHER:** Gabby Hartnett

ALL-TIME DEFENSIVE TEAM

OUTFIELD: Willie Mays, Joe DiMaggio, Terry Moore **1B:** George McQuinn **2B:** Joe Gordon **3B:** Ossie Bluege **SS:** Marty Marion **RH PITCHER:** Bob Gibson **LH PITCHER:** Bobby Shantz **CATCHER:** Al Lopez

MOST UNDERRATED BALL PLAYERS OF ALL TIME: Marty Marion, Frank Crosetti, Glenn Wright, Al Rosen
BEST CLUTCH HITTER EVER: Joe DiMaggio
BEST PINCH HITTER: Smoky Burgess
BEST SS-2B DOUBLE-PLAY COMBINATION EVER: Phil Rizzuto-Joe Gordon
GAME 7 WORLD SERIES PITCHER: Bob Gibson
BEST MANAGER OF ALL TIME: Joe McCarthy
THE BEST TEAM: Yankees (1939-1942)
FAVORITE STADIUM TO PLAY IN: Fenway Park
CITY WITH THE BEST FANS: Chicago (Cubs)
DESIGNATED HITTER: Oppose
BEST FASTBALL: Bob Feller
BEST CURVE: Bob Feller
BEST SCREWBALL: Carl Hubbell
BEST SPITBALL: Burleigh Grimes
BEST PICKOFF MOVE: Bill Wight
BEST SINKER/DROP: Bob Lemon
BEST CHANGE-UP: Johnny Rigney
BEST SLIDER: Bob Lemon
BEST BASE STEALER OF ALL TIME: Ty Cobb
BEST BUNTER: Travis Jackson
BEST THROWING ARM OF ALL TIME: Bob Kennedy
MOST KNOWLEDGEABLE BASEBALL BROADCASTERS: Vin Scully, Harry Heilmann
BEST UMPIRE YOU EVER SAW: Bill McGowan
BALL PLAYERS WHO NEVER PLAYED UP TO THEIR POTENTIAL: Hank Aaron, Larry Doby, Willie Davis
TOUGHEST PITCHER YOU EVER BATTED AGAINST: Spud Chandler
BALL PLAYER WHO DID THE MOST TO INSPIRE HIS TEAM: Joe DiMaggio
BEST TEAM OWNER YOU'VE KNOWN: Tom Yawkey
BASEBALL WRITER WHO UNDERSTOOD THE GAME THE BEST: Sam Greene

⊘ Bob Knepper ⊗

1976-1980: San Francisco Giants; 1981-1986: Houston Astros

Would you want a lefty who after several years in the bigs had won 15 or more games in four seasons? So would we. Knepper, in fact, has almost copped 20 wins twice (and look at his career shutouts). Though he picks many players from the

Mays-Aaron-Mantle era, only a few of his contemporaries make the Knepper all-time teams, and that's as it should be. Great ball players have to earn that title. Note that Bob picks the Astrodome as his favorite ballpark to play in. Even with the fences in a few feet, it's still a pitcher's paradise. Met broadcaster Ralph Kiner blurted out in exasperation during one game that guys don't hit well in the Dome "because they can't *see* the ball." He added that most writers (and most broadcasters, he implied) blame the bad hitting on the ball not carrying well indoors, or on the distant fences or high walls. But he pointed out that the fences aren't that deep anymore—and remarked there were many sets of lights in the stadium that weren't even *on* as he spoke. So we understand why Bob Knepper loves his Astrodome.

	W-L	PCT.	ERA	G
LIFETIME	97-106	.478	3.48	289
BEST COMPOSITE YEAR	17-15	.643	2.63	36

	IP	H	BB	SO	SHO.
LIFETIME	1888	1877	580	1063	22
BEST COMPOSITE YEAR	260			147	6

ALL-TIME ALL-STAR TEAM 1

OUTFIELD: Willie Mays, Babe Ruth, Ted Williams **3B:** Jim Davenport **SS:** Dave Concepcion **2B:** Bobby Richardson **1B:** Lou Gehrig **RH PITCHER:** Walter Johnson **LH PITCHER:** Sandy Koufax **CATCHER:** Johnny Bench **RELIEF PITCHER:** Bruce Sutter

ALL-TIME ALL-STAR TEAM 2

OUTFIELD: Roberto Clemente, Hank Aaron, Mickey Mantle **3B:** Mike Schmidt **SS:** Ernie Banks **2B:** Bill Mazeroski **1B:** Willie McCovey **RH PITCHER:** Bob Gibson **LH PITCHER:** Steve Carlton **CATCHER:** Gary Carter **RELIEF PITCHER:** Elroy Face

ALL TIME DEFENSIVE TEAM

OUTFIELD: Willie Mays, Andre Dawson, Joe DiMaggio **1B:** Gil Hodges **2B:** Bobby Richardson **3B:** Brooks Robinson **SS:** Ozzie Smith **RH PITCHER:** Bob Gibson **LH PITCHER:** Steve Carlton **CATCHER:** Gary Carter

MOST UNDERRATED BALL PLAYERS OF ALL TIME: Bill Buckner, Willie Montanez, Harvey Kuenn, Enos Slaughter

BEST CLUTCH HITTER EVER: Ted Williams
BEST PINCH HITTER: Manny Mota
GAME 7 WORLD SERIES PITCHER: Sandy Koufax
BEST MANAGER OF ALL TIME: Casey Stengel
FAVORITE STADIUM TO PLAY IN: Astrodome
DESIGNATED HITTER: Oppose
CITY WITH THE BEST FANS: Boston or Milwaukee
BEST FASTBALL: Walter Johnson
BEST CURVE: Sal Maglie
BEST SCREWBALL: Carl Hubbell
BEST SPITBALL: Gaylord Perry
BEST PICKOFF MOVE: Steve Carlton
BEST SINKER/DROP: Dale Murray
BEST CHANGE-UP: Mario Soto
BEST SLIDER: Tom Seaver
BEST BASE STEALER OF ALL TIME: Ty Cobb
BEST BUNTER: Rod Carew
BEST THROWING ARM OF ALL TIME: Willie Mays
MOST KNOWLEDGEABLE BASEBALL BROADCASTERS: Lindsay
  Nelson
BEST UMPIRE YOU EVER SAW: Dutch Rennert
**BALL PLAYERS WHO NEVER PLAYED UP TO THEIR POTEN-
TIAL:** Sam McDowell, Don Newcomb, Ryne Duren, Steve Dalkowski
HITTER YOU FOUND HARDEST TO GET OUT: Mike Schmidt
BALL PLAYER WHO DID THE MOST TO INSPIRE HIS TEAM: Pete
  Rose
**BASEBALL WRITER WHO UNDERSTOOD THE GAME THE
BEST:** None

⚾ Max Lanier ⚾

1938-1951: St. Louis Cardinals; 1953: St. Louis Browns; 1952-1953: N.Y. Giants
(Suspended in 1946-1949)

Before jumping to the ill-fated Mexican League during the 1946 season, St. Louis Cardinal left-hander Max Lanier had compiled a won-lost record of 74-47 (.612) and an ERA of 2.64, so you can see why the Pasquel brothers made him a big offer. New baseball commissioner Happy Chandler decreed that all the players who went to Mexico were to be banned from the majors for five years, but when the smoke cleared Lanier was back with the Redbirds in 1949, and he pitched for five more years. In more than 10% of his starts Max pitched a shutout, a better figure than many Hall of Fame hurlers. He was also outstanding in World Series competition, compiling a 2-1 record with a 1.71 ERA in seven appearances over 32 innings. He also hit four singles in nine Series at bats, driving in three runs.

	W-L	PCT.	ERA	G
LIFETIME	108-82	.568	3.01	327
BEST COMPOSITE YEAR	17-12	.682	1.90	37

	IP	H	BB	SO	SHO.
LIFETIME	1619	1490	611	821	21
BEST COMPOSITE YEAR	224			141	5

ALL-TIME ALL-STAR TEAM 1

OUTFIELD: Stan Musial, Willie Mays, Joe DiMaggio/Ted Williams **3B:** Brooks Robinson **SS:** Marty Marion **2B:** Frankie Frisch **1B:** Bill Terry **RH PITCHER:** Dizzy Dean **LH PITCHER:** Carl Hubbell **CATCHER:** Gabby Hartnett **RELIEF PITCHER:** Hoyt Wilhelm

ALL-TIME ALL-STAR TEAM 2

OUTFIELD: Enos Slaughter, Paul Waner, Mel Ott **3B:** Pie Traynor **SS:** Phil Rizzuto **2B:** Red Schoendienst **1B:** John Mize **RH PITCHER:** Early Wynn **LH PITCHER:** Warren Spahn **CATCHER:** Gus Mancuso **RELIEF**

ALL-TIME DEFENSIVE TEAM

OUTFIELD: Terry Moore, Willie Mays, Joe DiMaggio **1B:** Dolf Camilli **2B:** Red Schoendienst **3B:** Billy Cox **SS:** Pee Wee Reese **RH PITCHER:** Murry Dickson **LH PITCHER:** Harry Brecheen **CATCHER:** Mickey Owen

MOST UNDERRATED BALL PLAYERS OF ALL TIME: Arky Vaughan, Terry Moore, Enos Slaughter
BEST CLUTCH HITTER EVER: Paul Waner
BEST SS-2B DOUBLE-PLAY COMBINATION EVER: Bill Jurges-Billy Herman
GAME 7 WORLD SERIES PITCHER: Sandy Koufax
BEST MANAGER OF ALL TIME: Connie Mack
THE BEST TEAM: 1942 Cardinals
FAVORITE STADIUM TO PLAY IN: Wrigley Field
CITY WITH THE BEST FANS: St. Louis
DESIGNATED HITTER: Oppose
BEST FASTBALL: Van Lingle Mungo
BEST CURVE: Tommy Bridges

BEST SCREWBALL: Carl Hubbell
BEST SPITBALL: Preacher Roe
BEST PICKOFF MOVE: Steve Carlton
BEST SINKER/DROP: Hal Schumacher
BEST CHANGE-UP: Howie Pollet
BEST SLIDER: Bucky Walters
BEST BASE STEALER OF ALL TIME: Lou Brock
BEST BUNTER: Phil Rizzuto
BEST THROWING ARM OF ALL TIME: Carl Furillo
MOST KNOWLEDGEABLE BASEBALL BROADCASTERS: Dizzy Dean, Mel Allen
BEST UMPIRE YOU EVER SAW: There were many good ones; won't commit myself
BALL PLAYERS WHO NEVER PLAYED UP TO THEIR POTENTIAL: Rocky Nelson, Frank Crespi
TOUGHEST PITCHER YOU EVER BATTED AGAINST: Ewell Blackwell
HITTER YOU FOUND HARDEST TO GET OUT: Bob Elliott
BALL PLAYER WHO DID THE MOST TO INSPIRE HIS TEAM: Jimmy Brown
BEST TEAM OWNER YOU'VE KNOWN: Horace Stoneham
BASEBALL WRITER WHO UNDERSTOOD THE GAME THE BEST: Bob Broeg

⊘ Hal Lanier ◯

1964-1971: San Francisco Giants; 1972-1973: N.Y. Yankees

He didn't have much to brag about with his hitting, but this son of Max Lanier must have been doing something right. He was the regular Giant second baseman, then shortstop, for six seasons during the Mays-McCovey years. It stands to reason that he was an excellent fielder, something borne out by a look at his defensive stats. And by the way, he batted .274 his first season in the bigs.

Lanier coached the St. Louis Cardinals under Whitey Herzog before moving on to managership at Houston, where he pledged to install a Herzog-style team. Since he names Whitey as the best manager of all time, it will be interesting to watch events in the Astrodome, the perfect ballpark for a running club. Is Herzog inimitable, a genius? Perhaps, but there's probably room for competition, and Lanier has a reputation for shrewdness. He lived up to it in 1986.

It should be noted that Lanier filled out his ballot a few years ago—1984. So he may claim the right to make revisions. Things have changed since '84: Dwight Gooden, Vince Coleman, etc. And he has a new owner to embrace.

	AB	H	2B	3B	HR	R
LIFETIME	3703	843	111	20	8	297
BEST COMPOSITE YEAR	525	118	16	9	3	41

	RBI	BB	SB	BA	SLG.	OB%
LIFETIME	273	136	11	.228	.275	.255
BEST COMPOSITE YEAR	42	25	2	.274	.347	.284

Courtesy San Francisco Giants

Hal Lanier

ALL-TIME ALL-STAR TEAM 1

OUTFIELD: Willie Mays, Robert Clemente, Joe DiMaggio **3B:** Brooks Robinson **SS:** Marty Marion **2B:** Charles Gehringer **1B:** Lou Gehrig **RH PITCHER:** Dizzy Dean **LH PITCHER:** Carl Hubbell **CATCHER:** Johnny Bench

ALL-TIME ALL-STAR TEAM 2

OUTFIELD: Ted Williams, Babe Ruth, Stan Musial **3B:** Pie Traynor **SS:** Honus Wagner **2B:** Rogers Hornsby **1B:** Johnny Mize **RH PITCHER:** Bucky Walters **LH PITCHER:** Lefty Grove **CATCHER:** Roy Campanella

ALL-TIME DEFENSIVE TEAM

OUTFIELD: Willie Mays, Joe DiMaggio, Roberto Clemente **1B:** Gil Hodges **2B:** Jackie Robinson **3B:** Brooks Robinson **SS:** Ozzie Smith **RH PITCHER:** Bob Gibson **LH PITCHER:** Jim Kaat **CATCHER:** Johnny Bench

MOST UNDERRATED BALL PLAYERS OF ALL TIME: Jimmy Davenport, Ken Boyer
BEST CLUTCH HITTER EVER: Willie Mays
BEST PINCH HITTER: Manny Mota
BEST SS-2B DOUBLE-PLAY COMBINATION EVER: Gene Alley-Bill Mazeroski
GAME 7 WORLD SERIES PITCHER: Bob Gibson/Juan Marichal
BEST MANAGER OF ALL TIME: Whitey Herzog
THE BEST TEAM: N.Y. Yankees
FAVORITE STADIUM TO PLAY IN: Dodger Stadium
CITY WITH THE BEST FANS: Los Angeles (Dodgers)
DESIGNATED HITTER: Oppose
BEST FASTBALL: Bob Feller/Nolan Ryan
BEST CURVE: Sandy Koufax
BEST SCREWBALL: Carl Hubbell
BEST SPITBALL: Gaylord Perry
BEST PICKOFF MOVE: Don Drysdale
BEST SINKER/DROP: Don Drysdale
BEST CHANGE-UP: Stu Miller
BEST SLIDER: Steve Carlton
BEST BASE STEALER OF ALL TIME: Lou Brock/Rickey Henderson
BEST BUNTER: Maury Wills
BEST THROWING ARM OF ALL TIME: Roberto Clemente
MOST KNOWLEDGEABLE BASEBALL BROADCASTERS: Vin Scully, Jack Buck, Lou Simmons
BEST UMPIRE YOU EVER SAW: Doug Harvey
TOUGHEST PITCHER YOU EVER BATTED AGAINST: Don Drysdale
BALL PLAYER WHO DID THE MOST TO INSPIRE HIS TEAM: Willie Mays/Willie Stargell
BEST TEAM OWNER YOU'VE KNOWN: Augie Busch
BASEBALL WRITER WHO UNDERSTOOD THE GAME THE BEST: Dick Young

◇ Vance Law ◇

1980-1981: Pittsburgh Pirates; 1982-1984: Chicago White Sox; 1985-present: Montreal Expos

The young son of former Pirate ace Vernon Law (162-147, 3.77 ERA lifetime) came to the big leagues heralded, and he has had a tough time living up to expectations. But note that no team sends him back down to the minors. His statistics are respectable, though hardly enough to earn him All-Star berths. Law's survey picks are not the eyebrow raising sort. His selection of Dwight Gooden as the toughest pitcher he's faced would, we suspect, be seconded by three-quarters of active NL players.

	AB	H	2B	3B	HR	R
LIFETIME	1908	485	91	17	36	242
BEST COMPOSITE YEAR	519	138	30	6	17	75

	RBI	BB	SB	BA	SLG.	OB%
LIFETIME	213	209	20	.254	.376	.328
BEST COMPOSITE YEAR	59	86	6	.281	.405	.369

ALL-TIME ALL-STAR TEAM 1

OUTFIELD: Hank Aaron, Willie Mays, Ted Williams **3B:** Brooks Robinson **SS:** Ernie Banks **2B:** Jackie Robinson **1B:** Willie McCovey **RH PITCHER:** Bob Gibson **LH PITCHER:** Sandy Koufax **CATCHER:** Roy Campanella **RELIEF PITCHER:** Rollie Fingers

ALL-TIME ALL-STAR TEAM 2

OUTFIELD: Frank Robinson, Mickey Mantle, Roberto Clemente **3B:** Pete Rose **SS:** Phil Rizzuto, Pee Wee Reese **2B:** Nelson Fox **1B:** Stan Musial **RH PITCHER:** Tom Seaver **LH PITCHER:** Whitey Ford **CATCHER:** Yogi Berra, Thurman Munson **RELIEF PITCHER:** Bruce Sutter

ALL-TIME DEFENSIVE TEAM

OUTFIELD: Willie Mays, Paul Blair, Roberto Clemente, **1B:** Mike Squires **2B:** Bill Mazeroski **3B:** Brooks Robinson **SS:** Mark Belanger **RH PITCHER:** Vernon Law **LH PITCHER:** Jim Kaat **CATCHER:** Roy Campanella, Johnny Bench

BEST CLUTCH HITTER EVER: Harmon Killebrew
BEST PINCH HITTER: Manny Mota

BEST *PURE* HITTER: George Brett

BEST SS-2B DOUBLE-PLAY COMBINATION EVER: Gene Alley-Bill Mazeroski

GAME 7 WORLD SERIES PITCHER: Bob Gibson

BEST MANAGER OF ALL TIME: Billy Martin

THE BEST TEAM: Oakland A's (early 70s)

FAVORITE STADIUM TO PLAY IN: Dodger Stadium

CITY WITH THE BEST FANS: St. Louis

BEST FASTBALL: Nolan Ryan

BEST CURVE: Sandy Koufax

BEST SCREWBALL: Fernando Valenzuela

BEST SPITBALL: Gaylord Perry

BEST CHANGE-UP: Andy Messersmith

BEST SLIDER: Catfish Hunter

BEST BASE STEALER OF ALL TIME: Ricky Henderson, Tim Raines

BEST BUNTER: Rod Carew

BEST THROWING ARM OF ALL TIME: Dave Winfield

MOST KNOWLEDGEABLE BASEBALL BROADCASTERS: Jack Buck, Ernie Harwell

TOUGHEST PITCHER YOU EVER BATTED AGAINST: Dwight Gooden

BALL PLAYER WHO DID THE MOST TO INSPIRE HIS TEAM: Pete Rose

BASEBALL WRITER WHO UNDERSTOOD THE GAME THE BEST: Jerome Holtzman

---

Hank Greenberg's quest for the home run record:

Sam Harshaney, St. Louis Browns catcher (1937-1940), reveals this about the Detroit home run king's 1938 run at Ruth's record: "When Hank Greenberg hit his 58th home run, and inside-the-park shot, the umpire called Hank safe when I had him out. Hank admitted this to me later. Curious thing. Les Tietje was pitching for St. Louis and Hank's first two trips to the plate produced home runs. At the end of the inning of the second home run, Les and I had a conference in the dugout. 'Heck,' we said, 'let Hank try to tie Ruth's record.' So I called for just a straight lay-in pitch the next two plate appearances for Hank. Believe it or not, he just popped up to the infield on two fat pitches, medium speed."

⚾ Buck Leonard ⚾

Perhaps the most interesting of all the responses is this one by Hall of Famer Buck Leonard. Generally regarded as the greatest of all Negro League first basemen, he provides an expert's appraisal of black talent and its place in baseball history. Buck is too modest to vote for himself, but two other players chose him for their second team at first base. Moreover, when the color line was broken, Buck declined a major-league offer lest his deteriorating skills leave a bad impression for future blacks to live down. Such a sacrifice would likely be sneered at today.

Leonard hit for both average and power, and posted a .382 mark against major leaguers in those exhibition games that were recorded.

Note his choice of both Mickey Cochrane and Yogi Berra over longtime teammate Josh Gibson as catcher. But in the outfield, Oscar Charleston, perhaps the best all-around Negro League player of all, rates right up there with Babe Ruth and Willie Mays. Leonard rates Pop Lloyd, "the black Honus Wagner," ahead of the Flying Dutchman and every other shortstop but Joe Cronin. Both Charleston and Lloyd were later managers, as were nine other men on his all-time teams.

Although Buck pretty much sticks to his contemporaries in his ballot, he picks Fernando Valenzuela's screwball as superior to Carl Hubbell's. Hubbell himself was quoted to the effect that Fernando's scroogie is thrown and acts exactly like his own.

Other recent players Buck selected are Tug McGraw for best pickoff move and Lou Brock (with Ty Cobb) as the best base stealer. Comparing modern ball players to those of the 1930s and 1940s, Leonard told us, "They are more knowledgeable but not better players," a statement directly opposite the typical old-timer's view.

ALL-TIME ALL-STAR TEAM 1

OUTFIELD: Ty Cobb, Joe DiMaggio, Tris Speaker **3B:** Pie Traynor **SS:** Joe Cronin **2B:** Charlie Gehringer **1B:** Lou Gehrig **RH PITCHER:** Walter Johnson **LH PITCHER:** Lefty Grove **CATCHER:** Mickey Cochrane **RELIEF PITCHER:** Joe Page

ALL-TIME ALL-STAR TEAM 2

OUTFIELD: Oscar Charleston, Babe Ruth, Willie Mays **3B:** Brooks Robinson **SS:** Pop Lloyd **2B:** Eddie Collins **1B:** Bill Terry **RH PITCHER:** Satchel Paige **LH PITCHER:** Hal Newhouser **CATCHER:** Yogi Berra **RELIEF PITCHER:** Firpo Marberry

ALL-TIME DEFENSIVE TEAM

OUTFIELD: Roberto Clemente, Bob Meusel, Willie Mays **1B:** Joe Judge **2B:** Eddie Collins **3B:** Brooks Robinson **SS:** Marty Marion **RH PITCHER:** Hoyt Wilhelm **LH PITCHER:** Joe Page **CATCHER:** Muddy Ruel

BEST CLUTCH HITTER EVER: John Mize
BEST PINCH HITTER: John Mize
BEST SS-2B DOUBLE-PLAY COMBINATION EVER: Crosetti-Gordon
GAME 7 WORLD SERIES PITCHER: Walter Johnson
BEST MANAGER OF ALL TIME: Casey Stengel
THE BEST TEAM: 1927 Yankees

FAVORITE STADIUM TO PLAY IN: Yankee Stadium
CITY WITH THE BEST FANS: New York
BEST FASTBALL: Satchel Paige
BEST CURVE: Ted Trent
BEST SCREWBALL: Fernando Valenzuela
BEST SPITBALL: Burleigh Grimes
BEST PICKOFF MOVE: Tug McGraw
BEST CHANGE-UP: Rip Sewell
BEST KNUCKLEBALL: Hoyt Wilhelm
BEST BASE STEALER OF ALL TIME: Ty Cobb/Lou Brock
BEST BUNTER: Maury Wills
BEST THROWING ARM OF ALL TIME: Roberto Clemente
MOST KNOWLEDGEABLE BASEBALL BROADCASTERS: Lindsay
   Nelson, Joe Garagiola
BEST UMPIRE YOU EVER SAW: Jocko Conlan
TOUGHEST PITCHER YOU EVER BATTED AGAINST: Satchel Paige
BALL PLAYER WHO DID THE MOST TO INSPIRE HIS TEAM: Pepper
   Martin
BEST TEAM OWNER YOU'VE KNOWN: Jacob Ruppert
**BASEBALL WRITER WHO UNDERSTOOD THE GAME THE
   BEST:** Red Smith

⚾ Phil Linz ⚾

1962-1965: N.Y. Yankees; 1966-1967: Philadelphia Phillies; 1967-1968: N.Y.
Mets

"You can't get rich sitting on the bench—but I'm giving it a try," said
"Supersub" Phil Linz one lazy day at the ball park. Sit he did—but not in the 1964
World Series, when he played all seven games for the Yankees at shortstop and
belted two solo home runs, carding a nifty .452 slugging average with five runs
scored. Mostly, Linz filled in at short, third, and second, and his glove was
reliable. His career was unremarkable except for 1964, year of the now legendary
"harmonica incident." It happened aboard the Yankee team bus, he told us, during
a losing road trip. He began to play, and manager Yogi Berra told him to stop. "I
kept playing. He came back, and I threw the harmonica at him. He threw it back at
me, and I went into a whole thing about how I was giving 100%, but not all the
guys were. I think we won 28 of 31 games after that, and we went on to win the
pennant. Had we won the World Series, it would have been remembered." The
New York press played it up big. The authors were eight and nine years old at the
time, and *we* remember it.

Linz picks Sandy Koufax as his man to pitch the Game 7 of the World Series. He
picks Bob Gibson as the toughest pitcher he ever faced—though it was Gibson, in
Game 7 of the '64 Series, who tried to blow Linz away with an 0-2 fastball, only to
see it sail over the wall for a home run.

It was Joe Garagiola, then a Yankee broadcaster, who coaxed Linz into issuing his ultimatum, "Play me or keep me," to manager Ralph Houk aboard a Yankee plane in the early 1960s, Linz confesses. But that was when utility men were happy just to be on the roster. Today, they pull in salaries on a par with the President. What would Babe Ruth say?

	AB	H	2B	3B	HR	R
LIFETIME	1372	322	64	4	11	185
BEST COMPOSITE YEAR	368	92	21	3	5	63

	RBI	BB	SB	BA	SLG.	OB%
LIFETIME	96	112	13	.235	.311	.292
BEST COMPOSITE YEAR	25	43	6	.287	.372	.328

ALL-TIME ALL-STAR TEAM 1

OUTFIELD: Joe DiMaggio, Mickey Mantle, Babe Ruth **3B:** Brooks Robinson **SS:** Luis Aparicio **2B:** Jackie Robinson **1B:** Lou Gehrig **RH PITCHER:** Dwight Gooden **LH PITCHER:** Sandy Koufax **CATCHER:** Johnny Bench **RELIEF PITCHER:** Rich Gossage

ALL-TIME ALL-STAR TEAM 2

OUTFIELD: Roberto Clemente, Willie Mays, Hank Aaron **3B:** Graig Nettles **SS:** Pee Wee Reese **2B:** Bobby Richardson **1B:** Don Mattingly **RH PITCHER:** Bob Gibson **LH PITCHER:** Whitey Ford **CATCHER:** Yogi Berra **RELIEF PITCHER:** Ron Perranoski

ALL-TIME DEFENSIVE TEAM

OUTFIELD: Roberto Clemente, Willie Mays, Al Kaline **1B:** Keith Hernandez **2B:** Bobby Richardson **3B:** Brooks Robinson **SS:** Ozzie Smith **RH PITCHER:** Bob Gibson **LH PITCHER:** Bobby Shantz **CATCHER:** Gary Carter

MOST UNDERRATED BALL PLAYERS OF ALL TIME: Roger Maris, Carl Furillo
BEST CLUTCH HITTER EVER: Keith Hernandez
BEST PINCH HITTER: Smoky Burgess
BEST *PURE* HITTER: Ted Williams
BEST SS-2B DOUBLE-PLAY COMBINATION EVER: Luis Aparicio-Nellie Fox

GAME 7 WORLD SERIES PITCHER: Sandy Koufax
BEST MANAGER OF ALL TIME: Casey Stengel
THE BEST TEAM: 1927 Yankees
FAVORITE STADIUM TO PLAY IN: Fenway Park
CITY WITH THE BEST FANS: New York
DESIGNATED HITTER: Favor
BEST FASTBALL: Bob Gibson
BEST CURVE: Sandy Koufax
BEST SCREWBALL: Mike Cuellar
BEST SPITBALL: Gaylord Perry
BEST PICKOFF MOVE: Whitey Ford
BEST SINKER/DROP: Dan Quisenberry
BEST CHANGE-UP: Stu Miller
BEST SLIDER: Bob Gibson
BEST BASE STEALER OF ALL TIME: Rickey Henderson
BEST BUNTER: Phil Rizzuto
BEST HIT-AND-RUN MAN: Dick Groat
BEST THROWING ARM OF ALL TIME: Carl Furillo
MOST KNOWLEDGEABLE BASEBALL BROADCASTERS: Vin Scully,
    Red Barber
BEST UMPIRE YOU EVER SAW: Doug Harvey
**BALL PLAYERS WHO NEVER PLAYED UP TO THEIR POTEN-
    TIAL:** Richie Allen, Phil Linz, John Candelaria, Joe Pepitone
TOUGHEST PITCHER YOU EVER BATTED AGAINST: Bob Gibson
BALL PLAYER WHO DID THE MOST TO INSPIRE HIS TEAM: Pete
    Rose
**BASEBALL WRITER WHO UNDERSTOOD THE GAME THE
    BEST:** Maury Allen

⚾ Dale Long ⚾

1951: Pittsburgh Pirates, St. Louis Browns; 1955-1957: Pittsburgh Pirates; 1957-1959: Chicago Cubs; 1960: San Francisco Giants, N.Y. Yankees; 1961-1962: Washington Senators; 1962-1963: N.Y. Yankees

Mostly a part-time first baseman, Long distinguished himself on three counts: He is the only left-hander in modern times to have played behind the plate, catching in two games for the 1958 Cubs and manager Bob Scheffing. Secondly, he belted eight home runs in eight consecutive games for the 1956 Pirates, one off Warren Spahn and another off Carl Erskine. Not even the mighty Babe managed that. Thirdly, he hit nine career pinch-hit home runs.

	AB	H	2B	3B	HR	R
LIFETIME	3020	805	135	33	132	384
BEST COMPOSITE YEAR	517	135	26	13	27	68

	RBI	BB	SB	BA	SLG.	OB%
LIFETIME	467	353	10	.267	.464	.345
BEST COMPOSITE YEAR	91	66	6	.298	.513	.385

ALL-TIME ALL-STAR TEAM 1

OUTFIELD: Willie Mays, Mickey Mantle, Hank Aaron **3B:** Brooks Robinson **SS:** Tony Kubek **2B:** Bill Mazeroski **1B:** Gil Hodges **RH PITCHER:** Bob Feller **LH PITCHER:** Sandy Koufax **CATCHER:** Yogi Berra **RELIEF PITCHER:** Elroy Face

ALL-TIME ALL-STAR TEAM 2

OUTFIELD: Ted Williams, Frank Robinson, Stan Musial **3B:** Ken Boyer **SS:** Dick Groat **2B:** Bobby Richardson **1B:** Moose Skowron **RH PITCHER:** Bob Lemon **LH PITCHER:** Harvey Haddix **CATCHER:** Elston Howard **RELIEF PITCHER:** Goose Gossage

ALL-TIME DEFENSIVE TEAM

OUTFIELD: Willie Mays, Mickey Mantle, Bobby Del Greco **1B:** Gil Hodges **2B:** Nellie Fox **3B:** Clete Boyer **SS:** Tony Kubek **RH PITCHER:** Tom Seaver **LH PITCHER:** Harvey Haddix **CATCHER:** Roy Campanella

MOST UNDERRATED BALL PLAYERS OF ALL TIME: Frank Thomas, Gus Bell
BEST CLUTCH HITTER EVER: Smoky Burgess
BEST PINCH HITTER: John Blanchard
BEST SS-2B DOUBLE-PLAY COMBINATION EVER: Tony Kubek-Bobby Richardson
GAME 7 WORLD SERIES PITCHER: Whitey Ford
BEST MANAGER OF ALL TIME: Casey Stengel
THE BEST TEAM: 1962 Yankees
FAVORITE STADIUM TO PLAY IN: Municipal Stadium, old Kansas City A's park
CITY WITH THE BEST FANS: Pittsburgh
DESIGNATED HITTER: Oppose
BEST FASTBALL: Sandy Koufax
BEST CURVE: Harvey Haddix
BEST SCREWBALL: Warren Spahn
BEST SPITBALL: Lew Burdette

BEST PICKOFF MOVE: Warren Spahn
BEST CHANGE-UP: Carl Erskine
BEST SLIDER: Sal Maglie
BEST BASE STEALER OF ALL TIME: Lou Brock
BEST BUNTER: Nellie Fox
BEST THROWING ARM OF ALL TIME: Carl Furillo
MOST KNOWLEDGEABLE BASEBALL BROADCASTERS: Vin Scully, Mel Allen
BEST UMPIRE YOU EVER SAW: Jocko Conlan
BALL PLAYERS WHO NEVER PLAYED UP TO THEIR POTENTIAL: Joe Pepitone
TOUGHEST PITCHER YOU EVER BATTED AGAINST: Harvey Haddix
BALL PLAYER WHO DID THE MOST TO INSPIRE HIS TEAM: Mickey Mantle
BEST TEAM OWNER YOU'VE KNOWN: John Galbreath/Phil Wrigley
BASEBALL WRITER WHO UNDERSTOOD THE GAME THE BEST: Red Smith

⊘ Eddie Lopat ⊘

1944-1947: Chicago White Sox; 1947-1955: N.Y. Yankees; 1955: Baltimore Orioles

Edmund Lopatynski enjoyed his best years on the mound with the unstoppable N.Y. Yankees. Nicknamed "Steady Eddie" by broadcaster Mel Allen, for a good part of his career he wrestled with a temper that left him prone to throwing tantrums. Still active as a scout, Eddie was among the very best (indeed, steadiest) of AL pitchers for about 10 years. Pinpoint control and a superb change-up—voted eighth best by his peers here—were his tickets to a lifetime record of 166-112, with an ERA of 3.21 over the 1944-55 span. After going 50-49 in his first four seasons with a second-division White Sox club, Lopat had the good fortune to be traded to the Yanks, where his talents were better recognized. Casey Stengel saw in him the prototype Yankee Stadium southpaw, and he juggled his rotation to pitch Eddie there as often as possible. Lopat responded with seven years of 109 wins and only 51 losses (.681).

Lopat's best years were 1951 (21-9, 2.91 ERA) and 1953 (16-4, his ERA a league-leading 2.42). He also posted a World Series record of 4-1, with a 2.60 ERA in seven starts. Eddie received two players' votes as the best-fielding left-handed pitcher ever, and often helped himself with the bat, too, compiling a .211 career average with 5 home runs. He also managed the inept Kansas City Athletics in 1963 and 1964.

Eddie's choices are objective and well considered, as befits a veteran scout, running the historical gamut from Christy Mathewson to Rickey Henderson. You can see he had his pitching problems with (among others) Tiger center fielder Hoot Evers, a fine all-around ball player whose career started late due World War II.

Note too Lopat's batting problems with Alex Kellner, a tough lefty unfortunate enough to pitch for the Athletics in the 1950s. Usually cellar dwellers, the A's managed to finish over .500 in 1949; in that year Kellner went 20-12. Incidentally, Lopat proudly notes that Ted Williams "named me as his number one pitching nemesis. I moved the ball around on him, never threw to the same spot."

	W-L	PCT.	ERA	G
LIFETIME	166-112	.597	3.21	340
BEST COMPOSITE YEAR	21-13	.800	2.42	35

	IP	H	BB	S	SHO.
LIFETIME	2439	2464	650	859	28
BEST COMPOSITE YEAR	253			109	5

ALL-TIME ALL-STAR TEAM 1

OUTFIELD: Babe Ruth, Joe DiMaggio, Ted Williams **3B:** Eddie Mathews **SS:** Honus Wagner **2B:** Charlie Gehringer **1B:** Lou Gehrig **RH PITCHER:** Christy Mathewson **LH PITCHER:** Lefty Grove **CATCHER:** Bill Dickey **RELIEF PITCHER:** Rollie Fingers

ALL-TIME ALL-STAR TEAM 2

OUTFIELD: Ty Cobb, Stan Musial, Hank Aaron **3B:** Brooks Robinson **SS:** Joe Cronin **2B:** Rogers Hornsby **1B:** Jimmie Foxx **RH PITCHER:** Bob Feller **LH PITCHER:** Warren Spahn **CATCHER:** Mickey Cochrane **RELIEF PITCHER:** Johnny Murphy

ALL-TIME DEFENSIVE TEAM

OUTFIELD: Joe DiMaggio, Terry Moore, Carl Yastrzemski **1B:** Bill Terry **2B:** Jerry Coleman **3B:** Brooks Robinson **SS:** Luis Aparicio **RH PITCHER:** Bob Lemon **LH PITCHER:** Bobby Shantz **CATCHER:** Jim Hegan

BEST PINCH HITTER: Manny Mota
BEST *PURE* HITTER: Ted Williams
GAME 7 WORLD SERIES PITCHER: Allie Reynolds
BEST MANAGER OF ALL TIME: Casey Stengel
THE BEST TEAM: 1936 Yankees
FAVORITE STADIUM TO PLAY IN: Yankee Stadium

DESIGNATED HITTER: Favor
BEST FASTBALL: Allie Reynolds
BEST CURVE: Bob Feller
BEST SCREWBALL: Carl Hubbell
BEST SPITBALL: Burleigh Grimes
BEST PICKOFF MOVE: Bill Wight
BEST SINKER/DROP: Bob Lemon
BEST CHANGE-UP: Ellis Kinder
BEST SLIDER: Bob Gibson
BEST BASE STEALER OF ALL TIME: Rickey Henderson
BEST BUNTER: Phil Rizzuto
BEST THROWING ARM OF ALL TIME: Bob Kennedy
MOST KNOWLEDGEABLE BASEBALL BROADCASTERS: Mel Allen,
Red Barber
BEST UMPIRE YOU EVER SAW: Bill McGowan
TOUGHEST PITCHER YOU EVER BATTED AGAINST: Alex Kellner
HITTER YOU FOUND HARDEST TO GET OUT: Hoot Evers
BALL PLAYER WHO DID THE MOST TO INSPIRE HIS TEAM: Joe
DiMaggio
BEST TEAM OWNER YOU'VE KNOWN: Tom Yawkey

⊘ Rick Mahler ⊗

1979-1986: Atlanta Braves

Brother of Mickey Mahler, Rick has come into his own since being put into the Braves' starting rotation three years ago. His control has improved gradually, and with that, so has his W-L record (always, though, that's dependent on the starting eight, and the Braves have struggled the past couple of years). Three times Rick has been handed the ball on opening day, and three times he's responded with shutouts.

Obviously, Rick is a student of the game, blending players from every era into his survey and singling out Mel Stottlemyre as possessor of the best sinker of all time. Only a sophisticate would make that choice. Mel was stuck with some very bad Yankee teams, and, despite the New York press, didn't exactly suffer from overexposure. Arm trouble shortened his fine career, and yes, his ball *did* drop.

	W-L	PCT.	ERA	G
LIFETIME	47-41	.534	3.56	177
BEST COMPOSITE YEAR	17-15	.571	2.25	39

	IP	H	BB	SO	SHO.
LIFETIME	846.2	849	266	392	4
BEST COMPOSITE YEAR	267			107	2

ALL-TIME ALL-STAR TEAM 1

OUTFIELD: Babe Ruth, Hank Aaron, Willie Mays **3B:** Ed Mathews **SS:** Honus Wagner **2B:** Rogers Hornsby **1B:** Lou Gehrig **RH PITCHER:** Walter Johnson **LH PITCHER:** Cy Young **CATCHER:** Bill Dickey **RELIEF PITCHER:** Goose Gossage

ALL-TIME ALL-STAR TEAM 2

OUTFIELD: Ted Williams, Joe DiMaggio, Pete Rose **3B:** Mike Schmidt **SS:** Lou Boudreau **2B:** Nap Lajoie **1B:** George Sisler **RH PITCHER:** Bob Gibson **LH PITCHER:** Steve Carlton **CATCHER:** Johnny Bench **RELIEF PITCHER:** Dan Quisenberry

ALL-TIME DEFENSIVE TEAM

OUTFIELD: Willie Mays, Roberto Clemente, Gary Maddox **1B:** Chris Chambliss **2B:** Nap Lajoie **3B:** Brooks Robinson **SS:** Ozzie Smith **RH PITCHER:** Bob Gibson **LH PITCHER:** Ron Guidry **CATCHER:** Johnny Bench

BEST CLUTCH HITTER EVER: Reggie Jackson
BEST PINCH HITTER: Manny Mota
BEST SS-2B DOUBLE-PLAY COMBINATION EVER: Dave Concepcion-Joe Morgan
GAME 7 WORLD SERIES PITCHER: Jim (Catfish) Hunter
BEST MANAGER OF ALL TIME: Earl Weaver
THE BEST TEAM: 1927 Yankees
FAVORITE STADIUM TO PLAY IN: Dodger Stadium
CITY WITH THE BEST FANS: Los Angeles
DESIGNATED HITTER: Oppose
BEST FASTBALL: Nolan Ryan
BEST CURVE: Bert Blyleven
BEST SCREWBALL: Mike Marshall
BEST SPITBALL: Gaylord Perry
BEST PICKOFF MOVE: Tippy Martinez
BEST SINKER/DROP: Mel Stottlemyre
BEST CHANGE-UP: Mario Soto
BEST SLIDER: J.R. Richard
BEST BASE STEALER OF ALL TIME: Ty Cobb
BEST BUNTER: Pete Rose
BEST THROWING ARM OF ALL TIME: Roberto Clemente
MOST KNOWLEDGEABLE BASEBALL BROADCASTERS: Vin Scully
BEST UMPIRE YOU EVER SAW: Nick Colosi
TOUGHEST PITCHER YOU EVER BATTED AGAINST: Mario Soto

HITTER YOU FOUND HARDEST TO GET OUT: Al Oliver
BALL PLAYER WHO DID THE MOST TO INSPIRE HIS TEAM: Pete
Rose
BEST TEAM OWNER YOU'VE KNOWN: Ted Turner

⚾ Gus Mancuso ⚾

1928-1932: St. Louis Cardinals; 1933-1938: N.Y. Giants; 1939: Chicago Cubs;
1940: Brooklyn Dodgers; 1941-1942: St. Louis Cardinals; 1942-1944: N.Y.
Giants; 1945: Philadelphia Phillies

The late Gus Mancuso received seven votes (including his brother's) as the best
defensive catcher, and every few seasons he'd hit .366 or .348 as a platoon player.
He caught 1,360 games during 17 National League campaigns and called the
pitches for five pennant-winning teams in an eight-year stretch. Notice in his
responses a preference for his teammates on the Cardinals and Giants, like Frankie
Frisch and Travis Jackson. But especially interesting are Gus's choices of Carl
Hubbell and Lefty Gomez over Lefty Grove. Also noteworthy is his pick of Sam
Leslie as best pinch hitter; until his final season in 1938 Leslie had a pinch-hitting
batting average of .301. He also held the record for pinch hits in a season (22) from
1932 until it was first broken by Dave Philley in 1961.
    What city has the best fans? "All of them were good," this genial man told us.
R.I.P., Gus.

	AB	H	2B	3B	HR	R
LIFETIME	4505	1194	197	16	53	386
BEST COMPOSITE YEAR	519	156	23	3	9	55

	RBI	BB	SB	BA	SLG.	OB%
LIFETIME	543	418	8	.265	.351	.327
BEST COMPOSITE YEAR	63	48	2	.366	.551	.412

ALL-TIME ALL-STAR TEAM 1

OUTFIELD: Babe Ruth, Joe DiMaggio, Paul Waner **3B:** Pie Traynor **SS:** Phil
Rizzuto **2B:** Frank Frisch **1B:** Lou Gehrig **RH PITCHER:** Walter Johnson **LH
PITCHER:** Carl Hubbell **CATCHER:** Mickey Cochrane **RELIEF PITCHER:**
Adolfo Luque

ALL-TIME ALL-STAR TEAM 2

OUTFIELD: Mel Ott, Stan Musial, Ted Williams **3B:** Brooks Robinson **SS:** Travis Jackson **2B:** Rogers Hornsby **1B:** Jimmie Foxx **RH PITCHER:** Dizzy Dean **LH PITCHER:** Lefty Gomez **CATCHER:** Bill Dickey

ALL-TIME DEFENSIVE TEAM

OUTFIELD: Chick Hafey, Terry Moore, Mel Ott **1B:** Bill Terry **2B:** Frank Frisch **3B:** Brooks Robinson **SS:** Marty Marion **RH PITCHER:** Fred Fitzsimmons **LH PITCHER:** Carl Hubbell **CATCHER:** Jimmy Wilson

BEST CLUTCH HITTER EVER: Rogers Hornsby
BEST PINCH HITTER: Sam Leslie
GAME 7 WORLD SERIES PITCHER: Carl Hubbell
BEST MANAGER OF ALL TIME: John J. McGraw
THE BEST TEAM: 1930-31 St. Louis Cardinals
FAVORITE STADIUM TO PLAY IN: Polo Grounds
DESIGNATED HITTER: Oppose
BEST FASTBALL: Dazzy Vance
BEST CURVE: Adolf Luque
BEST SCREWBALL: Carl Hubbell
BEST SPITBALL: Burleigh Grimes
BEST SINKER/DROP: Hal Schumacher
BEST SLIDER: Roy Parmelee
BEST BASE STEALER OF ALL TIME: Max Carey
BEST THROWING ARM OF ALL TIME: Chick Hafey
MOST KNOWLEDGEABLE BASEBALL BROADCASTERS: Red Barber, Francis Laux, Sr.
BEST UMPIRE YOU EVER SAW: Bill Klem
BALL PLAYERS WHO NEVER PLAYED UP TO THEIR POTENTIAL: Chick Hafey, Homer Peel
TOUGHEST PITCHER YOU EVER BATTED AGAINST: Dazzy Vance
BALL PLAYER WHO DID THE MOST TO INSPIRE HIS TEAM: Gus Mancuso
BEST TEAM OWNER YOU'VE KNOWN: Wilbert Robinson
BASEBALL WRITER WHO UNDERSTOOD THE GAME THE BEST: Ken Smith

Marty Marion

1940-1950: St. Louis Cardinals; 1952-1953: St. Louis Browns

Marty Marion will not state flatly who is the best-fielding shortstop ever, only that "Luis Aparicio was as good as I ever saw." Of course, selecting the best glove man at short is a tough, tough call, but about 16% of the ball players who responded to our survey voted for Marion himself, placing him third all-time. It's fair to say that he is to shortstop what Joe DiMaggio is to center field—gliding to the ball, making it look easy. And Marty didn't hurt those great Cardinal teams of the 1940s with his bat, earning the nickname "Doubles" for his surprising ability to do just that. As a grizzled two-year veteran of 23, Marty was one of several Redbird players who advised the green Stan Musial to change his peculiar batting style. "His stance was horrible," Marion recalls. "We used to tell him he'd never stay in the big leagues with that kind of stance."

Marion's selection of Estel Crabtree as the best pinch hitter is backed by Crabtree's .319 lifetime average (37 for 116) in that role, close to the best ever....The choice of Bobby Doerr as the best second baseman with the glove is a minority viewpoint, but a thoroughly defensible one in view of the stats....The overwhelming majority of National League right-handed batters of the forties agree with Marion when he names Ewell (The Whip) Blackwell as "The Toughest Pitcher I Ever Faced." The crossfire fastballs of the six-foot, six-inch Blackwell made those hitters shudder like a schoolboy waiting for a whuppin'!

	AB	H	2B	3B	HR	R
LIFETIME	5506	1448	272	37	36	602
BEST COMPOSITE YEAR	567	147	38	6	6	70

	RBI	BB	SB	BA	SLG.	OB%
LIFETIME	624	470	35	.263	.345	.321
BEST COMPOSITE YEAR	74	59	9	.280	.375	.341

MANAGER
(Six years)

	W-L	PCT.
CARDINALS	81-73	.526
BROWNS	96-162	.372
WHITE SOX	179-138	.565

ALL-TIME ALL-STAR TEAM 1

OUTFIELD: Babe Ruth, Ted Williams, Joe DiMaggio **3B:** Brooks Robinson **SS:** Lou Boudreau **2B:** Rogers Hornsby **1B:** Lou Gehrig **RH PITCHER:** Bob Feller **LH PITCHER:** Sandy Koufax **CATCHER:** Yogi Berra

ALL-TIME ALL-STAR TEAM 2

OUTFIELD: Stan Musial, Willie Mays, Mickey Mantle **3B:** Mike Schmidt **SS:** Luis Aparicio **2B:** Charlie Gehringer **1B:** George Sisler **RH PITCHER:** Bob Gibson **LH PITCHER:** Steve Carlton **CATCHER:** Johnny Bench

ALL-TIME DEFENSIVE TEAM

OUTFIELD: Willie Mays, Terry Moore, Joe DiMaggio **1B:** Gil Hodges **2B:** Bobby Doerr **3B:** Brooks Robinson **SS:** Luis Aparicio **CATCHER:** Johnny Bench

BEST CLUTCH HITTER EVER: Marty Marion
BEST PINCH HITTER: Estel Crabtree
BEST *PURE* HITTER: Stan Musial
BEST SS-2B DOUBLE-PLAY COMBINATION EVER: Marty Marion-Red Schoendienst
GAME 7 WORLD SERIES PITCHER: Bob Gibson
BEST MANAGER OF ALL TIME: All the same
THE BEST TEAM: 1942 Cardinals
FAVORITE STADIUM TO PLAY IN: Sportsman's Park
CITY WITH THE BEST FANS: Brooklyn/St. Louis/Chicago
DESIGNATED HITTER: Favor
BEST FASTBALL: Bob Feller
BEST CURVE: Carl Erskine/Bob Feller
BEST SCREWBALL: Carl Hubbell
BEST PICKOFF MOVE: Steve Carlton
BEST SINKER/DROP: Eldon Auker
BEST CHANGE-UP: Howie Pollet
BEST SLIDER: Don Newcombe
BEST BASE STEALER OF ALL TIME: Ty Cobb/Lou Brock
BEST BUNTER: Phil Rizzuto/Nellie Fox
BEST HIT-AND-RUN MAN: Billy Herman
BEST THROWING ARM OF ALL TIME: Carl Furillo/Roberto Clemente
MOST KNOWLEDGEABLE BASEBALL BROADCASTERS: Harry Carey, Jack Buck
BEST UMPIRE YOU EVER SAW: Larry Goetz
TOUGHEST PITCHER YOU EVER BATTED AGAINST: Ewell Blackwell
BEST TEAM OWNER YOU'VE KNOWN: Phil Wrigley/Bill Veeck

BASEBALL WRITER WHO UNDERSTOOD THE GAME THE BEST: Red Smith/Roy Stockman

◐ Gil McDougald ◑

1951-1960: N.Y. Yankees

"He's the all-time best utility infielder the Yankees ever had," says Billy Martin of Gil McD. That would be damning with faint praise, but the Yanks have had potent benches since the Ruth era. And incidentally, to emphasize Martin's point, McDougald saw action in no fewer than 119 games in every one of the 10 seasons he spent with the Yanks. In five seasons, he went to bat over 500 times. In truth, he was a regular, but so versatile, and so tailored to the Stengel style of managing, that he was shifted around the diamond *like* a handyman infielder.

Indeed, Gil was a four-time All-Star, and he copped Rookie of the Year honors with a .306 BA in 1951. He topped that season with a grand slam in Game 5 of the World Series off Giant Larry Jansen.

McDougald shined in World Series play. Though only a .237 hitter lifetime in the Fall Classic, he ranks tenth all-time in Series home runs, eighth in runs and RBIs, ninth in walks, and seventh in hits. In the 1958 Series against the Milwaukee Braves, facing Warren Spahn and Lew Burdette, Gil and Hank Bauer sparked the Bronx Bombers to victory, McDougald carding a .321 BA and a .607 slugging average.

	AB	H	2B	3B	HR	R
LIFETIME	4676	1291	187	51	112	697
BEST COMPOSITE YEAR	555	156	27	9	14	87

	RBI	BB	SB	BA	SLG.	OB%
LIFETIME	576	559	45	.276	.410	.355
BEST COMPOSITE YEAR	83	68	14	.311	.488	.405

ALL-TIME ALL-STAR TEAM 1

OUTFIELD: Joe DiMaggio, Babe Ruth, Henry Aaron **3B:** Mike Schmidt **SS:** Luis Aparicio **2B:** Charlie Gehringer **1B:** Lou Gehrig **RH PITCHER:** Allie Reynolds **LH PITCHER:** Whitey Ford **CATCHER:** Yogi Berra **RELIEF PITCHER:** Goose Gossage

ALL-TIME ALL-STAR TEAM 2

OUTFIELD: Willie Mays, Roger Maris, Al Kaline **3B:** George Kell **SS:** Phil Rizzuto **2B:** Joe Gordon **1B:** John Mize **RH PITCHER:** Bob Feller **LH PITCHER:** Bobby Shantz **CATCHER:** Bill Dickey **RELIEF PITCHER:** Hoyt Wilhelm

ALL-TIME DEFENSIVE TEAM

OUTFIELD: Joe DiMaggio, Al Kaline, Carl Yastrzemski **1B:** Keith Hernandez **2B:** Joe Gordon **3B:** Graig Nettles **SS:** Luis Aparicio **LH PITCHER:** Bobby Shantz **CATCHER:** Roy Campanella

MOST UNDERRATED BALL PLAYERS OF ALL TIME: Roger Maris
BEST CLUTCH HITTER EVER: Yogi Berra
BEST PINCH HITTER: John Mize
BEST SS-2B DOUBLE-PLAY COMBINATION EVER: Phil Rizzuto-Jerry Coleman
GAME 7 WORLD SERIES PITCHER: Allie Reynolds
BEST MANAGER OF ALL TIME: Casey Stengel
THE BEST TEAM: 1951 Yankees
FAVORITE STADIUM TO PLAY IN: Fenway Park
CITY WITH THE BEST FANS: Boston
DESIGNATED HITTER: Favor
BEST FASTBALL: Bob Feller
BEST CURVE: Sandy Koufax
BEST SCREWBALL: Eddie Lopat
BEST PICKOFF MOVE: Bill Wight
BEST SINKER/DROP: Mike Garcia
BEST CHANGE-UP: Stu Miller
BEST SLIDER: Dick Donovan
BEST BASE STEALER OF ALL TIME: Rickey Henderson
BEST BUNTER: Luis Aparicio
BEST THROWING ARM OF ALL TIME: Rockey Colavito
MOST KNOWLEDGEABLE BASEBALL BROADCASTERS: Red Barber, Curt Gowdy
BEST UMPIRE YOU EVER SAW: Bill McGowan
BALL PLAYERS WHO NEVER PLAYED UP TO THEIR POTENTIAL: Billy Loes, Bob Kuzava
TOUGHEST PITCHER YOU EVER BATTED AGAINST: Sal Maglie
BALL PLAYER WHO DID THE MOST TO INSPIRE HIS TEAM: Joe DiMaggio
BEST TEAM OWNER YOU'VE KNOWN: Bobby "Doc" Brown
BASEBALL WRITER WHO UNDERSTOOD THE GAME THE BEST: John Drebinger

◎ Don McMahon ◎

1957-1962: Milwaukee Braves; 1962-1963: Houston Colt 45s (now Astros); 1964-1966: Cleveland Indians; 1966-1967: Boston Red Sox; 1967-1968: Chicago White Sox; 1968-1969: Detroit Tigers; 1969-1974: San Francisco Giants

In his 18-year career, Don McMahon started only two games. He was a relief specialist, as they say, and one of the best of that breed. He ranks seventh in the history of the game in appearances (874) and relief victories (90). He's in the top 15 (it changes almost annually) in career saves. Why, one might ask, did so many teams deal him to so many others? Was he a troublemaker? Former teammates would guffaw at any such suggestion.

McMahon was still pitching effectively into his early 40s, going 4-0 with a 1.50 ERA in 1973 (age 43) as a Giant. He is currently the "eye in the sky" for the L.A. Dodgers.

Who does this relief ace—who saw most of the best—pick for his top two? Fingers and Radatz. He wants Bob Gibson to start his hypothetical World Series Game 7. That's noteworthy because McMahon, as a Tiger in 1968, saw Bob *lose* Game 7. There was a mild debate over whose fault the loss was, but McMahon seems to confirm that it wasn't Gibson's: Curt Flood stumbled going after a routine, though hard-hit, Jim Northrup fly ball into the left-field gap, and the Tigers eked out a win.

	W-L	PCT.	ERA	G
LIFETIME	90-68	.570	2.96	874
BEST COMPOSITE YEAR	10-6	1.000	1.50	70

	IP	H	BB	SO	SHO.
LIFETIME	1310.2	1054	579	1002	0
BEST COMPOSITE YEAR	109.1			92	

ALL-TIME ALL-STAR TEAM 1

OUTFIELD: Willie Mays, Hank Aaron, Roberto Clemente **3B:** Ed Mathews **SS:** Ozzie Smith **2B:** Red Schoendienst **1B:** Willie McCovey **RH PITCHER:** Juan Marichal **LH PITCHER:** Warren Spahn **CATCHER:** Johnny Bench **RELIEF PITCHER:** Rollie Fingers

ALL-TIME ALL-STAR TEAM 2

OUTFIELD: Ted Williams, Stan Musial, Dave Winfield **3B:** Brooks Robinson **SS:** Luis Aparicio **2B:** Ryne Sandberg **1B:** Don Mattingly **RH PITCHER:** Bob Gibson **LH PITCHER:** Ron Guidry **CATCHER:** Del Crandall **RELIEF PITCHER:** Dick Radatz

ALL-TIME DEFENSIVE TEAM

OUTFIELD: Willie Mays, Rick Manning, Roberto Clemente **1B:** Frank Torre **2B:** Ryne Sandberg **3B:** Brooks Robinson **SS:** Ozzie Smith **RH PITCHER:** Bob Gibson **LH PITCHER:** Jim Kaat **CATCHER:** Johnny Bench

MOST UNDERRATED BALL PLAYERS OF ALL TIME: Ernie Lombardi, Roberto Clemente
BEST CLUTCH HITTER EVER: Willie McCovey
BEST PINCH HITTER: Manny Mota
BEST *PURE* HITTER: Stan Musial
BEST SS-2B DOUBLE-PLAY COMBINATION EVER: Dick Groat-Bill Mazeroski
GAME 7 WORLD SERIES PITCHER: Bob Gibson
BEST MANAGER OF ALL TIME: Eddie Stanky
THE BEST TEAM: 1957 Milwaukee Braves/1975 Cincinnati Reds
FAVORITE STADIUM TO PLAY IN: Wrigley Field
CITY WITH THE BEST FANS: New York
DESIGNATED HITTER: Favor
BEST FASTBALL: J.R. Richard/Dick Radatz
BEST CURVE: Camilo Pascual
BEST SCREWBALL: Juan Marichal
BEST SPITBALL: Gaylord Perry
BEST PICKOFF MOVE: Warren Spahn
BEST SINKER/DROP: Dan Quisenberry
BEST CHANGE-UP: Andy Messersmith
BEST SLIDER: Mark Littell
BEST BASE STEALER OF ALL TIME: Lou Brock/Vince Coleman
BEST BUNTER: Rod Carew
BEST HIT-AND-RUN MAN: Dick Groat
BEST THROWING ARM OF ALL TIME: Rockey Colavito
MOST KNOWLEDGEABLE BASEBALL BROADCASTERS: Don Drysdale, Red Barber
BEST UMPIRE YOU EVER SAW: Dutch Rennert
BALL PLAYERS WHO NEVER PLAYED UP TO THEIR POTENTIAL: Cesar Cedeno, Richie Allen
TOUGHEST PITCHER YOU EVER BATTED AGAINST: Don Drysdale
HITTER YOU FOUND HARDEST TO GET OUT: Joe Torre
BALL PLAYER WHO DID THE MOST TO INSPIRE HIS TEAM: Eddie Mathews
BEST TEAM OWNER YOU'VE KNOWN: Tom Yawkey
BASEBALL WRITER WHO UNDERSTOOD THE GAME THE BEST: Hal Liebowitz

Joe Oeschger

1914-1919: Philadelphia Phillies; 1919: N.Y. Giants; 1919-1923: Boston Braves; 1924: N.Y. Giants and Philadelphia Phillies; 1925: Brooklyn Dodgers

When the conversation turns to great feats of baseball endurance, the name of the late Joe Oeschger stands out. On May 1, 1920, he went the distance for Boston in the famous 26-inning 1-1 tie between Brooklyn and the Braves. Oeschger allowed but nine singles, the equivalent of three consecutive three-hitters, striking out seven and walking four before darkness halted the contest against Brooklyn's Leon Cadore. A sturdy right-hander, Oeschger had some good years for bad ball clubs, including a 20-14 season in 1921.

His all-time teams show a balance between his own and the modern eras, with a National League bias except for Luis Aparicio and Eddie Collins on the second team. In the "How 'Bout *That*" department is the somewhat astounding choice of Gary Matthews in the second outfield, but in a way it fits in with the hustling, inspirational type of ball player Joe prefers, and you can't argue with Matthews's post-season record (.323, 7 HR, 15 RBI in 65 AB). Also, note Joe's high regard for Eppa Rixey and Wilbur Cooper, two fine lefties from his own time.

National Baseball Library

Joe Osechger

	W-L	PCT.	ERA	G
LIFETIME	83-116	.417	3.81	365
BEST COMPOSITE YEAR	20-21	.588	2.75	46

	IP	H	BB	SO	SHO.
LIFETIME	1818	1936	651	535	18
BEST COMPOSITE YEAR	299			123	5

ALL-TIME ALL-STAR TEAM 1

OUTFIELD: Zack Wheat, Ed Roush, Ross Youngs **3B:** Pie Traynor **SS:** Rabbit Maranville **2B:** Rogers Hornsby/Joe Morgan **1B:** Hal Chase **RH PITCHER:** Grover Cleveland Alexander **LH PITCHER:** Eppa Rixey **CATCHER:** Chief Meyers

ALL-TIME ALL-STAR TEAM 2

OUTFIELD: Gary Matthews, Willie Mays **3B:** Mike Schmidt **SS:** Luis Aparicio **2B:** Eddie Collins **1B:** Pete Rose **RH PITCHER:** Dazzy Vance **LH PITCHER:** Sandy Koufax, Wilbur Cooper, Steve Carlton **CATCHER:** Johnny Bench

ALL-TIME DEFENSIVE TEAM

OUTFIELD: Zack Wheat, Ed Roush, Ross Youngs **1B:** Pete Rose **2B:** Joe Morgan **3B:** Mike Schmidt **SS:** Rabbit Maranville **RH PITCHER:** Grover Alexander **LH PITCHER:** Steve Carlton **CATCHER:** Johnny Bench

GAME 7 WORLD SERIES PITCHER: Grover Alexander
BEST MANAGER OF ALL TIME: John McGraw
THE BEST TEAM: N.Y. Giants
FAVORITE STADIUM TO PLAY IN: Polo Grounds (N.Y.)
CITY WITH THE BEST FANS: Los Angeles (Dodgers)
DESIGNATED HITTER: Oppose
BEST FASTBALL: Walter Johnson
BEST SCREWBALL: Fernando Valenzuela
BEST SPITBALL: Willie Doak
BEST PICKOFF MOVE: Sherry Smith
BEST SINKER/DROP: Grover Alexander
BEST SLIDER: Steve Carlton
BEST BASE STEALER OF ALL TIME: Ty Cobb

BEST BUNTER: Ty Cobb
MOST KNOWLEDGEABLE BASEBALL BROADCASTERS: Red Barber,
Vin Scully
BEST UMPIRE YOU EVER SAW: Bill Klem
TOUGHEST PITCHER YOU EVER BATTED AGAINST: Grover
Alexander
HITTER YOU FOUND HARDEST TO GET OUT: Zack Wheat
BALL PLAYER WHO DID THE MOST TO INSPIRE HIS TEAM: Rogers
Hornsby/Dave Bancroft
BEST TEAM OWNER YOU'VE KNOWN: W.F. Baker
**BASEBALL WRITER WHO UNDERSTOOD THE GAME THE
BEST:** Jack McDonald

⊘ Vic Power ⊘

1954-1958: Philadelphia/Kansas City Athletics; 1958-1961: Cleveland Indians;
1962-1964: Minnesota Twins; 1964: Los Angeles Angels & Philadelphia Phillies;
1965: California Angels

Author of a 22-game hitting streak while with the Indians, Power, known as a
hot dog, could play first, second, third, outfield, and even shortstop, though first
base was his best position and where he led the AL in fielding three times. The
players in our survey voted him #3 on the best defense first baseman list. In 1958,
Vic stole home twice in a game against the Tigers, the second time winning the
game in the 10th inning for the Indians. Old Power fans, and there are many indeed, will recall his peculiar batting stance: he held the bat down, pointing the
barrel almost straight into the ground.

It worked. Power, who never played in fewer than 105 games during any season
in his 12-year career, averaged 62 RBIs per season in his 10 most active years. He
was a free swinger—but struck out only once per 24.5 at bats, *way* below average.

Restricting his choices almost exclusively to men he saw play, Power shows a
bias toward good fielders like himself. How else to explain Clete Boyer over Eddie
Mathews on Team 2, or cannon-armed Rocky Colavito over, say, Frank
Robinson? Interestingly, Power thinks Willie Mays's arm was stronger than
Roberto Clemente's, an opinion not widely held.

	AB	H	2B	3B	HR	R
LIFETIME	6046	1716	290	49	126	765
BEST COMPOSITE YEAR	611	190	34	10	19	102

	RBI	BB	SB	BA	SLG.	OB%
LIFETIME	658	279	45	.284	.411	.315
BEST COMPOSITE YEAR	84	40	9	.319	.505	.357

ALL-TIME ALL-STAR TEAM 1

OUTFIELD: Henry Aaron, Willie Mays, Ted Williams **3B:** Brooks Robinson **SS:** Luis Aparicio **2B:** Nellie Fox **1B:** Mickey Vernon **RH PITCHER:** Early Wynn **LH PITCHER:** Whitey Ford **CATCHER:** Yogi Berra **RELIEF PITCHER:** Ryne Duren

ALL-TIME ALL-STAR TEAM 2

OUTFIELD: Roberto Clemente, Mickey Mantle, Rocky Colavito **3B:** Clete Boyer **SS:** Phil Rizzuto **2B:** Junior Gilliam **1B:** Joe Pepitone **RH PITCHER:** Bob Feller **LH PITCHER:** Sandy Koufax **CATCHER:** Roy Campanella **RELIEF PITCHER:** Dick Radatz

ALL-TIME DEFENSIVE TEAM

OUTFIELD: Roberto Clemente, Willie Mays, Al Kaline **1B:** Mickey Vernon **2B:** Nellie Fox **3B:** Brooks Robinson **SS:** Luis Aparicio **RH PITCHER:** Ruben Gomez **LH PITCHER:** Jim Kaat **CATCHER:** Yogi Berra

MOST UNDERRATED BALL PLAYERS OF ALL TIME: Richie Allen, Roger Maris
BEST CLUTCH HITTER EVER: Willie Mays
BEST PINCH HITTER: Dave Philley
BEST SS-2B DOUBLE-PLAY COMBINATION EVER: Luis Aparicio-Nellie Fox
GAME 7 WORLD SERIES PITCHER: Sandy Koufax
BEST MANAGER OF ALL TIME: Al Lopez
THE BEST TEAM: Yankees
FAVORITE STADIUM TO PLAY IN: Yankee Stadium
CITY WITH THE BEST FANS: New York
DESIGNATED HITTER: Favor
BEST FASTBALL: Ryne Duren
BEST CURVE: Camilo Pascual
BEST SCREWBALL: Mike Cuellar
BEST SPITBALL: Gaylord Perry
BEST PICKOFF MOVE: Bobby Shantz
BEST SINKER/DROP: Bob Turley
BEST CHANGE-UP: Stu Miller
BEST SLIDER: Early Wynn
BEST BASE STEALER OF ALL TIME: Luis Aparicio
BEST BUNTER: Phil Rizzuto
BEST THROWING ARM OF ALL TIME: Willie Mays
MOST KNOWLEDGEABLE BASEBALL BROADCASTERS: Mel Allen, Red Barber

BEST UMPIRE YOU EVER SAW: Joe Paparella
**BALL PLAYERS WHO NEVER PLAYED UP TO THEIR POTEN-
TIAL:** Richie Allen, Alex Johnson, Orlando Cepeda
TOUGHEST PITCHER YOU EVER BATTED AGAINST: Ryne Duren
BALL PLAYER WHO DID THE MOST TO INSPIRE HIS TEAM: Jim
Piersall
BEST TEAM OWNER YOU'VE KNOWN: Gene Autry
BASEBALL WRITER WHO UNDERSTOOD THE GAME THE BEST: Hal
Liebowitz

Oldtimer J.A. "Shag" Thompson, born 1893 (Philadelphia A's 1914-1916):

Your survey is filled out as best I am capable of doing at this late date in my life. I still have good reflexes, good health for a person of my age, for which I am thankful.... The game has changed in so many ways since I played 65 years ago that all one can say is it is still the good old American sport that will never give way to any other game. I still enjoy watching TV games, even though I am beyond the age of attending games with the large crowds on hand. But what a difference in the time consumed and the strategy employed by the managers. In our days we usually completed a game in an hour and a half to two hours, and in most cases our pitchers were able to go the distance, very seldom requiring relief. The teams in the major leagues were limited to 25 players—including manager and coaches, too. And the number of players required to operate the leagues was so small compared to today that one had to be good to hold onto his job. Then, too, the baseball gloves were so small that one did not have a basket for the ball to fall into. The balls were not nearly as lively then, and there was no rule against pitchers scuffing, discoloring, or using saliva to make it hard on the hitter. And one had to use both hands to catch a ball—or be fined. No one-handed catches, as is the rule today.

Well, it is still the good old American game, and the fans support it and enjoy the long, drawn out games with modern strategy. So be it....I have done my best in making selections, but there are so many players of high quality. Anyhow, I have enjoyed going back over the days that I would like to live over.

⚾ Dick Radatz ⚾

1962-1966: Boston Red Sox; 1966-1967: Cleveland Indians-Chicago Cubs; 1969: Detroit Tigers-Montreal Expos

Dick was king of the hill with the Sox in the early 1960s, twice ('62 and '64) winning the *Sporting News* Fireman of the Year Award, and picked for the All-Star team in '63 and '64, not typical then for a relief pitcher. He threw smoke, a la Goose Gossage, and his ball had wicked movement. At 6'6" and 230 lbs., he was every bit as scary as the Goose. "The Monster" ran into control problems, and his career was over after seven years. But he was one of the best ever:

1. He was 15-6, then 16-9, in 1963-64, all in relief.
2. He led *both* leagues in saves in 1962, '63 and '64, and of course in relief victories in '63 and '64.
3. He averaged more than one strikeout per inning.

Boston fans thrilled to The Monster, and he responds in kind in the survey, picking that city's fans as the best, choosing their stadium as his preferred (along with the House That Ruth Built), and naming Tom Yawkey "the best team owner I've known."

	W-L	PCT.	ERA	G
LIFETIME	52-43	.547	3.13	381
BEST COMPOSITE YEAR	16-11	.714	1.97	79

	IP	H	BB	SO	SHO.
LIFETIME	693.2	532	296	745	0
BEST COMPOSITE YEAR	157			181	

ALL-TIME ALL-STAR TEAM 1

OUTFIELD: Babe Ruth, Ty Cobb, Willie Mays **3B:** Brooks Robinson **SS:** Honus Wagner **2B:** Charlie Gehringer **1B:** Lou Gehrig **RH PITCHER:** Cy Young **LH PITCHER:** Sandy Koufax **CATCHER:** John Bench **RELIEF PITCHER:** Hoyt Wilhelm

ALL-TIME ALL-STAR TEAM 2

OUTFIELD: Ted Williams, Joe DiMaggio, Tris Speaker **3B:** Mike Schmidt **SS:** Luis Aparicio **2B:** Bobby Doerr **1B:** Willie McCovey **RH PITCHER:** Bob Gibson **LH PITCHER:** Whitey Ford **CATCHER:** Bill Dickey **RELIEF PITCHER:** Rollie Fingers

ALL-TIME DEFENSIVE TEAM

OUTFIELD: Joe DiMaggio, Willie Mays, Al Kaline **1B:** Vic Power/George Scott **2B:** Bill Mazeroski **3B:** Brooks Robinson **SS:** Luis Aparicio **RH PITCHER:** Bob Gibson **LH PITCHER:** Jim Kaat **CATCHER:** John Bench

MOST UNDERRATED BALL PLAYERS OF ALL TIME: Tony Oliva, Billy Williams, Roger Maris, Johnny Pesky
BEST CLUTCH HITTER EVER: Tony Perez
BEST PINCH HITTER: Gates Brown

BEST *PURE* HITTER: Ted Williams
BEST SS-2B DOUBLE-PLAY COMBINATION EVER: Luis Aparicio and anybody
GAME 7 WORLD SERIES PITCHER: Sandy Koufax
BEST MANAGER OF ALL TIME: Joe McCarthy
THE BEST TEAM: 1927 Yankees
FAVORITE STADIUM TO PLAY IN: Fenway Park/Yankee Stadium
CITY WITH THE BEST FANS: Boston/Detroit
DESIGNATED HITTER: Oppose
BEST FASTBALL: Sam McDowell
BEST CURVE: Camilo Pascual
BEST SCREWBALL: Willie Hernandez
BEST SPITBALL: Gaylord Perry
BEST SINKER/DROP: Bruce Sutter
BEST CHANGE-UP: Jack Morris
BEST SLIDER: Bob Gibson
BEST BASE STEALER OF ALL TIME: Lou Brock
BEST HIT-AND-RUN MAN: Bobby Richardson
BEST THROWING ARM OF ALL TIME: Roberto Clemente
MOST KNOWLEDGEABLE BASEBALL BROADCASTERS: Ernie Harwell, Vin Scully
BEST UMPIRE YOU EVER SAW: Nestor Chylak/Doug Harvey
TOUGHEST PITCHER YOU EVER BATTED AGAINST: Sandy Koufax
HITTER YOU FOUND HARDEST TO GET OUT: Tony Kubek
BALL PLAYER WHO DID THE MOST TO INSPIRE HIS TEAM: Pete Rose
BEST TEAM OWNER YOU'VE KNOWN: Tom Yawkey
BASEBALL WRITER WHO UNDERSTOOD THE GAME THE BEST: Peter Gammons

⚾ Paul Richards ⚾

1932: Brooklyn Dodgers; 1933-1935: N.Y. Giants; 1935: Philadelphia Athletics; 1943-1946: Detroit Tigers

Good-field-no-hit, former catcher Richards was renowned for his baseball brain. He managed for the Chicago White Sox and the Baltimore Orioles and served as a general manager when not in charge of the lineup card. But on the field he did help to win the 1945 World Series for the Tigers, hitting two doubles with four RBIs in game seven against the Cubs.

Richards restricted his survey to major leaguers, but he told us: "Satchel Paige ranks right up there with the all-time great pitchers. He was just something you don't see: pinpoint control, velocity, knowledge of pitching, ability to hit and field and bunt—he could do *everything*, and I didn't see him in his prime."

	AB	H	2B	3B	HR	R
LIFETIME	1417	321	51	5	15	140
BEST COMPOSITE YEAR	313	71	13	1	5	32

	RBI	BB	SB	BA	SLG.	OB%
LIFETIME	155	157	15	.227	.301	.241
BEST COMPOSITE YEAR	37	38	8	.256	.355	.325

ALL-TIME ALL-STAR TEAM 1

OUTFIELD: Babe Ruth, Joe DiMaggio, Tris Speaker **3B:** Brooks Robinson **SS:** Luis Aparicio **2B:** Charlie Gehringer **1B:** Lou Gehrig **RH PITCHER:** Bob Feller **LH PITCHER:** Carl Hubbell **CATCHER:** Bill Dickey **RELIEF PITCHER:** Hoyt Wilhelm

ALL-TIME ALL-STAR TEAM 2

OUTFIELD: Al Kaline, Roberto Clemente, Terry Moore **3B:** Pie Traynor **SS:** Lou Boudreau **2B:** Nellie Fox **1B:** Billy Terry **RH PITCHER:** Ted Lyons **LH PITCHER:** Sandy Koufax **CATCHER:** Gabby Hartnett **RELIEF PITCHER:** Joe Page

ALL-TIME DEFENSIVE TEAM

OUTFIELD: Joe Moore, Joe DiMaggio, Al Kaline **1B:** Jim Spencer **2B:** Charlie Gehringer **3B:** Brooks Robinson **SS:** Mark Belanger **RH PITCHER:** Fred Fitzsimmons **LH PITCHER:** Bobby Shantz **CATCHER:** Bill Dickey

MOST UNDERRATED BALL PLAYERS OF ALL TIME: Bob Elliott, Joe Moore
BEST CLUTCH HITTER EVER: Bob Elliott
BEST PINCH HITTER: Dave Philley
BEST SS-2B DOUBLE-PLAY COMBINATION EVER: Phil Rizzuto-Joe Gordon
GAME 7 WORLD SERIES PITCHER: Carl Hubbell
BEST MANAGER OF ALL TIME: Walter Alston
THE BEST TEAM: 1926 Yankees
FAVORITE STADIUM TO PLAY IN: Fenway Park
CITY WITH THE BEST FANS: Chicago (White Sox)
DESIGNATED HITTER: Oppose
BEST FASTBALL: Bill Zuber

BEST CURVE: Tommy Bridges
BEST SCREWBALL: Carl Hubbell
BEST SPITBALL: Burleigh Grimes
BEST PICKOFF MOVE: Phil Niekro
BEST SINKER/DROP: Wilcy Moore
BEST CHANGE-UP: Hal Newhouser
BEST SLIDER: Johnny Allen
BEST BASE STEALER OF ALL TIME: Ty Cobb
BEST BUNTER: Nellie Fox
BEST THROWING ARM OF ALL TIME: Al Kaline
MOST KNOWLEDGEABLE BASEBALL BROADCASTERS: Vin Scully,
   J. Doggert
BEST UMPIRE YOU EVER SAW: Bill McGowan
**BALL PLAYERS THAT NEVER PLAYED UP TO THEIR POTEN-
TIAL:** Jackie Brandt, Bill Nicholson
TOUGHEST PITCHER YOU EVER BATTED AGAINST: Bob Feller
BALL PLAYER WHO DID THE MOST TO INSPIRE HIS TEAM: Babe
   Ruth
BEST TEAM OWNER YOU'VE KNOWN: Walter Briggs
**BASEBALL WRITER WHO UNDERSTOOD THE GAME THE
BEST:** Warren Brown

✪ George "Twinkle Toes" Selkirk ✪

1934-1942: N.Y. Yankees

Selkirk is best known as the Yankee who replaced Babe Ruth in right field. He typified the lefty-swinging slugger the Bombers have long been known for, averaging 20 homers and 105 RBIs per *154* games. Platooned much of his career, George also did the other things winning players do. He had a strong arm, good speed, and an exceptional batting eye, walking an average of 88 times per full season. Twice he drove in eight runs in one game, and his RBI totals are all the more impressive for his having batted sixth or seventh most of the time in a potent Yank lineup.

His selections here lean toward the great Yankee squads of the 1930s, but let's not quibble. The choice of Lou Gehrig as the best clutch hitter of all time can hardly draw boos; Lou batted behind the most pitched-around hitter in history, the Babe, and averaged 142 RBIs per season over his career. Isn't this what they call "bringing home the bacon?"

An interesting Selkirk pick is "Broadway" Charlie Wagner in the best change-up category. Wagner was a Red Sox right-hander who was taking his place as a top AL moundsman, going 26-19, with a 3.19 ERA in 1941-42, before the war interrupted his progress.

	AB	H	2B	3B	HR	R
LIFETIME	2790	810	131	41	108	503
BEST COMPOSITE YEAR	493	153	28	12	21	103

	RBI	BB	SB	BA	SLG.	OB%
LIFETIME	576	486	49	.290	.483	.396
BEST COMPOSITE YEAR	107	103	13	.328	.629	.443

ALL-TIME ALL-STAR TEAM

OUTFIELD: Babe Ruth, Ty Cobb, Joe DiMaggio **3B:** Pie Traynor **SS:** Honus Wagner **2B:** Charlie Gehringer **1B:** Lou Gehrig **RH PITCHER:** Red Ruffing **LH PITCHER:** Lefty Grove **CATCHER:** Bill Dickey **RELIEF PITCHER:** Johnny Murphy

BEST CLUTCH HITTER EVER: Lou Gehrig
BEST SS-2B DOUBLE-PLAY COMBINATION EVER: Phil Rizzuto-Joe Gordon
GAME 7 WORLD SERIES PITCHER: Red Ruffing
BEST MANAGER OF ALL TIME: Joe McCarthy
THE BEST TEAM: 1927 Yankees
FAVORITE STADIUM TO PLAY IN: Tiger Stadium,
DESIGNATED HITTER: Oppose
BEST FASTBALL: Lefty Grove
BEST SCREWBALL: Carl Hubbell
BEST CHANGE-UP: "Broadway" Charlie Wagner
BEST THROWING ARM OF ALL TIME: Bob Meusel
TOUGHEST PITCHER YOU EVER BATTED AGAINST: Lefty Grove
BALL PLAYER WHO DID THE MOST TO INSPIRE HIS TEAM: Lou Gehrig
BEST TEAM OWNER YOU'VE KNOWN: Col. Ruppert

Joe Sewell

1920-1930: Cleveland Indians; 1931-1933: N.Y. Yankees

Debuting after regular shortstop Ray Chapman was killed by a Carl Mays fastball, Hall of Famer Joe Sewell was the toughest man to strike out in baseball history. In no season did he whiff more than 20 times, and once he struck out just four times in 608 at bats. In 10 of 14 seasons he struck out fewer than 10 times. It's always impressive to hear that Joe DiMaggio had seasons with more home runs than strikeouts, but Sewell had years with more *triples* than Ks, and he didn't hit too many triples.

Although he was a small man (about five feet, six inches) playing the demanding shortstop position, Sewell was there for 1,103 consecutive games, the fifth longest such streak ever. He also flashed an excellent glove both at short and later at third base, had good speed and was a noted hit-and-run artist. Ten times Sewell batted over .300, and he drove in 109 and 104 runs during seasons in which he hit four and three homers, respectively.

Joe voted for his brother Luke as the best fielding catcher ever, one of three players to so choose. A third brother, Tommy, played in one game for the Cubs in 1927.

We've tried to keep our opinions in the background, but we can't fathom Joe's selection of Hank Aaron as a player who never lived up to his potential. Possibly Hank was underrated, but with the most homers ever, he surely did all he could with his talent.

	AB	H	2B	3B	HR	R
LIFETIME	7132	2226	436	68	49	1141
BEST COMPOSITE YEAR	608	204	48	12	11	102

	RBI	BB	SB	BA	SLG.	OB%
LIFETIME	1051	844	74	.312	.413	.378
BEST COMPOSITE YEAR	109	98	17	.353	.479	.450

ALL-TIME ALL-STAR TEAM 1

OUTFIELD: Ty Cobb, Tris Speaker, Babe Ruth **3B:** Pie Traynor **SS:** Honus Wagner **2B:** Charlie Gehringer **1B:** Lou Gehrig **RH PITCHER:** Walter Johnson **LH PITCHER:** Lefty Grove **CATCHER:** Bill Dickey **RELIEF PITCHER:** Wilcy Moore

ALL-TIME ALL-STAR TEAM 2

OUTFIELD: Joe DiMaggio, Mickey Mantle, Willie Mays **3B:** George Kell **SS:** Joe Cronin **2B:** Frankie Frisch **1B:** George Sisler **RH PITCHER:** Charlie Ruffing **LH PITCHER:** Lefty Gomez **CATCHER:** Mickey Cochrane **RELIEF PITCHER:** Fred Marberry

ALL-TIME DEFENSIVE TEAM

OUTFIELD: Charlie Jamieson, Tris Speaker, Ty Cobb **1B:** George Sisler **2B:** Charlie Gehringer **3B:** Willie Kamm **SS:** Marty Marion **RH PITCHER:** Ted Lyons **LH PITCHER:** Warren Spahn **CATCHER:** Luke Sewell

MOST UNDERRATED BALL PLAYERS OF ALL TIME: Enos Slaughter
BEST CLUTCH HITTER EVER: Ty Cobb
BEST PINCH HITTER: Johnny Mize
BEST SS-2B DOUBLE-PLAY COMBINATION EVER: Tinker-Evers
GAME 7 WORLD SERIES PITCHER: Charlie Ruffing
BEST MANAGER OF ALL TIME: Tris Speaker/Joe McCarthy
THE BEST TEAM: 1932 Yankees
FAVORITE STADIUM TO PLAY IN: Yankee Stadium
CITY WITH THE BEST FANS: New York/Boston
DESIGNATED HITTER: Oppose
BEST FASTBALL: Walter Johnson
BEST CURVE: Mel Harder
BEST SCREWBALL: Jim Bagby
BEST SPITBALL: Burleigh Grimes
BEST PICKOFF MOVE: Sherrod Smith
BEST SINKER/DROP: Wilcy Moore
BEST CHANGE-UP: Waite Hoyt
BEST SLIDER: George Blaeholder
BEST BASE STEALER OF ALL TIME: Ty Cobb
BEST BUNTER: Ty Cobb
BEST THROWING ARM OF ALL TIME: Babe Ruth
BEST UMPIRE YOU EVER SAW: Tommy Connelley
BALL PLAYERS THAT NEVER PLAYED UP TO THEIR POTENTIAL: Hank Aaron
TOUGHEST PITCHER YOU EVER BATTED AGAINST: Dutch Leonard
BALL PLAYER WHO DID THE MOST TO INSPIRE HIS TEAM: Ty Cobb/ Babe Ruth
BEST TEAM OWNER YOU'VE KNOWN: Jake Ruppert
BASEBALL WRITER WHO UNDERSTOOD THE GAME THE BEST: Ford Frick

⊘Luke Sewell⊘

1921-1932: Cleveland Indians; 1933-1934: Washington Senators; 1935-1938: Chicago White Sox; 1939: Cleveland Indians; 1942: St. Louis Browns

From his first game in 1921 to his last game as a manager in 1952, Luke Sewell's reputation was that of an excellent receiver and a keen student of the game.

Although he usually batted seventh or eighth, Sewell was adept at doing the little things: he was a good bunter and hit-and-run man, didn't strike out much, and had good speed, especially for a catcher. As a manager, he finished with a .485 winning percentage over 10 years and maneuvered the St. Louis Browns to their first and only pennant in 1944. In his choices, he sticks to his own era and isn't shy about picking himself on the defensive team or as an underrated ball player. And don't snicker, for Luke played 20 years and ranks 13th on the all-time list of games caught and 11th on the lifetime double-plays chart. He also caught three no-hitters.

Cleveland Indians

Luke Sewell

	AB	H	2B	3B	HR	R
LIFETIME	5383	1393	272	56	20	653
BEST COMPOSITE YEAR	474	138	30	9	5	65

	RBI	BB	SB	BA	SLG.	OB%
LIFETIME	696	486	65	.259	.341	.320
BEST COMPOSITE YEAR	73	54	11	.294	.384	.336

ALL-TIME ALL-STAR TEAM

OUTFIELD: Ty Cobb, Babe Ruth, Tris Speaker **3B:** Ossie Bluege **SS:** None **2B:** Charlie Gehringer **1B:** George Sisler **RH PITCHER:** George Uhle **LH PITCHER:** Lefty Grove **CATCHER:** None **RELIEF PITCHER:** Firpo Marberry

ALL-TIME DEFENSIVE TEAM

OUTFIELD: Charlie Jamieson, Dom DiMaggio **1B:** George Sisler **2B:** Charlie Gehringer **3B:** Ossie Bluege **SS:** Lou Boudreau **RH PITCHER:** None **LH PITCHER:** None **CATCHER:** Myself

MOST UNDERRATED BALL PLAYERS OF ALL TIME: Ossie Bluege, Myself
BEST CLUTCH HITTER EVER: Babe Ruth
GAME 7 WORLD SERIES PITCHER: Lefty Grove
THE BEST TEAM: 1926 Yankees
FAVORITE STADIUM TO PLAY IN: Comiskey Park (Chicago)
CITY WITH THE BEST FANS: Probably Boston
DESIGNATED HITTER: Oppose
BEST FASTBALL: Lefty Grove
BEST CURVE: George Uhle
BEST SCREWBALL: Carl Hubbell
BEST SPITBALL: Stan Coveleski
BEST PICKOFF MOVE: Sherry Smith
BEST BASE STEALER OF ALL TIME: Ty Cobb
BEST UMPIRE YOU EVER SAW: Bill Summers, Bill McGowan
TOUGHEST PITCHER YOU EVER BATTED AGAINST: Lefty Grove
HITTER YOU FOUND HARDEST TO GET OUT: Ty Cobb
BALL PLAYER WHO DID THE MOST TO INSPIRE HIS TEAM: Ty Cobb
BEST TEAM OWNER YOU'VE KNOWN: Probably Tom Yawkey

Rip Sewell

1932: Detroit Tigers; 1938-1949: Pittsburgh Pirates

In his 12 years with the Pirates, Rip Sewell's winning percentage was 100 points higher than the ball club's (.596/.496). His absurd "Eephus pitch," often imitated but never duplicated, caused great humiliation and embarrassment among hitters and ranks sixth on the players' best change-up list. Yes, Ted Williams tattooed the pitch in the 1946 All-Star game, but Sewell is hardly alone there. Rip was a three-time National League All-Star, and can often be found among the pitching leaders in various categories during his career.

When in doubt, Rip will lean toward a Pirate on his top teams, but hell, it's about time someone voted for Ralph Kiner. His choices on the whole reflect a knowledge of baseball history as well as an appreciation of today's players. Note the unusual choice of Cy Blanton for best curveball. A teammate of Sewell's, Blanton led the NL in ERA in 1935 and shutouts in both '35 and 36. You can also see that Rip has a high opinion of his own change-up and slider; 19 respondents agree with him about the off-speed pitch, but Rip stands alone in rating his slider the best.

	W-L	PCT.	ERA	
LIFETIME	143-97	.596	3.48	
BEST COMPOSITE YEAR	21-17	.813	2.54	

	IP	H	BB	SO	SHO.
LIFETIME	2119	2101	748	636	20
BEST COMPOSITE YEAR	286			87	5

ALL-TIME ALL-STAR TEAM 1

OUTFIELD: Joe DiMaggio, Paul Waner, Mickey Mantle **3B:** Pie Traynor **SS:** Honus Wagner **2B:** Charlie Gehringer **1B:** Johnny Mize **RH PITCHER:** Bob Feller **LH PITCHER:** Lefty Grove **CATCHER:** Mickey Cochrane **RELIEF PITCHER:** Bruce Sutter

ALL-TIME ALL-STAR TEAM 2

OUTFIELD: Roger Maris, Ralph Kiner, Willie Mays **3B:** Brooks Robinson **SS:** Pee Wee Reese **2B:** Billy Herman **1B:** Lou Gehrig **RH PITCHER:** Walter Johnson **LH PITCHER:** Warren Spahn **CATCHER:** Johnny Bench **RELIEF PITCHER:** Rollie Fingers

ALL-TIME DEFENSIVE TEAM

OUTFIELD: Joe DiMaggio, Willie Mays, Pete Reiser **1B:** Keith Hernandez **2B:** Billy Herman **3B:** Graig Nettles **SS:** Honus Wagner **RH PITCHER:** Bob Gibson **LH PITCHER:** Bobby Shantz **CATCHER:** Mickey Cochrane

BEST CLUTCH HITTER EVER: Dusty Rhodes
BEST PINCH HITTER: Manny Mota
BEST SS-2B DOUBLE-PLAY COMBINATION EVER: Tinker to Evers
GAME 7 WORLD SERIES PITCHER: Bob Feller

BEST MANAGER OF ALL TIME: Connie Mack
THE BEST TEAM: Yankees
FAVORITE STADIUM TO PLAY IN: Polo Grounds
CITY WITH THE BEST FANS: Chicago
DESIGNATED HITTER: Oppose
BEST FASTBALL: Walter Johnson
BEST CURVE: Cy Blanton
BEST SCREWBALL: Carl Hubbell
BEST SPITBALL: Burleigh Grimes
BEST PICKOFF MOVE: Steve Carlton
BEST SINKER/DROP: Tommy Bridges
BEST CHANGE-UP: Rip Sewell
BEST SLIDER: Rip Sewell
BEST BASE STEALER OF ALL TIME: Rickey Henderson
BEST BUNTER: Phil Rizzuto
BEST THROWING ARM OF ALL TIME: Ron Northey
MOST KNOWLEDGEABLE BASEBALL BROADCASTERS: Joe
   Garagiola, Red Barber
BEST UMPIRE YOU EVER SAW: Babe Pinelli
TOUGHEST PITCHER YOU EVER BATTED AGAINST: Carl Hubbell
HITTER YOU FOUND HARDEST TO GET OUT: Stan Musial
BALL PLAYER WHO DID THE MOST TO INSPIRE HIS TEAM: Pete
   Rose
BEST TEAM OWNER YOU'VE KNOWN: Tom Yawkey
**BASEBALL WRITER WHO UNDERSTOOD THE GAME THE
   BEST:** Grantland Rice

⚾ Larry Sherry ⚾

1958-1963: Los Angeles Dodgers; 1964-1967: Detroit Tigers; 1967: Houston
Astros; 1968: California Angels

Brother of Norm Sherry, the Dodger back-up backstop (who caught his brother
on many an occasion), Larry pitched almost exclusively in relief for the Dodgers
and played a key role in their 1959 and 1960 efforts. He won two World Series
games against the White Sox in '59 ... and saved the other two. In short, he was the
Series MVP.

	W-L	PCT.	ERA	G
LIFETIME	53-44	.546	3.67	416
BEST COMPOSITE YEAR	14-10	.778	2.19	58

	IP	H	BB	SO	SHO.
LIFETIME	799.1	747	374	606	1
BEST COMPOSITE YEAR	142.1			114	1

ALL-TIME ALL-STAR TEAM 1

OUTFIELD: Hank Aaron, Willie Mays, Roberto Clemente **3B:** Brooks Robinson **SS:** Luis Aparicio **2B:** Pete Rose **1B:** Willie Stargell **RH PITCHER:** Don Drysdale **LH PITCHER:** Whitey Ford **CATCHER:** Roy Campanella **RELIEF PITCHER:** Rich Gossage

ALL-TIME ALL-STAR TEAM 2

OUTFIELD: Mickey Mantle, Stan Musial, Ted Williams **3B:** Ken Boyer **SS:** Dave Concepcion **2B:** Nellie Fox **1B:** Gil Hodges **RH PITCHER:** Bob Gibson **LH PITCHER:** Sandy Koufax **CATCHER:** Johnny Bench **RELIEF PITCHER:** Rollie Fingers

ALL-TIME DEFENSIVE TEAM

OUTFIELD: Mickey Stanley, Ken Berry, Roberto Clemente **1B:** Vic Power **2B:** Bill Mazeroski **3B:** Brooks Robinson **SS:** Roy McMillan **RH PITCHER:** Bob L. Miller **LH PITCHER:** Bobby Shantz **CATCHER:** Johnny Bench

MOST UNDERRATED BALL PLAYERS OF ALL TIME: Al Kaline
BEST PINCH HITTER: Smoky Burgess
GAME 7 WORLD SERIES PITCHER: Don Drysdale
BEST MANAGER OF ALL TIME: Billy Martin
THE BEST TEAM: Dodgers
FAVORITE STADIUM TO PLAY IN: Dodger Stadium
CITY WITH THE BEST FANS: Los Angeles (Dodgers)/Cincinnati
DESIGNATED HITTER: Oppose
BEST FASTBALL: Rex Barney
BEST SCREWBALL: Jim Brewer
BEST SPITBALL: Gaylord Perry
BEST PICKOFF MOVE: Danny McDevitt
BEST SINKER/DROP: Clem Labine
BEST CHANGE-UP: Johnny Padres
BEST SLIDER: Bob Gibson
BEST BASE STEALER OF ALL TIME: Lou Brock
BEST BUNTER: Rod Carew
BEST THROWING ARM OF ALL TIME: Carl Furillo

MOST KNOWLEDGEABLE BASEBALL BROADCASTERS: Vin Scully
BEST UMPIRE YOU EVER SAW: Al Barlick
BALL PLAYERS WHO NEVER PLAYED UP TO THEIR POTENTIAL:
Willie Davis, Al Kaline
BALL PLAYER WHO DID THE MOST TO INSPIRE HIS TEAM: Gil
Hodges
BEST TEAM OWNER YOU'VE KNOWN: Walter O'Malley

Dick Sisler

1946-1947: St. Louis Cardinals; 1948-1951: Philadelphia Phillies; 1952:
Cincinnati Reds; 1952-1953: St. Louis Cardinals

There are no real surprises on Dick Sisler's ballot, just extremely well-thought-out responses, spanning the years from Cy Young to Rickey Henderson. The only hints of bias are the (100% justifiable) choices of his father, the immortal George Sisler, as the best first baseman and pure hitter. It's hard to believe that *anyone* could leave out a fabulous-fielding .420 hitter who led his league in stolen bases four times. For your pleasure, we include George's stats here too.

Let's not forget that Dick was a good ball player too. Adept at both first base and the outfield, his major-league debut wasn't until after WW II at the age of 26. His three-run homer off Don Newcombe in the 10th inning of the last game of the 1950 season won the pennant for the Phillies, and had it been hit for a N.Y. team it would be as famous as Bobby Thomson's "Shot heard 'round the world." Dick also managed Cincinnati for a year and a half in 1964 and 1965; he took over from Freddy Hutchinson in mid-'64 and missed the pennant by only one game. His overall winning percentage as a manager was .563 (121-94).

Dick Sisler	AB	H	2B	3B	HR	R
LIFETIME	2606	720	118	28	55	302
BEST COMPOSITE YEAR	523	155	29	6	13	79

	RBI	BB	SB	BA	SLG.	OB%
LIFETIME	360	226	6	.276	.406	.334
BEST COMPOSITE YEAR	83	64	3	.296	.442	.373

George Sisler	AB	H	2B	3B	HR	R
LIFETIME	8267	2812	425	165	100	1284
BEST COMPOSITE YEAR	649	257	49	18	19	137

	RBI	BB	SB	BA	SLG.	OB%
LIFETIME	1175	472	375	.340	.468	.376
BEST COMPOSITE YEAR	122	49	51	.420	.632	.465

ALL-TIME ALL-STAR TEAM 1

OUTFIELD: Babe Ruth, Ty Cobb, Joe DiMaggio/Tris Speaker **3B:** Pie Traynor **SS:** Honus Wagner **2B:** Rogers Hornsby **1B:** George Sisler/Lou Gehrig **RH PITCHER:** Walter Johnson **LH PITCHER:** Lefty Grove **CATCHER:** Mickey Cochrane **RELIEF PITCHER:** Cy Young

ALL-TIME ALL-STAR TEAM 2

OUTFIELD: Mickey Mantle, Willie Mays, Ted Williams **3B:** Brooks Robinson **SS:** Pee Wee Reese **2B:** Charlie Gehringer **1B:** Stan Musial **RH PITCHER:** Bob Gibson **LH PITCHER:** Warren Spahn **CATCHER:** Johnny Bench **RELIEF PITCHER:**Rich Gossage

ALL-TIME DEFENSIVE TEAM

OUTFIELD: Terry Moore, Dom DiMaggio, Roberto Clemente **1B:** George Sisler **2B:** Red Schoendienst **3B:** Brooks Robinson **SS:** Marty Marion **RH PITCHER:** Bob Gibson **LH PITCHER:** Jim Kaat **CATCHER:** Rick Ferrell

MOST UNDERRATED BALL PLAYERS OF ALL TIME: Enos Slaughter, Terry Moore, Phil Rizzuto
BEST PINCH HITTER: Smoky Burgess
BEST *PURE* HITTER: Ted Williams/George Sisler
BEST SS-2B DOUBLE-PLAY COMBINATION EVER: Marty Marion-Red Schoendienst
GAME 7 WORLD SERIES PITCHER: Bob Gibson
BEST MANAGER OF ALL TIME: Joe McCarthy
THE BEST TEAM: 1927 Yankees
FAVORITE STADIUM TO PLAY IN: Ebbets Field/Wrigley Field
CITY WITH THE BEST FANS: Same as above
DESIGNATED HITTER: Oppose
BEST FASTBALL: Walter Johnson
BEST CURVE: Bob Feller
BEST SCREWBALL: Carl Hubbell/Fred Fitzsimmons
BEST SPITBALL: Burleigh Grimes
BEST PICKOFF MOVE: Warren Spahn/Bill Wight
BEST CHANGE-UP: Carl Erskine

BEST SLIDER: Robin Roberts
BEST BASE STEALER OF ALL TIME: Rickey Henderson
BEST BUNTER: Phil Rizzuto
BEST HIT-AND-RUN MAN: Luke Appling/Dick Groat
BEST THROWING ARM OF ALL TIME: Roberto Clemente
MOST KNOWLEDGEABLE BASEBALL BROADCASTERS: Red Barber, Ernie Harwell
BEST UMPIRE YOU EVER SAW: Al Barlick
TOUGHEST PITCHER YOU EVER BATTED AGAINST: Curt Simmons
BALL PLAYER WHO DID THE MOST TO INSPIRE HIS TEAM: Enos Slaughter
BEST TEAM OWNER YOU'VE KNOWN: Bob Carpenter/Gene Autry
BASEBALL WRITER WHO UNDERSTOOD THE GAME THE BEST: Bob Broeg

◐ Enos Slaughter ◑

1938-1942 & 1946-1953: St. Louis Cardinals; 1954-1955: N.Y. Yankees; 1955-1956: Kansas City Athletics; 1956-1959: N.Y. Yankees; 1959: Milwaukee Braves

The easy #1 choice as the most underrated player ever, Hall of Famer Enos "Country" Slaughter, the tobacco farmer from North Carolina, was a ball player's ball player, great on defense and always an offensive threat. Slaughter was a line-drive hitter with extra-base power to all fields, a world-class base runner, and a disciplined swinger with nearly two walks for every strikeout. As an outfielder he was superb, with a shotgun arm. Last but not least, his hustling style was an inspiration to those who saw or played with him (including a young fan named Pete Rose)—he garnered 6 1/2 votes as the player who did the most to inspire his team. Slaughter's lifetime numbers are impressive enough, but the war robbed him of the very prime of his career (military service at ages 27 through 29). He led the league in hits and triples in 1942, and in RBIs when he returned in 1946. World War II cost Country Slaughter lifetime totals of over 500 doubles, 200 home runs, and nearly 200 triples, not to mention 3,000 hits.

His picks in our survey reflect a kind of consensus, spanning the generations. Note his choice of the 1942 Cardinals as the best team ever; they were a superb squad, for sure, winning 106 games while scoring the most runs and allowing the fewest in the league. They came from behind to beat a great Dodger club down the stretch, then stunned the baseball world by disposing of the mighty Yankees in five Series games.

	AB	H	2B	3B	HR	R
LIFETIME	7946	2383	413	148	169	1247
BEST COMPOSITE YEAR	609	193	52	17	18	100

Whitey Ford and Enos Slaughter after starring in Game 3 of the 1956 World Series.

	RBI	BB	SB	BA	SLG.	OB%
LIFETIME	1304	1019	71	.300	.453	.379
BEST COMPOSITE YEAR	130	88	9	.336	.511	.417

ALL-TIME ALL-STAR TEAM 1

OUTFIELD: Babe Ruth, Joe DiMaggio, Ty Cobb **3B:** Pie Traynor **SS:** Honus Wagner **2B:** Charlie Gehringer **1B:** Lou Gehrig **RH PITCHER:** Cy Young **LH PITCHER:** Lefty Grove **CATCHER:** Gabby Hartnett **RELIEF PITCHER:** Hoyt Wilhelm

ALL-TIME ALL-STAR TEAM 2

OUTFIELD: Ted Williams, Mickey Mantle, Henry Aaron **3B:** Brooks Robinson **SS:** Joe Cronin **2B:** Rogers Hornsby **1B:** George Sisler **RH PITCHER:** Grover Alexander **LH PITCHER:** Warren Spahn **CATCHER:** Bill Dickey **RELIEF PITCHER:** Rollie Fingers

ALL-TIME DEFENSIVE TEAM

OUTFIELD: Joe DiMaggio and Terry Moore **1B:** Hal Chase **2B:** Eddie Collins **3B:** Brooks Robinson **SS:** None **RH PITCHER:** None **LH PITCHER:** Bobby Shantz **CATCHER:** Johnny Bench

MOST UNDERRATED BALL PLAYERS OF ALL TIME: Enos Slaughter
BEST PINCH HITTER: Johnny Mize
GAME 7 WORLD SERIES PITCHER: Whitey Ford
BEST MANAGER OF ALL TIME: John McGraw
THE BEST TEAM: 1942 Cardinals
CITY WITH THE BEST FANS: Brooklyn
DESIGNATED HITTER: Favor
BEST FASTBALL: Bob Feller
BEST CURVE: Tommy Bridges
BEST SCREWBALL: Carl Hubbell
BEST SPITBALL: Burleigh Grimes
BEST PICKOFF MOVE: Whitey Ford
BEST BASE STEALER OF ALL TIME: Lou Brock
BEST UMPIRE YOU EVER SAW: Bill Klem
BASEBALL WRITER WHO UNDERSTOOD THE GAME THE BEST: Red Smith

⚾ Tracy Stallard ⚾

1960-1962: Boston Red Sox; 1963-1964: N.Y. Mets; 1965-1966: St. Louis Cardinals

It didn't lengthen Tracy's career to get stuck on three lousy teams in his six years in the majors. Best known for giving up Roger Maris's 61st home run in 1961, Stallard should have won an award for losing only 20 games—the most in the NL—in 1964 with the New York Mets, who were 53-109. Truth is, his 10-20 won-lost season was his *best*—because his ERA that grotesque year was just 3.79. He yielded only 213 hits in 225.2 innings pitched and kept his sanity (e.g., only 73 walks allowed) while the hapless Mets tried to look like major leaguers.

But the Met front office shipped him off to the world champion St. Louis Cardinals, with whom Stallard went 11-8, 3.38 ERA in 1965. That was the year the Cards collapsed, however.

National Baseball Library

Met catcher Jesse Gonder congratulating Tracy Stallard after a 1964 shutout of Cardinals.

	W-L	PCT.	ERA	G
LIFETIME	30-57	.345	4.17	183
BEST COMPOSITE YEAR	11-20	.579	3.38	43

	IP	H	BB	SO	SHO.
LIFETIME	764.2	716	343	477	3
BEST COMPOSITE YEAR	225.2			118	2

ALL-TIME ALL-STAR TEAM 1

OUTFIELD: Mickey Mantle, Willie Mays, Al Kaline **3B:** Brooks Robinson **SS:** Phil Rizzuto **2B:** Bobby Richardson **1B:** Rod Carew **RH PITCHER:** Juan Marichal **LH PITCHER:** Sandy Koufax **CATCHER:** Johnny Bench **RELIEF PITCHER:** Rich Gossage

ALL-TIME ALL-STAR TEAM 2

OUTFIELD: Ted Williams, Joe DiMaggio, Pete Reiser **3B:** Graig Nettles **SS:** Mark Belanger **2B:** Julian Javier **1B:** Gil Hodges **RH PITCHER:** Bob Feller **LH PITCHER:** Whitey Ford **CATCHER:** Yogi Berra **RELIEF PITCHER:** Bruce Sutter

ALL-TIME DEFENSIVE TEAM

OUTFIELD: Al Kaline, Willie Mays, Mickey Mantle **1B:** Rod Carew/Gil Hodges **2B:** Bobby Richardson **3B:** Brooks Robinson **SS:** Phil Rizzuto **RH PITCHER:** Don Drysdale **LH PITCHER:** Bobby Shantz **CATCHER:** Johnny Bench

MOST UNDERRATED BALL PLAYERS OF ALL TIME: Al Kaline, Rod Carew
BEST CLUTCH HITTER EVER: Gil Hodges
BEST PINCH HITTER: Smoky Burgess
GAME 7 WORLD SERIES PITCHER: Sandy Koufax
BEST MANAGER OF ALL TIME: Walter Alston
THE BEST TEAM: Yankees
FAVORITE STADIUM TO PLAY IN: Dodger Stadium
CITY WITH THE BEST FANS: Los Angeles (Dodgers)
DESIGNATED HITTER: Oppose
BEST FASTBALL: Herb Score/Nolan Ryan
BEST CURVE: Sandy Koufax

BEST SCREWBALL: Whitey Ford
BEST SPITBALL: Don Drysdale
BEST PICKOFF MOVE: Roger Craig
BEST CHANGE-UP: Stu Miller
BEST SLIDER: Bob Gibson
BEST BASE STEALER OF ALL TIME: Maury Wills
BEST THROWING ARM OF ALL TIME: Rocky Colavito
MOST KNOWLEDGEABLE BASEBALL BROADCASTERS: Vin Scully,
Lindsay Nelson
BEST UMPIRE YOU EVER SAW: Tom Gorman
HITTER YOU FOUND HARDEST TO GET OUT: Tony Kubek
BALL PLAYER WHO DID THE MOST TO INSPIRE HIS TEAM: Mickey
Mantle
BEST TEAM OWNER YOU'VE KNOWN: Tom Yawkey
**BASEBALL WRITER WHO UNDERSTOOD THE GAME THE
BEST:** Red Smith

⚾ Virgil Trucks ⚾

1941-1952: Detroit Tigers; 1953: St. Louis Browns; 1953-1955: Chicago White
Sox; 1956: Detroit Tigers; 1957-1958: Kansas City Athletics; 1958: N.Y. Yankees

Virgil Trucks pitched his first major-league game at the age of 21 and his last at
39. In between he had a losing record only twice, and it can be said with confidence
that World War II cost him lifetime totals of 200 wins and 40 shutouts. As it is, his
stats of 177 and 35 aren't shabby. Pitching amid trade rumors all season with the
last-place Tigers of 1952, Virgil earned his share of baseball immortality by twirling two no-hitters, 1-0 blankings of the Senators and Yankees. Detroit did trade
him at the end of the year, and he proceeded to win 39 games in the next two years.
Trucks was the right-handed half of one of the really good lefty-righty duos (with
Hal Newhouser); between them they won 298 games for the Tigers, exactly the
same total that Christy Mathewson and Rube Marquard won for the Giants.
  In his selections, Virgil chooses Detroit Tigers where reasonable and shows a
clear preference for recent ball players on his second team. Surprise picks are Billy
Hunter as best defensive shortstop and Dick Conger for best change-up. Conger
was a right-hander who got his first late-season look with Detroit at the age of 19 in
1940 but never got a chance after the war.

	W-L	PCT.	ERA	G
LIFETIME	177-235	.567	3.39	517
BEST COMPOSITE YEAR	20-19	.667	2.74	48

	IP	H	BB	SO	SHO.
LIFETIME	2682	2416	1088	1534	35
BEST COMPOSITE YEAR	275			161	6

ALL-TIME ALL-STAR TEAM 1

OUTFIELD: Babe Ruth, Ty Cobb, Joe DiMaggio **3B:** George Kell **SS:** Luke Appling **2B:** Charlie Gehringer **1B:** Hank Greenberg **RH PITCHER:** Bob Feller **LH PITCHER:** Steve Carlton **CATCHER:** Mickey Cochrane **RELIEF PITCHER:** Johnny Murphy

ALL-TIME ALL-STAR TEAM 2

OUTFIELD: Willie Mays, Hank Aaron, Ted Williams **3B:** Mike Schmidt **SS:** Frank Crosetti **2B:** Pete Rose **1B:** Steve Garvey **RH PITCHER:** Tom Seaver **LH PITCHER:** Whitey Ford **CATCHER:** Gary Carter **RELIEF PITCHER:** Rollie Fingers

ALL-TIME DEFENSIVE TEAM

OUTFIELD: Tris Speaker, Dom DiMaggio, Willie Mays **1B:** Lou Gehrig **2B:** Bill Mazeroski **3B:** Red Rolfe **SS:** Billy Hunter **RH PITCHER:** Allie Reynolds **LH PITCHER:** Warren Spahn **CATCHER:** Bill Dickey

MOST UNDERRATED BALL PLAYERS OF ALL TIME: Steve Garvey
BEST CLUTCH HITTER EVER: Ted Williams
BEST PINCH HITTER: Smoky Burgess
BEST SS-2B DOUBLE-PLAY COMBINATION EVER: Dick Groat-Bill Mazeroski
GAME 7 WORLD SERIES PITCHER: Whitey Ford
BEST MANAGER OF ALL TIME: Walt Alston
THE BEST TEAM: Yankees
FAVORITE STADIUM TO PLAY IN: Detroit
CITY WITH THE BEST FANS: New York (Yankees)
DESIGNATED HITTER: Oppose
BEST FASTBALL: Bob Feller
BEST CURVE: Bob Feller
BEST SCREWBALL: Carl Hubbell
BEST SPITBALL: Lew Burdette
BEST PICKOFF MOVE: Whitey Ford
BEST SINKER/DROP: Carl Hubbell
BEST CHANGE-UP: Dick Conger
BEST SLIDER: Robin Roberts

BEST BASE STEALER OF ALL TIME: Ty Cobb
BEST BUNTER: Phil Rizzuto
BEST THROWING ARM OF ALL TIME: Roberto Clemente
MOST KNOWLEDGEABLE BASEBALL BROADCASTERS: Harry Heilmann, Mel Allen
BEST UMPIRE YOU EVER SAW: Bill Summers
BALL PLAYERS WHO NEVER PLAYED UP TO THEIR POTEN-TIAL: Johnny Groth, Dick Wakefield
TOUGHEST PITCHER YOU EVER BATTED AGAINST: All of them
HITTER YOU FOUND HARDEST TO GET OUT: Ted Williams
BALL PLAYER WHO DID THE MOST TO INSPIRE HIS TEAM: Dizzy Trout
BEST TEAM OWNER YOU'VE KNOWN: Walter O. Briggs, Sr.
BASEBALL WRITER WHO UNDERSTOOD THE GAME THE BEST: Sam Greene

◯ Billy Wambsganss ◯

1914-1923: Cleveland Indians; 1924-1925: Boston Red Sox; 1926: Philadelphia Athletics

The late Billy Wambsganss was the oldest player to send us a ballot; he broke in with Cleveland in 1914. Primarily a second baseman, he is best remembered for an unassisted triple play in game five of the 1920 World Series. (That game also featured the first World Series grand slam, by the Indians' Elmer Smith.) Wamby was fine afield and a decent dead-ball hitter with excellent speed.

	AB	H	2B	3B	HR	R
LIFETIME	5241	1359	215	59	7	710
BEST COMPOSITE YEAR	636	174	41	11	2	93

	RBI	BB	SB	BA	SLG.	OB%
LIFETIME	519	490	142	.259	.327	.323
BEST COMPOSITE YEAR	60	60	18	.295	.393	.369

ALL-TIME ALL-STAR TEAM 1

OUTFIELD: Babe Ruth, Ty Cobb, Tris Speaker **3B:** Home Run Baker **SS:** Honus Wagner **2B:** Eddie Collins **1B:** Lou Gehrig **RH PITCHER:** Walter Johnson **LH PITCHER:** Sandy Koufax **CATCHER:** Ray Schalk **RELIEF PITCHER:** Rollie Fingers

National Baseball Library

Bill Wambsganss completes his unassisted triple play in the 1920 World Series by tagging Brooklyn Dodger Otto Miller. Pete Kilduff of the Dodgers, who had been doubled off second, looks back from third base, as does Cleveland third baseman Larry Gardner.

ALL-TIME ALL-STAR TEAM 2

OUTFIELD: Joe Jackson, Zack Wheat, Rube Oldring **3B:** Larry Gardner **SS:** Lou Boudreau **2B:** Rogers Hornsby **1B:** Hal Trosky **RH PITCHER:** Joe Wood **LH PITCHER:** Bob (Lefty) Grove **CATCHER:** Jimmy Archer **RELIEF PITCHER:** Willie Hernandez

ALL-TIME DEFENSIVE TEAM

OUTFIELD: Tris Speaker, Joe Jackson, Max Carey **1B:** Hal Chase **2B:** Jimmy Dykes, Rogers Hornsby **3B:** Brooks Robinson **SS:** Honus Wagner **RH PITCHER:** Joe Wood **LH PITCHER:** Jim Kaat **CATCHER:** Jim Hegan

MOST UNDERRATED BALL PLAYERS OF ALL TIME: Donie Bush, Everett Scott, Harry Steinfeldt

BEST CLUTCH HITTER EVER: Babe Ruth
BEST PINCH HITTER: Babe Ruth
BEST SS-2B DOUBLE-PLAY COMBINATION EVER: Lou Boudreau-Joe Gordon
GAME 7 WORLD SERIES PITCHER: Walter Johnson
BEST MANAGER OF ALL TIME: Connie Mack
THE BEST TEAM: 1914 Philadelphia Athletics
FAVORITE STADIUM TO PLAY IN: Polo Grounds
CITY WITH THE BEST FANS: Boston
DESIGNATED HITTER: Oppose
BEST FASTBALL: Walter Johnson
BEST CURVE: Joe Wood
BEST SCREWBALL: Jim Bagby
BEST SPITBALL: Stan Coveleski
BEST PICKOFF MOVE: Sherry Smith
BEST SINKER/DROP: Carl Hubbell
BEST CHANGE-UP: Jean Dubuc
BEST SLIDER: Early Wynn
BEST BASE STEALER OF ALL TIME: Max Carey
BEST BUNTER: Bill Wambsganss
BEST THROWING ARM OF ALL TIME: Tris Speaker
MOST KNOWLEDGEABLE BASEBALL BROADCASTERS: Red Barber, Herb Score
BEST UMPIRE YOU EVER SAW: Billy Evans
TOUGHEST PITCHER YOU EVER BATTED AGAINST: Walter Johnson
BALL PLAYER WHO DID THE MOST TO INSPIRE HIS TEAM: Joe Sewell, Tris Speaker
BEST TEAM OWNER YOU'VE KNOWN: Jim Dunn
BASEBALL WRITER WHO UNDERSTOOD THE GAME THE BEST: Grantland Rice

⊘Sammy White⊘

1951-1959: Boston Red Sox; 1961: Milwaukee Braves; 1962: Philadelphia Phillies

Originally, we planned to give Sammy this page because his brother, Bill, used to live next door to one of us. But then we took a close look at his stats. He was, in the words of former teammate Johnny Pesky, "a good receiver." Fine on defense, he's one of only 27 catchers in AL history to pull off an unassisted double play, and he caught in 1,027 games during his career. He also poked most of his 66 home runs over the Green Monster at Fenway Park, and in general used that ball park to its best advantage. In the seasons he wasn't hurt or platooned, he averaged 63 RBIs.

Note that Sammy nominates Mel Parnell for the best pickoff move. White was behind the plate for Parnell's no-hitter in 1956 against the White Sox. And, putting modesty aside, Sammy picks himself as the best defensive catcher ever. Maybe you can think of other candidates, but White *was* unnoticed when he played. Let's give him his due, starting with a look at his statistics:

	AB	H	2B	3B	HR	R
LIFETIME	3502	916	167	20	66	324
BEST COMPOSITE YEAR	544	142	34	4	14	65

	RBI	BB	SB	BA	SLG.	OB%
LIFETIME	421	218	14	.262	.377	.305
BEST COMPOSITE YEAR	75	44	4	.284	.435	.325

ALL-TIME ALL-STAR TEAM 1

OUTFIELD: Ted Williams, Mickey Mantle, Joe DiMaggio **3B:** Brooks Robinson **SS:** Cal Ripken **2B:** Nellie Fox **1B:** Gil Hodges **RH PITCHER:** Bob Lemon **LH PITCHER:** Warren Spahn **CATCHER:** Johnny Bench **RELIEF PITCHER:** Ellis Kinder

ALL-TIME ALL-STAR TEAM 2

OUTFIELD: Duke Snider, Willie Mays, Al Kaline **3B:** George Kell **SS:** Honus Wagner **2B:** Rogers Hornsby **1B:** Lou Gehrig **RH PITCHER:** Don Drysdale **LH PITCHER:** Sandy Koufax **CATCHER:** Roy Campanella **RELIEF PITCHER:** Hoyt Wilhelm

ALL-TIME DEFENSIVE TEAM

OUTFIELD: Richie Ashburn, Jackie Jensen, Hank Bauer **1B:** Mickey Vernon **2B:** Frank Bolling **3B:** Brooks Robinson **SS:** Marty Marion **RH PITCHER:** Don Larsen **LH PITCHER:** Whitey Ford **CATCHER:** Sammy White

BEST CLUTCH HITTER EVER: Al Rosen
BEST PINCH HITTER: Manny Mota
BEST *PURE* HITTER: Stan Musial
BEST SS-2B DOUBLE-PLAY COMBINATION EVER: Tinker-Evers
GAME 7 WORLD SERIES PITCHER: Warren Spahn
BEST MANAGER OF ALL TIME: Darrell Johnson
THE BEST TEAM: 1957 Yankees

FAVORITE STADIUM TO PLAY IN: Detroit (Tiger Stadium)
CITY WITH THE BEST FANS: Detroit
DESIGNATED HITTER: Favor
BEST FASTBALL: Bob Turley
BEST CURVE: Bob Lemon
BEST SCREWBALL: Warren Spahn
BEST SPITBALL: Ellis Kinder
BEST PICKOFF MOVE: Mel Parnell
BEST SINKER/DROP: Frank Sullivan
BEST CHANGE-UP: Whitey Ford
BEST SLIDER: Bob Lemon
BEST BASE STEALER OF ALL TIME: Rickey Henderson
BEST BUNTER: Billy Goodman
BEST HIT-AND-RUN MAN: George Kell
BEST THROWING ARM OF ALL TIME: Rocky Colavito
MOST KNOWLEDGEABLE BASEBALL BROADCASTERS: Mel Allen, Curt Gowdy
BEST UMPIRE YOU EVER SAW: Bill Summers
BALL PLAYERS THAT NEVER PLAYED UP TO THEIR POTENTIAL: Walt Dropo, Jim Piersall, Haywood Sullivan
TOUGHEST PITCHER YOU EVER BATTED AGAINST: Bob Lemon
BALL PLAYER WHO DID THE MOST TO INSPIRE HIS TEAM: Don Zimmer
BEST TEAM OWNER YOU'VE KNOWN: Bill Veeck
BASEBALL WRITER WHO UNDERSTOOD THE GAME THE BEST: None

⚾ Glenn Wright ⚾

1924-1928: Pittsburgh Pirates; 1929-1933: Brooklyn Dodgers; 1935: Chicago White Sox

The late Glenn "Buckshot" Wright, so-called because of his rifle arm, was also called "flawless" by Arthur Daley of the *New York Times*. Ranked 18th by the players on the all-time list, he rates fifth among shortstops of the 1921-1945 era, and he also received 12 votes as an underrated ball player. Had there been a Rookie of the Year award in 1924, Glenn would have been a strong contender for the honor, breaking in with the Pirates with a .287 average and 111 RBIs and playing shortstop in all 153 games that season. During his 11-year career with Pittsburgh and Brooklyn, Wright hit over .300 four times, and four times drove in over 100 runs. As a shortstop, he set a record that stood for 51 years with 601 assists, leading the league in that department twice, in double plays twice, and in putouts once. Wright got the thrill of a lifetime on May 7, 1925. In the ninth inning vs. the Cardinals, with Jimmy Cooney on second and Rogers Hornsby on first, Sunny Jim

Bottomley ripped a liner up the middle with the hit-and-run on. Wright speared the drive, stepped on second, then tagged Hornsby running from first, thus completing that rarest of rare plays, the unassisted triple play.

Wright's all-time team is notable for its National League slant, for the great throwing arms in the outfield, and for the choice of Al Lopez, brilliant on defense, as the catcher, bypassing several other Hall of Fame receivers.

	AB	H	2B	3B	HR	R
LIFETIME	4153	1219	203	76	93	584
BEST COMPOSITE YEAR	616	189	32	18	22	97

	RBI	BB	SB	BA	SLG.	OB%
LIFETIME	723	209	38	.294	.446	.327
BEST COMPOSITE YEAR	126	39	14	.321	.543	.360

ALL-TIME ALL-STAR TEAM 1

OUTFIELD: Babe Ruth, Paul Waner, Chick Hafey **3B:** Pie Traynor **SS:** Travis Jackson **2B:** Rogers Hornsby **1B:** Bill Terry **RH PITCHER:** Brover Cleveland Alexander **LH PITCHER:** Lefty Grove **CATCHER:** Al Lopez **RELIEF PITCHER:** None

BEST CLUTCH HITTER EVER: Rogers Hornsby
GAME 7 WORLD SERIES PITCHER: Grover Cleveland Alexander
BEST MANAGER OF ALL TIME: Joe McCarthy
THE BEST TEAM: 1927 Yankees
DESIGNATED HITTER: Favor
BEST FASTBALL: Walter Johnson
BEST CURVE: Too many
BEST SCREWBALL: Carl Hubbell
BEST SPITBALL: Burleigh Grimes
BEST PICKOFF MOVE: Can't remember
BEST SINKER/DROP: Wilcy Moore
BEST CHANGE-UP: Grover C. Alexander
BEST SLIDER: Not sure
BEST BASE STEALER OF ALL TIME: Pepper Martin
BEST BUNTER: Rabbit Maranville
BEST THROWING ARM OF ALL TIME: Bob Meusel
MOST KNOWLEDGEABLE BASEBALL BROADCASTERS: Red Barber
BEST UMPIRE YOU EVER SAW: Bill Klem

TOUGHEST PITCHER YOU EVER BATTED AGAINST: Grover Cleveland
Alexander
BALL PLAYER WHO DID THE MOST TO INSPIRE HIS TEAM: Babe
Ruth
BEST TEAM OWNER YOU'VE KNOWN: Barney Dreyfus
**BASEBALL WRITER WHO UNDERSTOOD THE GAME THE
BEST:** Dan Daniels

How Much Are You Worth Today?

"If you were playing today, how much should your annual salary be?" We asked
this of selected old-timers. Jim Bunning told us, "It's not important." That
wasn't what most of the rest said. Some answers:

Eddie Lopat: "Around $1 million"
Marty Marion: "$1 million"
Vinegar Bend Mizell: "$500,000"
Johnny Pesky: "350-400,000"
Harry Eisenstat: "500,000"

Phil Linz deadpanned, "I gotta think at least thirty thousand a year." Then he
added, soberly, that he'd probably have a contract of three years at $300,000
per.

In every case, as we see it, the old-timers came in on the low side.

⚾ Whitlow Wyatt ⚾

1929-1933: Detroit Tigers; 1933-1936: Chicago White Sox; 1937: Cleveland Indians; 1939-1944: Brooklyn Dodgers; 1945: Philadelphia Phillies

Whit Wyatt struggled as a relief pitcher through the 1930s with the Tigers,
White Sox, and Indians. The problem: control of a sharp-breaking slider, one good
enough to garner six votes as the best ever. With the Brooklyn Dodgers in 1939,
Leo Durocher put Wyatt in the starting rotation and he responded by becoming a
star. In that season Brooklyn jumped from seventh to third place and finished no
lower during Wyatt's five prime years with the club. His record over that span was
78-39, with a 2.71 ERA in tiny Ebbets Field. He and Kirby Higbe each won 22
games for the 1941 Bums, and Wyatt went on to beat the Yankees in the series that
year, the only Brooklyn pitcher to do so. He also coached in the majors and minors
until 1964.

	W-L	PCT.	ERA	G	
LIFETIME	106-95	.527	3.78	360	
BEST COMPOSITE YEAR	22-14	.737	2.34	43	
	IP	H	BB	SO	SHO.
LIFETIME	1762	1684	642	872	17
BEST COMPOSITE YEAR	288			176	7

ALL-TIME ALL-STAR TEAM 1

OUTFIELD: Joe DiMaggio, Babe Ruth, Ted Williams **3B:** Brooks Robinson **SS:** Pee Wee Reese **2B:** Charlie Gehringer **1B:** Lou Gehrig **RH PITCHER:** Bob Feller **LH PITCHER:** Warren Spahn **CATCHER:** Bill Dickey

BEST MANAGER OF ALL TIME: Leo Durocher
THE BEST TEAM: 1929-1931 Yankees
FAVORITE STADIUM TO PLAY IN: County Stadium, Milwaukee
CITY WITH THE BEST FANS: Brooklyn
DESIGNATED HITTER: Oppose
BEST FASTBALL: Bob Feller
BEST CURVE: Bob Feller/Tommy Bridges
BEST SCREWBALL: Carl Hubbell
BEST SPITBALL: Red Faber/Burleigh Grimes
BEST PICKOFF MOVE: Warren Spahn
BEST SINKER/DROP: Bob Lemon
BEST CHANGE-UP: Elroy Face
BEST SLIDER: George Blaeholder
BEST BASE STEALER OF ALL TIME: Ty Cobb/Lou Brock
BEST BUNTER: Maury Wills
BEST THROWING ARM OF ALL TIME: Bob Meusel
MOST KNOWLEDGEABLE BASEBALL BROADCASTERS: Red Barber
BEST UMPIRE YOU EVER SAW: Babe Pinelli
TOUGHEST PITCHER YOU EVER BATTED AGAINST: Bob Feller
HITTER YOU FOUND HARDEST TO GET OUT: Slap hitters
BEST TEAM OWNER YOU'VE KNOWN: Lew Perini/Larry MacPhail
BASEBALL WRITER WHO UNDERSTOOD THE GAME THE BEST: Roscoe McGowan

⬤Don Zimmer⬤

1954-1959: Brooklyn/L.A. Dodgers; 1960-1961: Chicago Cubs; 1962: N.Y. Mets-Cincinnati Reds; 1963: Los Angeles Dodgers; 1963-1965: Washington Senators

Don Zimmer was nearly killed when beaned by a pitch in the minors in 1953 and was hit in the face three years later by a Hal Jeffcoat pitch, suffering a fractured cheekbone. The scrappy infielder was much slimmer, we assure you, than the figure you've seen on the screen with the Yanks, the Red Sox, or the Cubs.

Zim was something more than a utility man, something less than a regular at any of the infield positions. He averaged 91 games per season and scored or knocked in a run every three games. And in 1961, he made the NL All-Star team.

Few ball players have seen as much talent in the last 30 years as Zim (or as many umpires he didn't like; look at his ballot). His nine years as a manager have been moderately successful, the best of them coming when he was at the Red Sox helm; each year he was frustrated by either the Yankees or the Orioles, but each year was respectable. What we noticed, however, is that he didn't nominate *one* ball player he's managed to any of the top spots.

	AB	H	2B	3B	HR	R
LIFETIME	3283	773	130	22	91	353
BEST COMPOSITE YEAR	477	120	25	7	17	57

	RBI	BB	SB	BA	SLG.	OB%
LIFETIME	352	246	45	.235	.372	.289
BEST COMPOSITE YEAR	60	37	14	.262	.443	.304

ALL-TIME ALL-STAR TEAM 1

OUTFIELD: Joe DiMaggio, Ty Cobb, Babe Ruth **3B:** Brooks Robinson **SS:** Luis Aparicio **2B:** Charlie Gehringer **1B:** Lou Gehrig **RH PITCHER:** Bob Feller **LH PITCHER:** Lefty Grove **CATCHER:** Johnny Bench **RELIEF PITCHER:** Johnny Murphy

ALL-TIME ALL-STAR TEAM 2

OUTFIELD: Tris Speaker, Joe Jackson, Mickey Mantle **3B:** Ken Boyer **SS:** Dave Concepcion **2B:** Rogers Hornsby **1B:** Gil Hodges **RH PITCHER:** Don Drysdale **LH PITCHER:** Sandy Koufax **CATCHER:** Mickey Cochrane **RELIEF PITCHER:** Hoyt Wilhelm

ALL-TIME DEFENSIVE TEAM

OUTFIELD: Joe DiMaggio, Tris Speaker, Willie Mays **1B:** Vic (Pellot) Power
2B: Bill Mazeroski **3B:** Brooks Robinson **SS:** Luis Aparicio **RH PITCHER:**
None **LH PITCHER:** Howie Pollet **CATCHER:** Johnny Bench

MOST UNDERRATED BALL PLAYERS OF ALL TIME: Carl Furillo, Enos
Slaughter
BEST CLUTCH HITTER EVER: Frank Robinson
GAME 7 WORLD SERIES PITCHER: Bob Feller
BEST MANAGER OF ALL TIME: Al Lopez
THE BEST TEAM: 1975 Cincinnati Reds
CITY WITH THE BEST FANS: Detroit
DESIGNATED HITTER: Oppose
BEST FASTBALL: Bob Feller
BEST CURVE: Tommy Bridges
BEST SCREWBALL: Ruben Gomez
BEST SPITBALL: Gaylord Perry
BEST PICKOFF MOVE: Bill Wight
BEST SINKER/DROP: Don Drysdale
BEST CHANGE-UP: Carl Erskine
BEST SLIDER: Harry Dorish
BEST BASE STEALER OF ALL TIME: Jack Cassini
BEST BUNTER: Jack Cassini
BEST THROWING ARM OF ALL TIME: Johnny Bench
MOST KNOWLEDGEABLE BASEBALL BROADCASTERS: Ty Tyson,
Ernie Harwell
BEST UMPIRE YOU EVER SAW: Never saw a good one
**BALL PLAYERS THAT NEVER PLAYED UP TO THEIR POTEN-
TIAL:** Larry Doby, Vada Pinson, Tim Manning
TOUGHEST PITCHER YOU EVER BATTED AGAINST: Mickey
McDermott
BALL PLAYER WHO DID THE MOST TO INSPIRE HIS TEAM: Pete
Rose
BEST TEAM OWNER YOU'VE KNOWN: John Fetzer

CLOSER LOOKS II

Baltimore Orioles

Courtesy Detroit Tigers

Charlie Lau and Johnny Sain, unorthodox batting and pitching coaches, respectively. Prize pupils: George Brett and Jim Kaat, among others.

The Best Ever:
The Verdict Of the Managers and Coaches

FIRST BASE

1.	Lou Gehrig	39.6%	5.	Stan Musial		5.0
2-3.	Willie McCovey	10.8	6.	Hank Greenberg		4.5
2-3.	Jimmie Foxx	10.8	7.	Gil Hodges		2.7
4.	George Sisler	9.5				

SECOND BASE

1.	Rogers Hornsby	24.5%	6-7.	Nellie Fox	3.9
2.	Charlie Gehringer	23.5	6-7.	Joe Gordon	3.9
3.	Bill Mazeroski	15.7	8-10.	Eddie Collins	2.9
4.	Joe Morgan	7.8	8-10.	Jackie Robinson	2.9
5.	Bobby Doerr	4.9	8-10.	Bobby Richardson	2.9

THIRD BASE

1.	Brooks Robinson	43.6%	4.	Mike Schmidt	9.1
2.	Pie Traynor	18.2	5-6.	George Brett	2.7
3.	Eddie Mathews	10.0	5-6.	Graig Nettles	2.7

SHORTSTOP

1.	Honus Wagner	19.4%	5-6.	Dave Concepcion	7.4
2.	Luis Aparicio	15.7	7.	Lou Boudreau	6.5
3-4.	Luke Appling	8.3	8.	Ozzie Smith	5.6
3-4.	Ernie Banks	8.3	9-10.	Robin Yount	4.6
5-6.	Phil Rizzuto	7.4	9-10.	Marty Marion	4.6

CATCHER

1.	Johnny Bench	34.6%	5-6.	Gabby Hartnett	6.5
2.	Bill Dickey	18.7	5-6.	Roy Campanella	6.5
3.	Yogi Berra	17.8	7.	Gary Carter	2.8
4.	Mickey Cochrane	8.4	8.	Thurman Munson	1.9

OUTFIELDERS

1.	Babe Ruth	13.2%	9.	Stan Musial	5.5
2-3.	Willie Mays	12.9	10.	Tris Speaker	3.1
2-3.	Joe DiMaggio	12.9	11-12.	Frank Robinson	1.8
4.	Ted Williams	11.6	11-12.	Al Kaline	1.8
5.	Hank Aaron	8.6	13-15.	Billy Williams	.9
6.	Mickey Mantle	7.3	13-15	Reggie Jackson	.9
7.	Ty Cobb	6.3	13-15.	Carl Yastrzemski	.9
8.	Roberto Clemente	5.8			

RIGHT-HANDED PITCHERS

1.	Bob Gibson	21.3%	6-7.	Cy Young	3.7
2.	Bob Feller	19.4	6-7.	Allie Reynolds	3.7
3.	Walter Johnson	17.1	8-11.	Dizzy Dean	2.8
4-5.	Grover Cleveland		8-11.	Christy Mathewson	2.8
	Alexander	4.6	8-11.	Jim Palmer	2.8
4-5.	Juan Marichal	4.6	8-11.	Bob Lemon	2.8

LEFT-HANDED PITCHERS

1.	Sandy Koufax	33.8%	5.	Carl Hubbell	7.2
2.	Warren Spahn	18.9	6.	Whitey Ford	3.6
3.	Lefty Grove	17.6	7.	Hal Newhouser	2.7
4.	Steve Carlton	8.1			

RELIEF PITCHERS

1.	Goose Gossage	21.1%	6-8.	Wilcy Moore	4.2
2.	Bruce Sutter	16.8	6-8.	Dan Quisenberry	4.2
3.	Rollie Fingers	15.8	6-8.	Dick Radatz	4.2
4.	Hoyt Wilhelm	7.4	9.	Johnny Murphy	3.7
5.	Elroy Face	6.3	10.	Joe Page	3.2

What Player Did the Most to Inspire His Team?

1.	Pete Rose	23.7%	14.	Pee Wee Reese	1.7
2.	Joe DiMaggio	5.1	15.	Mickey Cochrane	1.6
3.	Willie Mays	3.8	16-17.	Ernie Banks	1.5
4-5.	Jackie Robinson	3.3	16-17.	Lou Boudreau	1.5
4-5.	Mickey Mantle	3.3	18-19.	Eddie Stanky	1.3
6.	Lou Gehrig	2.8	18-19.	Ted Williams	1.3
7.	Pepper Martin	2.5	20-21.	Enos Slaughter	1.2
8-9.	Babe Ruth	2.3	20-21.	Billy Martin	1.2
8-9.	Willie Stargell	2.3	22.	Thurman Munson	1.1
10.	Roberto Clemente	2.1	23.	Dick Bartell	1.0
11.	Frank Robinson	2.0	24.	Don Hoak	.9
12.	Stan Musial	1.9	25.	Ty Cobb	.8
13.	Nellie Fox	1.8			

With the exception of Ernie "Lets Play Two" Banks, every man on this list played on at least one pennant winner, and most led their teams to many more than one. But then what is the purpose of inspiration if not victory?

Pete Rose received more votes than the next seven on the list combined. He was the easy #1 choice of players from each era. Many have called Rose a throwback, and the voters obviously agree. He leads the group of "scrappers" that is well-represented here: Jackie Robinson, Pepper Martin, Nellie Fox, Pee Wee Reese, Eddie Stanky, Don Hoak, Enos Slaughter, Billy Martin, Dick Bartell, and Ty Cobb. That's fully half the list, and represents a helluva lot of hard-nosed baseball, and more especially some of the most sensational World Series performances ever: Slaughter's mad dash from first to home in the 1946 classic, Jackie Robinson's steal of home in 1955, Billy Martin's one-man show in 1953, and Pepper Martin's in 1931.

Looking at the rest of the list, you'll notice other pretty fair Series performers, guys named Gehrig, Ruth, Stargell, Clemente, Mantle, and Munson.

It seems that the ability to inspire others would be a prime ingredient for a successful manager or even a coach. Eight of the 25 did manage in the bigs (and Willie Stargell remains a distinct possibility), but with surprisingly little success. They total 59 years of managing but only five pennants and three world championships. Only Mickey Cochrane and Billy Martin, with two pennants each, can be said to be at the top of the managing profession. The jury is still out on Pete Rose, though he has started strongly—and, we predict, he'll keep that pace more or less throughout his career. Of course, we don't mean to knock the other men but it's clear that inspiration starts from the barrel of a bat.

Besides the scrappers, the other large group on this list is the strong, silent (or not so silent) type—you shouldn't have any trouble picking them out. Also, we must consider the special cases, like Mickey Mantle, performing heroically despite crippling injuries. Who that saw it will ever forget Mantle standing on first base with blood oozing out of his uniform leg in the 1961 World Series? Then again, how about Jackie Robinson breaking down the barriers, seething all the while at abuse from fans and an occasional player? It's not so much that no one ever was slandered, cursed, or spiked, or spit at on a ball field—in the earliest days of the game, it happened day in and day out. But Jackie took it all without the satisfaction of giving it back, and he did it alone, performing brilliantly in the process. It inspired his teammates, that's for sure.

St. Louis Cardinals

Stan the Man

The Best *Pure* Hitter				
1. Ted Williams	53.0%	7.	Rod Carew	3.5
2. Stan Musial	7.3	8.	Hank Aaron	3.2
3. George Brett	5.1	9.	Wade Boggs	2.6
4-6. Rogers Hornsby	3.8	10-11.	Pete Rose	1.9
4-6. Roberto Clemente	3.8	10-11.	Tony Oliva	1.9
4-6. Billy Williams	3.8	12.	Ty Cobb	1.6

This question was a late addition to our survey, which we refined twice over the course of the polling period (1982-1986). Only 160 players gave their opinions, and of these, 85 picked the Splendid Splinter, a whopping 53%. A larger sampling would be necessary to get an accurate ranking of the also-rans (if Stan Musial and Ty Cobb will excuse the expression). But although the results of places 2 through 12 are not statistically valid, they do give a definite picture of the type of hitter the players prefer. The finalists are all great students of hitting—many were or are great *teachers*, too—with thousands of hours of practice to their credit despite the greatest natural hitting ability. Eight of the 12 are lefty swingers. There is one switch hitter, Mr. Peter Rose, who conversely and by his own admission did *not* have an easy time being great.

To our minds the most remarkable thing about these responses is that not one tally went to Babe Ruth. Perhaps the term "pure hitter" implies batting average rather than power, but isn't there something to be said for the Babe's alma mater, the Pick-One-Out-And-Cream-It School?

Pittsburgh Pirates

Roberto Clemente

The Top 20 Throwing Arms
(Not Including Pitchers)

1.	Roberto Clemente	29.7%	11.	Al Kaline	1.6
2.	Rocky Colavito	14.8	12.	Johnny Bench	1.5
3.	Carl Furillo	14.6	13.	Dave Parker	1.4
4.	Joe DiMaggio	5.0	14.	Reggie Smith	1.2
5.	Bob Meusel	4.8	15.	Dwight Evans	1.1
6-7.	Ellis Valentine	2.9	16.	Dave Winfield	1.0
6-7.	Willie Mays	2.9	17-20.	Gabby Hartnett	.8
8.	Chick Hafey	2.8	17-20.	Tris Speaker	.8
9.	Ollie Brown	2.5	17-20.	Cesar Geronimo	.8
10.	Bob Kennedy	2.2	17-20.	Babe Ruth	.8

As you might expect, right fielders dominate the top 20 throwing arms, led by the incomparable shotgun of Roberto Clemente. The next time someone tells you that outfielders with good arms don't get assists because no one challenges them, invite him to check out the totals of these 20 fellows. For example, during his 18-year career Clemente averaged over 17 assists per 154 games and was still leading the league at age 33. To a lesser extent, the same is true of all the other outfielders, even the center fielders. One unfortunate side effect of those extra outs is a few more errors on throws, but this can be misleading. Many times the scoring rules demand an error be charged on the near-perfect throw that hits an arriving base runner and squirts away. But the outfielder has done his job.

Perhaps a little surprising is that besides Johnny Bench (12th) and Gabby Hartnett (17th), only two other catchers received votes: Jerry Grote of Mets fame and Tony Pena, the Pirate phenom who may just have the best catcher's arm ever. Pena's standing can only improve if he keeps picking off runners with what looks like a flick of the wrist, but he and Jerry got only two votes apiece.

The Best Umpire	
1. Bill Klem	12.1%
2. Al Barlick	9.4
3. Jocko Conlan	9.0
4. Bill McGowan	8.4
5. Doug Harvey	7.9
6. Nestor Chylak	6.7
7. Cal Hubbard	4.0
8. Bill Summers	3.3
9. Paul Runge	3.0
10. Augie Donatelli	2.5

Others with votes: Babe Pinelli, Bill Haller, Bill Evans, Dutch Rennert, Steve Palermo, Chis Pelekoudas, Ron Luciano, Ed Vargo, Shag Crawford, Bob Engel, Tom Gorman, and Larry Goetz.

Didn't someone once say, "Never give an umpire an even break"? The reason we ask is that when we got comments along with umpire picks, they went typically like this: "I'd have to say _____ is the best—but what a jerk." Or: "Most umpires today are too worried about someone showing them up rather than doing a good job." Or how about this one: "None is the best. All had moments of brilliance and stupidity.: That's probably the most sensible remark about umps we read. Theirs is a high-risk job, you'd have to say.

They Never Played Up To Their Potential

RAW VOTES

1. Cesar Cedeno	32	3. Bobby Bonds	24
2. Richie Allen	29	4. Dick Wakefield	22

5.	Dave Parker	19	16-18.	Lou Novikoff	7
6.	Joe Pepitone	16	19-22.	Dick Stuart	6
7.	Ellis Valentine	15	19-22.	Reggie Smith	6
8.	Dave Nicholson	14	19-22.	Reggie Jackson	6
9.	Sam McDowell	13	19-22.	Jimmy Piersall	6
10.	Alex Johnson	12	23-30.	Tom Tresh	5
11-12.	Clint Hurdle	10	23-30.	Bobby Murcer	5
11-12.	Dave Kingman	10	23-30.	Jack Clark	5
13-14.	Mickey Mantle	9	23-30.	Mickey McDermott	5
13-14.	Clint Hartung	9	23-30.	Mike Ivie	5
15.	Herb Score	8	23-30.	Cleon Jones	5
16-18.	Jim Gentile	7	23-30.	Fred Lynn	5
16-18.	Willie Davis	7	23-30.	Jeff Heath	5

A difficult question, one that many players chose not to answer. We purposely inserted the phrase "for one reason or another never lived up to their potential" in order to get the broadest possible interpretation. But it's unfair in a sense to lump Mickey Mantle, Herb Score, and the other injury cases together with Cesar Cedeno, Richie Allen, Joe Pepitone, and the other, well, squanderers.

It's a sad category, and the list is filled top to bottom with every degree of human tragedy, self-inflicted and otherwise. Besides injuries, here are tales of drink, drugs, womanizing, mental breakdown, and the blameless inability to live up to hype. In the cases of Bobby Bonds and Dick (Dr. Strangelove) Stuart, their glaring weaknesses—strikeouts and defense, respectively—were glossed over when they came up amid reports of "the next Willie Mays" and "the minor league's Babe Ruth." Both went on to have fine careers, but only Willie Mays and Babe Ruth could live up to those expectations.

Cedeno was victimized by his advance billing and more directly by that pitcher's paradise, the Astrodome, but his alleged attitude problem didn't exactly put him on the path to glory.

Nearly all of Dave Parker's votes were drawn before his outstanding 1985 season; perhaps he will reclaim superstar status and fade off the list.

Note that of the 30 players listed here, 26 played after 1950. Only Dick Wakefield, Clint Hartung, Lou Novikoff (a sensational minor-league hitter), and Jeff Heath played earlier. This might be a commentary on the attitude of many moderns; it might also be a reflection of the Age of Hype ushered in by TV.

Speaking of hype, it was first discovered in New York, and unsurprisingly, fully one-third of the finalists in this unenviable category played for either the Yankees or Mets.

Interestingly, Sam McDowell, Herb Score, and Mickey McDermott—all lefties—are the only pitchers here, unless you count Clint Hartung. Much of Hartung's inability to fulfill his promise can be attributed to the Giants' indecision on where to play him: in the outfield or on the mound. The "Hondo Hurricane" was ineffective as a hurler, posting a 29-29, 5.02 ERA record in 112 games. As a hitter, he batted a mere .238, but showed power, with 14 HRs in just 378 at bats.

One type of hitter who keeps popping up here is the lots-of-homers, lots-of-strikeouts, lots-of-streaks basher, the type who looks like the next Babe Ruth during a hot streak—before the arrival of the cold light of day. Which brings to mind the old baseball maxim: "You're never as good as you look when you win, and never as bad as you look when you lose"—a perfect encapsulation of the career of, say, Dave Kingman.

The All-Time Great Double-Play Combos

1.	Tinker-Evers	15.3%	12.	Jurges-Herman	2.5
2.	Aparicio-Fox	12.0	13-14.	McMillan-(Johnny) Temple	1.4
3.	Rizzuto-Gordon	8.8	13-14.	Trammell-Whitaker	1.4
4.	Mazeroski-Groat	6.9	15.	Smith-Herr	1.3
5.	Boudreau-Gordon	6.0	16-17.	Rizzuto-Coleman	1.2
6.	Reese-Robinson	5.9	16-17.	Belanger-Grich	1.2
7.	Alley-Mazeroski	5.8	18-21.	Rizzuto-Priddy	.9
8.	Concepcion-Morgan	4.6	18-21.	Crosetti-Lazzeri	.9
9.	Marion-Schoendienst	3.8	18-21.	Belanger-D. Johnson	.9
10.	Kubek-Richardson	3.2	18-21.	Kessinger-Beckert	.9
11.	Boudreau-Red Mack	2.7			

Individually Rated: The Best Double-Play Men Ever

(Numbers in parentheses represent the number of different keystone partners each man received votes with, if more than one.)

SHORTSTOPS

1.	Joe Tinker	15.0%
2.	Luis Aparicio	12.3
3.	Phil Rizzuto (4)	9.6
4.	Lou Boudreau (2)	8.4
5.	Dick Groat	7.0
6.	Pee Wee Reese (2)	6.7
7.	Gene Alley	5.9
8.	Dave Concepcion	4.5
9.	Marty Marion (3)	4.2
10.	Tony Kubek	3.2

SECOND BASEMEN

1.	Johnny Evers	15.0%
2.	Joe Gordon (3)	14.9
3.	Bill Mazeroski (2)	12.9
4.	Nellie Fox (2)	12.5
5.	Jackie Robinson	6.0
6.	Joe Morgan	4.5
7.	Red Schoendienst (2)	4.0
8.	Billy Herman (3)	3.4
9.	Bobby Richardson	3.2
10.	Red Mack	2.6

Frankie Crosetti (right) stops Walker Cooper's infield hit in Game 4 of the 1943 World Series, forcing Stan Musial to hold at second and protecting the Yankees' 2-1 victory. Joe Gordon looks on.

Obviously, the Tinker-Evers legend made them the automatic pick of many who never saw the Cub pair in action. True, but then no one has written a poem about "Bowa to Trillo to Rose is a Rose is a Rose." But poetry aside, they do deserve serious consideration as the premier twosome. Joe Tinker could loosely be described as Marty Marion with 25-30 stolen bases a year added, and Johnny Evers was similar to Nellie Fox-the-player and Billy Martin-the-battler.

Joe Gordon received more votes than any other second baseman except Evers, and he *was* spectacular on the pivot, but his standing surely gets a boost from teammates Rizzuto and Boudreau. On the other hand, Bill Mazeroski got six solo votes—which say, in effect, "Maz and *Anybody*." Only one other player was so honored: Ozzie Smith. Perhaps Ozzie's two such tallies are as impressive as Maz's six, for the shortstop is usually considered the bottom half of the exacta. But Mazeroski's domination of the all-time double-play columns certainly removes all doubt as to which second baseman was best on the pivot. He holds three of the ten best single-season DP totals ever (no one else has two) and his career mark of 1,706 double plays is 87 more than Nellie Fox, who is in second place. And Maz played 201 fewer games at second. That said, a majority of players seemed to reason that whatever Fox yields to Mazeroski, White Sox teammate Aparicio takes back at shortstop over Dick Groat and Gene Alley.

An example of how opinions can change over time is Pee Wee Reese and Jackie Robinson finishing ten votes ahead of Marty Marion and Red Schoendienst. In 1950 it would very likely have been the other way around. It also feels a little suspect because on the "Best Defensive Second Baseman" list, the Redhead edges Jackie, and at shortstop, Marion wallops Reese by 66 votes.

Of the active combos, only Ozzie Smith and Tommy Herr (six) and Alan Trammell and Lou Whitaker (six) received any votes. Both pairs stand a good chance to move up, especially with more playoff and World Series exposure.

Many of these middle infielders were mentioned with more than one partner, making conclusions doubly difficult. Phil Rizzuto, for example, was the shortstop entry with Joe Gordon (37 1/2 votes), Jerry Coleman (five votes), Gerry Priddy (four), and Billy Martin (one). This is a less emphatic way of saying "Rizzuto and Anybody." The Scooter's four different partners were the most, but Marty Marion (with Schoendienst, Emil Verban, and Don Gutteridge), Joe Gordon (with Rizzuto, Boudreau, and Frank Crosetti), and Billy Herman (with Reese, Jurges, and Woody English) all received votes with three. For a different angle on the results, see the breakdown of double-play men individually rated.

The Best Clutch Hitter

1.	Ted Williams	14.6%	13-15.	George Brett	1.8
2.	Yogi Berra	7.7	13-15.	Paul Waner	1.8
3.	Joe DiMaggio	6.6	13-15.	Pete Rose	1.8
4.	Stan Musial	6	16.	Mickey Mantle	1.6
5.	Babe Ruth	4.2	17-20.	Joe Cronin	1.5
6.	Lou Gehrig	4	17-20.	Roberto Clemente	1.5
7.	Rogers Hornsby	3.5	17-20.	Johnny Mize	1.5
8.	Willie Mays	2.9	17-20.	Hank Aaron	1.5
9-10.	Tommy Henrich	2.7	21-23.	Tony Perez	1.3
9-10.	Ty Cobb	2.7	21-23.	Smoky Burgess	1.3
11.	Frank Robinson	2.4	21-23.	Manny Mota	1.3
12.	Reggie Jackson	2.2	24.	Thurman Munson	.9

FOUR VOTES EACH: Hack Wilson, Bill Dickey, Jackie Robinson, Tony Oliva, Eddie Murray, and Carl Yastrzemski

Right off the bat, notice that the top eight selections are better hitters than any other eight hitters anyone can name as a group. Don't even try.

It seems a prerequisite for being a ranking clutch hitter that a guy be a great hitter, period. That certainly makes sense and, paradoxically, it lends credence to the theory that consistent clutch hitters don't even exist. To such theorists, all the great "money" feats can be explained by luck *or given ability.* They produce statistics—often confusing and even contradictory—"proving" their contention. But some simple evidence supporting the "There's No Such Thing As a Clutch Hitter" School would be the World Series record of the top four finishers in the "Best Clutch Hitter" sweepstakes. The combined World Series batting average of Williams, Berra, Joe D., and Musial is .267, with 21 home runs in 156 games. That's fine for a Jim Hickman but not what you'd expect from the best player ever at his position, as all four might well be. On the other hand, Ruth, Gehrig, and Hornsby have some credentials too, and their combined Series totals are .327 with 25 homers in 87 games. They slugged .670.

But the skeptics might press on, saying that even a reputation as exalted as Tommy "Ol' Reliable" Henrich's is stared down by the cold fact of a .262 World Series average, 20 points below career. (Of course, the playoffs and Series are far from the only measures of clutch hitting, but they're useful if only because the pressure is on maximum. And in most of the cases we have before us, these men had more than a couple of chances to prove their worth under fire.)

But what does it all mean? Who among us doesn't have a particular player (or two or three) whom we want up there at the showdown? We suspect even diehard disbelievers have their secret favorites. Sometimes stats are deceiving. If, for example, you look at Tommy Henrich's 1949 World Series line you see he was five for 19 with only one home run and one RBI in five games. Look again. That homer came in the ninth inning of Game 1, breaking up a 0-0 gut-wrencher that some say was the best pitching duel in Series history. Henrich, in the ninth slot on the players' all-time list, is the only one of the top 20 who is not or will not be in the Hall of Fame. This being so, he would fit the classic definition of the clutch hitter: a good hitter who becomes great under pressure. He would fit, except that he *was* a great hitter, much better than his statistics show. For starters, Tommy missed three-plus prime years because of World War II. Secondly, it took some time for him to return to form in 1946; it was easily the worst year of his career: .251 BA and .411 slugging. Eliminate this season and his lifetime slugging average is .502, higher than Ernie Banks and Goose Goslin. Thirdly, he didn't start playing organized hardball until he was 20 years old, and consequently did not reach the majors until he was 24, having hit over .325 at every minor-league stop. And finally, of course, those who saw him play every day thought he was a great hitter, as a look at the "Best Outfielder" list will confirm. Henrich and everyone else down to the last Honorable Mention on the clutch-hitter list have this common trait: they're all cool customers, waiting to take advantage of an opening.

What about the aforementioned .267 BA for the top four guys? It could easily be attributed to a natural baseball tendency, the inclination to have better pitchers on the mound when the game or the pennant or the world championship is on the line. Question: What happens, over time, when clutch hitters face clutch pitchers?

The Best Hit-And-Run Men

1.	Dick Groat	17.8%	7-8.	Bobby Richardson	3.8
2.	Billy Herman	10.2	9-10.	Pete Rose	3.0
3.	Luke Appling	9.1	9-10.	Roberto Clemente	3.0
4.	Alvin Dark	5.3	11-13.	Lou Boudreau	2.3
5.	Nellie Fox	4.5	11-13.	Junior Gilliam	2.3
6.	Rod Carew	4.2	11-13.	Rogers Hornsby	2.3
7-8.	Manny Mota	3.8	14.	George Kell	1.9

Saying that John McGraw didn't invent the hit and run is like saying that Elvis Presley didn't invent rock 'n' roll. Technically true but irrelevant. The popularity of the play has ebbed and flowed since its introduction in the early 1890s. At first, critics preferred advancing base runners via the sacrifice bunt and the stolen base. Then the home run became a preferred method.

Hitting behind the runner is back in style now, particularly in the big artificial-turf ball parks of the National League. But even during the biggest home run years there were always bat-control artists like Billy Herman, Luke Appling, and Paul Waner. This is partly because the mere threat of a hit and run can create an advantage for the offense. Too, hitting behind the runner is a skill that can be *learned* by hitters—mainly those without power, of course—seeking an added weapon for their game.

Every single man on this list was a known student of the game, and few hit many homers. Including Pete Rose and Rod Carew, 11 of the 14 on the list were middle infielders. Several of them could be called "underrated" in the sense that they are not talked about much these days. Dick Groat and Alvin Dark are two examples. Both were fine shortstops who made consistent offensive contributions to at least two pennant-winning teams. In Dark's first seven years with the Braves and Giants, he averaged .297 with 34 doubles, 13 homers, and 95 runs scored per year. Some bat control! A look at his stats for 1948, 1951, and 1954 gives a pretty good idea why his teams won pennants all three years. Besides his usual first-rate glove work, Dark's average for those years was .306, with 106 two-baggers and 37 home runs—and tack on fine speed with good instincts and the leadership qualities that later helped make him a world champion manager. Also, in three World Series (65 at bats) he hit .323.

Groat didn't have power or speed, but the Duke University basketball star hit .293 over his first 11 major-league seasons with Pittsburgh and St. Louis, throwing in an MVP award and a batting title in 1960 (name the last shortstop to do *that*). Traded to the Cardinals before 1963, Groat was a major reason the Cards jumped from sixth place to second, then won it all in '64. With help from second basemen Bill Mazeroski and Julian Javier, Groat ranks fifth all-time in double plays by a shortstop, with 1,237.

The Best "Money" Pitcher

("You are the manager of a team in the 7th game of the World Series. What pitcher would you pick to start the game?")

1.	Sandy Koufax	26.4%	12.	Catfish Hunter	2.0
2.	Bob Gibson	15.8	13.	Grover C. Alexander	1.9
3.	Whitey Ford	8.2	14-15.	Red Ruffing	1.6
4.	Walter Johnson	5.9	14-15.	Don Drysdale	1.6
5.	Carl Hubbell	4.6	16.	Dwight Gooden	1.5
6.	Steve Carlton	3.3	17-18.	Tom Seaver	1.3
7.	Lefty Grove	3.1	17-18.	Bob Lemon	1.3
8.	Bob Feller	2.9	19.	Juan Marichal	1.2
9.	Allie Reynolds	2.3	20.	Cy Young	1.0
10.	Dizzy Dean	2.2	21.	Vic Raschi	.9
11.	Warren Spahn	2.1			

The flip side of the clutch hitter question. In fact, it's really the A-side, because when clutch pitchers face clutch hitters, the pitchers usually win. Usually. You wouldn't want to bet against George Brett facing Catfish Hunter, but the World

Series records of these pitchers are almost always better than their regular season accomplishments. The same thing cannot be said about the best clutch hitters, in part because they faced these hurlers.

As with all the more subjective questions in our survey, many pre-1920 players are frozen out because so few respondents (six, to be precise) actually played against them. Three-Finger Brown, Mathewson, et al. were also frozen out by Walter Johnson, arguably the best pitcher of all time. The Big Train's fourth-place finish (33 votes) on this list doesn't tell the whole story: among those who played with him, he received 68% of the vote. To emphasize his greatness, in Johnson's 13 seasons before the Babe Ruth era, his 1.65 ERA was 17 points lower than Ed Walsh's all-time career best. Then after 1919, with something gone off his fastball, from ages 32 to 39, smack dab in the hardest-hitting era ever, with good teams *and* pitiful ones, Walter was 120-88 with a 3.34 ERA. His 110 career shutouts are 20 more than anyone else's, and that feat looks untouchable today. It's always dangerous to say a record is untouchable, but if Dwight Gooden, say, averaged seven shutouts a year for 15 years, he'd still be five short of Johnson. Speaking of Gooden, at this writing he had not pitched one post-season inning, yet he still received eight and a half votes—in anticipation, no doubt.

One interesting aspect about the list of the greatest money pitchers is the difference between it and the lists of the greatest righties and lefties. Koufax is no surprise here, nor are any other top finishers, even Allie Reynolds. One eyebrow-raiser might be Bob Feller, who as the players' second choice for all-time-right-hander drew 146 votes, while drawing only 17 as the best money-moundsman. Rapid Robert's World Series record is not good (0-2, 5.02 ERA), but one of those losses was a two-hit, 1-0 heartbreaker decided after a disputed call on a pickoff attempt. And it wouldn't be fair to hold 1948 against him, especially since by that time his super-strikeout days were behind him.

Another way to look at the question of who you'd like to see on the mound in the seventh game of the Series is to forget all about analysis and go with the pitcher you just plain enjoy watching the most. Of the contemporary masters, Gooden of course comes to mind, or Fernando Valenzuela (three votes), or Nolan Ryan when he's on (also three votes). It depends on whether you'd prefer watching the fireballing, read-'em-and-weep style of a Koufax or Gibson, or the "comfortable 0-for-4" string-pulling of the Ford-Hubbell variety.

Last but not least, there's the pragmatic school. Three ball players answered the "7th game of the Series" question this way: "I would throw in my two best relievers," each for half a game. "The pitcher who pitched best so far" in the Series was the second answer. And Dave Wickersham, who had some good years on the mound with Detroit in the 1960s, decided that "it depends on the ball park ... Lefty Grove in Yankee stadium."

The Best Base Stealer

1.	Lou Brock	43.3%	6.	Vince Coleman	1.7
2.	Rickey Henderson	17.6	7.	Jackie Robinson	1.5
3.	Ty Cobb	15.1	8.	Max Carey	1.0
4.	Maury Wills	12.9	9.	Luis Aparicio	.9
5.	George Case	2.6	10.	Joe Morgan	.8

Stolen Bases Through 1985

	STOLEN BASES THROUGH 1985	STOLEN BASE SUCCESS RATE THROUGH 1985
Aparicio	506	.788
Brock	938	.756
Carey	738	NA
Case	349	NA
Cobb	892	NA
Coleman	110	.815
Henderson	573	.796
Morgan	689	.810
Robinson	197	NA
Wills	586	.738

Despite Lou Brock's overwhelming lead, it is by no means certain that in 10 years he will still be Number One. By that time, barring injury, Rickey Henderson will be comfortably past him in total stolen bases. And then there are Tim Raines and Vince Coleman, and probably one or two more somewhere in the minor leagues, all barking at Sweet Lou's winged heels.

The question "Who is the best base stealer of all time?" was not asked to find out only who stole the most bases, obviously. Rather, we wanted to know who was the most *effective* pilferer. Stolen base percentage would be the prime indicator, but total stolen bases and expert "situation" basestealing should also come into play. Tim Raines is, to this point, the best base thief with an 85% success ratio. He averages 75 stolen bases a year, and one is hard pressed to think of anyone better, yet Raines received only two votes. This must be because (a) he hasn't challenged the single-season record, (b) he hasn't been in a World Series, and (c) he plays in far-off Montreal. Vince Coleman, on the other hand, got 10 votes after just one year in the bigs, both because as a rookie he did for a time make a run at Henderson's record and because he enjoyed post-season TV exposure in 1985. In Raines's rookie season, strike-shortened 1981, he stole 71 bases in 88 games, which would project to 131 in a normal season. Of course, projecting isn't *doing*, especially since base stealers tend to wear down as the season wears on.

The question for Henderson, Coleman, and Raines is: Can they buck the odds and keep it up long enough to pass Brock, the endurance champ? Bear in mind that of all athletic skills running speed is the first to go, and it doesn't take much to turn a stolen base into a "caught stealing." And then there is the increased chance of injury due to more running and sliding and more contact with elbows, mitts, and baseballs. Not too long ago people were nominating Cesar Cedeno, Willie Wilson, and Ron LeFlore, even Omar Moreno and Billy North, as candidates for all kinds of stolen base records. Only Wilson and Moreno remain, and both are decided longshots now.

By contrast, Joe Morgan didn't really begin to steal until he came back from a broken kneecap at the age of 25. From age 28 on, Morgan stole 534 bases—more than three-quarters of his career total. When compared with the similar figures for Brock, Maury Wills, Honus Wagner, and others, Morgan's numbers indicate that the true greats more than compensate for the loss of speed with greater knowledge of the basestealing craft. So for the time being, the jury must remain out on the newcomers, though Henderson's prospects look particularly bright. Baseball sage Paul Richards was particularly high on Rickey. "That center fielder for the Yankees could do great things," he told us. And another old-timer agrees, picking "Henderson or Brock—one of the moderns" to lead the basestealing list. "But," he adds, "this says something about artificial turf and a lack of pitcher-catcher fundamentals."

St. Louis Cardinals

Lou Brock

The Best Fans In Baseball

1.	Los Angeles	19.1%		8.	Kansas City	3.3
2.	Chicago	16.7		9.	Cincinnati	2.9
3.	New York	15.9		10-11.	Philadelphia	1.8
4.	Boston	15.5		10-11.	Baltimore	1.8
5.	Detroit	6.7		12.	Montreal	1.4
6.	St. Louis	4.9		13.	Toronto	1.0
7.	Milwaukee	3.8				

There are four yardsticks for taking the measure of a city's fans. First and foremost, do they come out to the park, even when the team is down, as Cubs fans have? Second, do they know the intricacies of baseball, or will they, for example, boo the batter who advances base runners while making an out? Third, do they have the enthusiasm to breathe life into the home team or to intimidate the opposition—and we *don't* mean can they pull off a good wave, which is one of the more absurd things for fans to do at a baseball game. No, we're thinking of San Diego's fans in the 1984 playoffs and the way they spooked the Cubs.

Finally, are the fans civilized enough to make a ball game suitable for the kids and appreciative enough to give a decent round of applause to an opponent's outstanding performance? (One old-timer listed Detroit as the best city. The fans there, he explained, "are the most loyal and the most dangerous." Praising with faint damns.)

New York Mets

Tug McGraw: Met and Philly fans worshipped the cheerleader-pitcher.

Dodger fans have taken much abuse for their laid-back ways and for leaving in the sixth inning, but they do come out in droves and they don't murder each other at the drop of a pop-up. The players' preference for L.A. rooters is stronger than it looks, because about half the respondents never played there. Naturally, players show a bias toward cities they called home. The bias comes out in the wash, however, because most of them played for at least two teams. (If the hometown tendencies *didn't* even out, New York would easily be first instead of third, and Philadelphia, Cleveland, and Pittsburgh would place higher than relative newcomers Milwaukee and Kansas City.) Royals and Brewers fans can be rightfully proud of the high regard in which they are held; by all the aforementioned yardsticks they more than make the grade.

On the other hand, residents of Houston, Oakland, and Seattle should hang their heads in shame, for the minor-league city of Louisville beat them all with 2 1/2 votes. That might not be statistically significant, but by topping the million mark for Triple-A baseball, there's no doubt that Louisville would strongly support a big-league franchise. (How's this for a great May weekend? Saturday afternoon at the Kentucky Derby, then a Sunday morning drive through bluegrass country, and on over to a doubleheader at the ball park.)

By Era: The Greatest at Each Position

CATCHER 1900-1920
1. Ray Schalk
2. Roger Bresnahan
3. Johnny Kling
4. Chief Meyers
5. Hank Gowdy

CATCHER 1946-1968
1. Yogi Berra
2. Roy Campanella
3. Walker Cooper
4. Jim Hegan
5. Elston Howard

CATCHER 1921-1945
1. Bill Dickey
2. Mickey Cochrane
3. Gabby Hartnett
4. Ernie Lombardi
5. Josh Gibson/Jimmy Wilson

CATCHER 1969-1985
1. Johnny Bench
2. Gary Carter
3. Thurman Munson
4. Carlton Fisk
5. Ted Simmons

RIGHT-HANDED PITCHER 1900-1920
1. Walter Johnson
2. Cy Young
3. Christy Mathewson
4. Grover Cleveland Alexander
5. Ed Walsh

RIGHT-HANDED PITCHER 1946-1968
1. Bob Gibson
2. Don Drysdale
3. Juan Marichal
4. Robin Roberts
5. Bob Lemon

RIGHT-HANDED PITCHER 1921-1945
1. Bob Feller
2. Dizzy Dean
3. Red Ruffing
4. Ewell Blackwell
5. Dazzy Vance

RIGHT-HANDED PITCHER 1969-1985
1. Tom Seaver
2. Nolan Ryan
3. Jim Palmer
4. Dwight Gooden
5. Catfish Hunter

LEFT-HANDED PITCHER 1900-1920
1. Rube Waddell
2. Babe Ruth
3. Eddie Plank
4. Rube Marquard
5. Nap Rucker

LEFT-HANDED PITCHER 1921-1945
1. Lefty Grove
2. Carl Hubbell
3. Lefty Gomez
4. Herb Pennock
5. Johnny Vander Meer

LEFT-HANDED PITCHER 1946-1968
1. Sandy Koufax
2. Warren Spahn
3. Whitey Ford
4. Bob Newhouser
5. Herb Score

LEFT-HANDED PITCHER 1969-1985
1. Steve Carlton
2. Ron Guidry
3. Fernando Valenzuela
4. Mickey Lolich
5. Jerry Koosman

"Who Is The Best Team Owner You've Known?"

1.	Tom Yawkey	19.6%
2.	Walter O'Malley	7.9
3.	Phil K. Wrigley	4.9
4.	Connie Mack	4.8
5.	Gene Autry	4.7
6.	Bill Veeck	4.6
7.	Gussie Busch, Sr.	4.0
8.	Horace Stoneham	3.8
9.	John Galbraith	2.8
10.	Clark Griffith	2.7
11.	Peter O'Malley	2.2
12-13.	Ruly Carpenter	2.1
12-13.	NONE	2.1
14.	Walter Briggs	1.9
15.	Jacop Ruppert	1.7
16.	Charles Comiskey	1.6
17-18.	Joan Payson	1.5
17-18.	Bob Carpenter	1.5

SHORTSTOP 1900-1920
1. Honus Wagner
2. Rabbit Maranville
3. Dave Bancroft
4. Roger Peckinpaugh
5. Joe Tinker

SHORTSTOP 1921-1945
1. Luke Appling
2. Joe Cronin
3. Lou Boudreau
4. Travis Jackson
5. Glenn Wright

SHORTSTOP 1946-1968
1. Luis Aparicio
2. Ernie Banks
3. Marty Marion
4. Pee Wee Reese
5. Phil Rizzuto

SHORTSTOP 1969-1985
1. Ozzie Smith
2. Dave Concepcion
3. Robin Yount
4. Cal Ripken
5. Mark Belanger

THIRD BASE 1900-1920
1. Jimmy Collins
2. Frank Baker
3. Buck Weaver
4. Art Devlin
5. Larry Gardner

THIRD BASE 1921-1945
1. Pie Traynor
2. Red Rolfe
3. Stan Hack
4. Ken Keltner
5. Joe Dugan

THIRD BASE 1946-1968
1. Brooks Robinson
2. Eddie Mathews
3. George Kell
4. Ken Boyer
5. Jackie Robinson

THIRD BASE 1969-1985
1. Mike Schmidt
2. George Brett
3. Graig Nettles
4. Pete Rose
5. Buddy Bell

SECOND BASE 1900-1920
1. Eddie Collins
2. Napoleon Lajoie
3. Johnny Evers
4. Larry Doyle
5. Miller Huggins

SECOND BASE 1921-1945
1. Charlie Gehringer
2. Rogers Hornsby
3. Joe Gordon
4. Frankie Frisch
5. Bobby Doerr

SECOND BASE 1946-1968
1. Jackie Robinson
2. Bill Mazeroski
3. Nellie Fox
4. Bobby Richardson
5. Red Schoendienst

SECOND BASE 1969-1985
1. Joe Morgan
2. Pete Rose
3. Rod Carew
4. Ryne Sandberg
5. Bobby Grich

FIRST BASE 1900-1920
1. Hal Chase
2. Frank Chance
3. Stuffy McInnis
4. Jake Daubert
5. Harry Davis

FIRST BASE 1921-1945
1. Lou Gehrig
2. Jimmie Foxx
3. George Sisler
4. Bill Terry
5. Hank Greenberg

FIRST BASE 1946-1968
1. Stan Musial
2. Gil Hodges
3. Willie McCovey
4. Johnny Mize
5. Mickey Vernon

FIRST BASE 1969-1985
1. Willie Stargell
2. Pete Rose
3. Eddie Murray
4. Rod Carew
5. Steve Garvey

National Baseball Library

Bill Wambsganss, Pete Kilduff, Clarence Mitchell, and Otto Miller (left to right) model the uniform of the day.

OUTFIELD 1900-1920
1. Ty Cobb
2. Tris Speaker
3. Joe Jackson
4. Willie Keeler
5. Fred Clarke
6. Clarence Beaumont
7. Sam Crawford
8. Max Carey
9. Zack Wheat
10. Elmer Flick
11. Duffy Lewis
12. Harry Hooper

OUTFIELD 1921-1945
1. Joe DiMaggio
2. Babe Ruth
3. Paul Waner
4. Al Simmons
5. Mel Ott
6. Tommy Henrich
7. Terry Moore
8. Harry Heilmann
9. Joe Medwick
10. Earle Combs
11. Lloyd Waner
12. Chick Hafey

OUTFIELD 1946-1968
1. Willie Mays
2. Ted Williams
3. Mickey Mantle
4. Hank Aaron
5. Stan Musial
6. Roberto Clemente
7. Al Kaline
8. Frank Robinson
9. Duke Snider
10. Enos Slaughter
11. Roger Maris
12. Carl Furillo

OUTFIELD 1969-1985
1. Carl Yastrzemski
2. Reggie Jackson
3. Pete Rose
4. Lou Brock
5. Dale Murphy
6. Fred Lynn
7. Dave Winfield
8. Andre Dawson
9. Dave Parker
10. Rickey Henderson
11. Willie McGee
12. Jim Rice

Franchise-By-Franchise:
All-Time Greats

We culled these teams from the grand totals at each position. In order to qualify for a particular franchise, a player must have played at least two years for the club at or near his peak. By these standards, for example, Rogers Hornsby does not qualify as a Giant, a Cub, or a Brave, but Steve Carlton does make the grade as a Cardinal.

National Baseball Library

Spring training, 1949: Joe DiMaggio, Phil Rizzuto, and Charley Keller soak up some sun.

AMERICAN LEAGUE

NEW YORK YANKEES

Bill Dickey	C
Lou Gehrig	1B
Joe Gordon	2B
Graig Nettles	3B
Phil Rizzuto	SS
Babe Ruth	OF
Joe DiMaggio	OF
Mickey Mantle	OF
Allie Reynolds	RHP
Whitey Ford	LHP
Goose Gossage	RP

Probably the strongest team listed, the outfielders alone could take a pennant—even with the '62 Mets as supporting cast. How would you like to face this lineup:

1.	Mickey Mantle	LF
2.	Joe DiMaggio	CF
3.	Babe Ruth	RF
4.	Lou Gehrig	1B
5.	Bill Dickey	C
6.	Joe Gordon	2B
7.	Graig Nettles	3B
8.	Phil Rizzuto	SS
9.	Whitey Ford	P

Just to give a manager something to do, he could flip-flop Dickey and Gordon if a lefty were pitching. Other than that, leave the thing on automatic pilot.

WASHINGTON SENATORS/MINNESOTA TWINS

Muddy Ruel	C
Mickey Vernon	1B
Rod Carew	2B
Harmon Killebrew	3B
Joe Cronin	SS
Goose Goslin	OF
Tony Oliva	OF
Heinie Manush	OF
Walter Johnson	RHP
Jim Kaat	LHP
Fred Marberry	RP

With the exception of Muddy Ruel, a brainy defensive specialist, this team is a real offensive powerhouse. Mickey Vernon, Rod Carew, Goose Goslin, Tony Oliva, and Heinie Manush account for 14 batting titles among them.

PHILADELPHIA-KANSAS CITY-OAKLAND ATHLETICS

Mickey Cochrane	C
Jimmie Foxx	1B
Eddie Collins	2B
Frank Baker	3B
Bert Campaneris	SS
Al Simmons	OF
Rickey Henderson	OF
Reggie Jackson	OF
Catfish Hunter	RHP
Lefty Grove	LHP
Rollie Fingers	RP

Here's an interesting squad, combining the very old and the brand new. This team might give the Yankees a run for their money; they have five players (Cochrane, Collins, Foxx, Grove, and Fingers) who are arguably the best ever at their positions, plus Rickey Henderson, probably the best leadoff man ever (remember, however, that Mickey Mantle batted first at the beginning of his career and would claim the leadoff title if he hadn't started hitting 40 or 50 homers a season).

CHICAGO WHITE SOX

Ray Schalk/Carlton Fisk	C
Joe Kuhel	1B
Nellie Fox	2B
Buck Weaver/Willie Kamm	3B
Luis Aparicio	SS
Al Simmons	OF
Joe Jackson	OF
Harold Baines	OF
Early Wynn	RHP
Billy Pierce	LHP
Goose Gossage	RP

The presence of Joe Kuhel might raise a few eyebrows, but he was on a par with Keith Hernandez: fewer walks, but many more stolen bases to go with a great glove, a good average, and medium-range power. Willie Kamm is also largely forgotten outside Chicago, yet from 1924 to 1934 he towered over his competition at the hot corner—and compiled a lifetime .370 on-base average.

BOSTON RED SOX

Carlton Fisk	C
Jimmie Foxx	1B
Bobby Doerr	2B
Jimmy Collins	3B
Joe Cronin	SS
Ted Williams	OF
Tris Speaker	OF
Carl Yastrzemski	OF
Cy Young	RHP
Lefty Grove	LHP
Dick Radatz	RP

These Red Sox starting pitchers are probably the best of any American League team, with Grove finishing second and Young sixth in the all-time voting. Overall, these "Best Bosox" could also challenge the Bronx Bombers—as they each have in the past, come to think of it.

ST. LOUIS BROWNS/BALTIMORE ORIOLES

Rollie Hemsley	C
George Sisler	1B
Bobby Grich	2B
Brooks Robinson	3B
Luis Aparicio	SS
Frank Robinson	OF
Paul Blair	OF
Heinie Manush	OF
Jim Palmer	RHP
Dave McNally	LHP
Hoyt Wilhelm	RP

Mostly Orioles here. Although the Browns won the pennant in 1944, their best team was the 1922 club led by George Sisler and Urban Shocker (whose name sounds like a *New York Post* headline). That team lost the flag to the Yanks by one game in a final heart-stopping series to end the season.

CLEVELAND INDIANS

Jim Hegan	C
Hal Trosky	1B
Joe Gordon	2B
Ken Keltner	3B
Lou Boudreau	SS
Joe Jackson	OF
Tris Speaker	OF
Earl Averill	OF
Bob Feller	RHP
Herb Score	LHP
Satchel Paige	RP

Unfortunately, there is room for only one right-handed starter. The Tribe has a long history of great righties. Besides Feller, Indian righties receiving votes include Bob Lemon, Early Wynn, Gaylord Perry, Mel Harder, and Luis Tiant. Also note Big Hal Trosky at first base; a career batting average of .302 with a .522 slugging average and 116 RBIs per 154 games are his sterling credentials.

DETROIT TIGERS

Mickey Cochrane	C
Hank Greenberg	1B
Charlie Gehringer	2B
George Kell	3B
Alan Trammell	SS
Harry Heilmann	OF
Ty Cobb	OF
Al Kaline	OF
Jim Bunning	RHP
Hal Newhouser	LHP
Fred Marberry	RP

Another proud franchise. There is nothing remotely resembling a weak link in this team, which is peppered with greats from every era since Ty Cobb. The only question is whether Jack Morris will eclipse Jim Bunning as right-handed starter.

"What Was Your Favorite Stadium To Play Or Manage Or Coach In?"	
1. Yankee Stadium	16.2%
2. Wrigley Field	13.7
3. Tiger Stadium	12.8
4. Fenway Park	9.9
5. Dodger Stadium	9.5
6. Comiskey Park	5.2
7. Polo Grounds (New York)	3.6
8. Forbes Field (Pittsburgh)	2.8
9. Ebbets Field (Brooklyn, NY)	2.2
10. Sportsman's Park (St. Louis)	2.1
11. Milwaukee County Stadium	2.0
12-13. Crosley Field (Cincinnati)	1.6
12-13. Kansas City Municipal	1.6
14. Shibe Park (Philadelphia)	1.5
15. Royals Stadium	1.4
16. Cleveland Municipal	1.3
17. Baltimore Memorial	1.2
18-20. Astrodome	1.1
18-20. Anaheim	1.1
18-20. Jack Murphy (San Diego)	1.1

Franchise-By-Franchise: All Time Greats

NATIONAL LEAGUE

BOSTON/MILWAUKEE/ATLANTA BRAVES

Del Crandall	C
Orlando Cepeda	1B
Red Schoendienst	2B
Eddie Mathews	3B
Rabbit Maranville	SS

Hank Aaron	OF
Dale Murphy	OF
Dusty Baker	OF
Johnny Sain	RHP
Warren Spahn	LHP
Don McMahon	RP

It's not customary to think of Orlando Cepeda as a Brave, but before he came to Atlanta in a trade for Joe Torre they were a .500 team; with Cha-Cha at first, virtually the same team won the NL West in 1969. Following that, in 1970 he hit .305 with 34 homers and 111 RBIs.

Fairly slim pickings, relatively speaking, for the third outfield spot, with Dusty Baker's competition coming from Wally Berger, Tommy Holmes, and Sid Gordon.

BROOKLYN/LOS ANGELES DODGERS

Roy Campanella	C
Gil Hodges	1B
Jackie Robinson	2B
Billy Cox	3B
Pee Wee Reese	SS
Duke Snider	OF
Carl Furillo	OF
Willie Keeler	OF
Don Drysdale	RHP
Sandy Koufax	LHP
Ron Perranoski	RP

You will notice that, minus Wee Willie Keeler and the pitchers, every player is from the great Dodger squads of the early fifties. Keeler does belong on a Brooklyn team, though, because he hit .359 over four seasons (1899-1902) for them. Also, we can't help but wonder where Steve Howe would have placed had he not messed himself up with drugs.

CHICAGO CUBS

Gabby Hartnett	C
Frank Chance	1B
Billy Herman	2B
Stan Hack	3B
Ernie Banks	SS
Billy Williams	OF
Hack Wilson	OF
Kiki Cuyler	OF
Pete Alexander	RHP
Larry French	LHP
Bruce Sutter	RP

As a Cub from 1935-1940, Larry French had a record of 90-70, with an ERA of 3.43, twice tying for the league lead in shutouts. It is testimony to the Cubs' bygone status as a perennial power that the franchise, not having won a pennant in over 40 years, can still boast a team this strong.

CINCINNATI REDS

Johnny Bench	C
Ted Kluszewski	1B
Joe Morgan	2B
Pete Rose	3B
Dave Concepcion	SS
Frank Robinson	OF
Edd Roush	OF
Vada Pinson	OF
Ewell Blackwell	RHP
Johnny Vander Meer	LHP
Ted Abernathy	RP

Ted Kluszewski's career batting and slugging averages are just short of the glamour marks at .298 and .498, respectively, and there is little doubt that another victim of the Great American Back Problem can be chalked up: Ted's slipped disk cost him a plaque in the Hall of Fame. During his four-year peak from 1953-1957 he averaged .315 with 43 home runs. He still holds the record with 10 RBIs in a six-game World Series in 1959.... Except for the pitchers, this club is drawn largely from the dominating Big Red Machine teams of the mid-1970s, as one might expect.

NEW YORK/SAN FRANCISCO GIANTS

Roger Bresnahan	C
Willie McCovey	1B
Frankie Frisch	2B
Freddie Lindstrom	3B
Travis Jackson	SS
Willie Mays	OF
Mel Ott	OF
Ross Youngs	OF
Christy Mathewson	RHP
Carl Hubbell	LHP
Lindy McDaniel	RP

Sadly, there are only the Willies here after 1940. Al Rosen is a respected G.M.; perhaps he can help recapture the lustre on the faded crown of what was once the flagship franchise of the National League.

PHILADELPHIA PHILLIES

Jimmie Wilson	C
Pete Rose	1B
Manny Trillo	2B
Mike Schmidt	3B
Larry Bowa	SS
Chuck Klein	OF
Richie Ashburn	OF
Irish Meusel	OF
Pete Alexander	RHP
Steve Carlton	LHP
Jim Konstanty	RP

Long a doormat in the National League, the Phillies emerged in the 1970s as an annual contender, largely due to the efforts of the five players listed here from that era. And shouldn't it be six players? It's difficult to understand the preference for Jim Konstanty over Tug McGraw, whatever one thought of the latter's histrionics. Konstanty had only two good years, one for the Phillies, while McGraw of course had many over his career and ranks in the top 10 all-time in appearances, saves, and relief wins.

PITTSBURGH PIRATES

Tony Pena	C
Willie Stargell	1B
Bill Mazeroski	2B
Pie Traynor	3B
Honus Wagner	SS
Roberto Clemente	OF
Paul Waner	OF
Lloyd Waner	OF
Burleigh Grimes	RHP
Wilbur Cooper	LHP
Elroy Face	RP

Not that these guys are slouches with the stick, but this club is strictly top drawer on defense. Mazeroski and Clemente are unquestionably the best ever at their positions, and Pena, Wagner, Traynor, and the Waners are right up there at theirs. Don't overlook left-hander Wilbur Cooper, who as a Pirate from 1912-1924 was 202-159 (.560) with an ERA of 2.74 and 34 shutouts.
Where is Ralph Kiner?

ST. LOUIS CARDINALS

Walker Cooper	C
Johnny Mize	1B
Rogers Hornsby	2B
Ken Boyer	3B

Marty Marion	SS
Stan Musial	OF
Enos Slaughter	OF
Lou Brock	OF
Bob Gibson	RHP
Steve Carlton	LHP
Bruce Sutter	RP

It's funny how a particular team, playing in different ball parks and eras, can acquire and maintain a certain style of play. From the mid-1920s to the Gashouse Gang to the great "St. Louis Swifties" clubs, from "El Birdos" of the 1960s to the current "Whitey's Rabbits," the Redbirds have been an aggressive, speedy team consistently near the top in doubles, triples, and stolen bases.

Since the lively ball era began in 1920, the Cards have led the league in home runs only three times, and not since 1944 at that. This all-time outfit has good power, though. Another point about the Redbirds is the depth of stars, especially at second base with Frisch, Red Schoendienst, and Tommy Herr; and in the outfield with Joe Medwick, Chick Hafey, Terry Moore, and even Curt Flood.

Cub fans might be amused to know that in the teens and early twenties it was widely held that St. Louis could never win the pennant because the Midwestern heat burned out the players by September.

1946 All Star Game, Municipal Stadium, Cleveland: Charley Keller crosses the plate after his home run in the first inning. Bobby Doerr (L) congratulates him. Catcher Walker Cooper looks on.

The Top Managers

1.	Casey Stengel	19.4%
2.	Joe McCarthy	15.4
3.	Walter Alston	14.0
4.	John McGraw	8.7
5.	Connie Mack	7.7
6.	Earl Weaver	6.9
7.	Al Lopez	2.7
8.	Billy Martin	2.5
9.	Miller Huggins	2.3
10-11.	Whitey Herzog	1.8
10-11.	Sparky Anderson	1.8
12.	Ralph Houk	1.7
13.	Bucky Harris	1.6
14-15.	Leo Durocher	1.4
14-15.	Fred Hutchinson	1.4
16-17.	Gene Mauch	1.1
16-17.	Gil Hodges	1.1
18.	Danny Murtaugh	1.0
19.	Paul Richards	.9

National Baseball Library Collection

Miller Huggins: Babe Ruth's skipper ranks ninth on the all-time manager list.

The oldest and truest cliché of managing, one that has been uttered by virtually every field general since the beginning, is, "You gotta have the horses if you wanna make a run." The perfect symmetry in the won-lost record of Casey Stengel is the best case in point. In his first nine years, with Brooklyn and the Boston Braves, his teams' overall winning percentage was .437 (602-777). Only once in Casey's early days did a squad of his finish over .500, eking out a 77-75 mark with Boston in 1938, and only twice in nine seasons did he place as high as fifth. Immediately after shifting his talents to New York, though, the Old Perfesser's teams reeled off 10 pennants in 12 seasons, posting a .621 figure over that span, the most dominant dynasty in baseball history. In *sports* history.

The thing is, of course, that Casey didn't change his idiosyncratic managing style one iota after switching to the Yanks. He'd go with "the book," deep into the book, against the book; he'd hold his pitchers back to go against a particular team or in a particular ball park. He would shift men all over the diamond during the course of a game as no manager does today, not even his protegés Billy Martin and Whitey Herzog. Only Mickey Mantle and Yogi Berra regularly batted 500 + times on his teams, though Gil McDougald would slip in there once in a while, shifting from second to third to short. Whitey Ford, arguably the league's best pitcher in the 1950s, in nine years under Casey finished only in the top five once in games started, because Stengel would hold him back to pitch in Yankee Stadium as often as possible. When the Old Perfesser was fired, Ford won 66 games in three years, after not winning 20 in *any* season under Stengel. His innings pitched had jumped about 50 per season—and the Yankees kept winning pennants because they had the horses. Casey then took the same style across the river, and got a lot of laughs if few victories with the hapless Mets for three and a half seasons.

Now Joe McCarthy had some horses, and he knew what to do with them. In 24 years as skipper for the Cubs, Yankees, and Red Sox, not once—repeat, not once—did one of his teams finish in the second division. His .614 lifetime winning percentage is the all-time best, .021 better than his nearest modern competition, Billy Southworth. That's 99 wins per 162-game season—over 24 years! Marse Joe was a man with a memory; he disdained charts and statistical minutiae, claiming to have it all in his head.

Tommy Henrich tells a story in Donald Honig's *Baseball Between the Lines* to illustrate McCarthy's vast memory. Minor-league batting sensation (and friend of Henrich's) Jimmy Wasdell had just been called up by the Washington Senators and the talk in the Yankee clubhouse turned to how to pitch to the newcomer. As Henrich tells it, "Well, as far as I knew, I was the only one on the club who had ever played with Wasdell, who knew anything about him. But I'm not that dumb; I'm not going to tell these wise guys how to pitch to Jimmy Wasdell. I've seen too many outfielders give well-meaning advice that exploded in somebody's face. But while I'm keeping quiet, McCarthy says, 'I know who he is. He's that kid that pinch-hit against us in Chattanooga when we came through there in the spring. He can't hit a change-up.' I looked at him. I couldn't believe it....The truth was Wasdell *couldn't* hit a change-up...and went 0 for 4 that day."

Newspapermen didn't care for the reticent Walter Alston because, as Dick Young put it, "He didn't write their stories for them." But look at the record. Twenty-three years, seven pennants and eight second-place finishes, an average of 90 wins a year—that's the formula for Alston's third-place showing. He was patient with his young players (like all the managers on this list) and would never berate a player in public (unlike some of the guys on this list). He was known for his explosive temper (like many here), hence his nickname "Smokey"—you could see it blowing out his ears. He was straight-laced and down-home. As Jim Murray of the *Los Angeles Times* said, "The only guy in the game who could look Billy Graham in the face without blushing…who would order corn on the cob in a Paris restaurant." Alston was hired to finally beat the Yankees and win the first world championship for the Bums. After a second-place finish in 1954, he did just that. Cries of "Walter Who?" greeted his arrival in Brooklyn, but his popular predecessor Charlie Dressen received a mere two and a half votes in this survey, again giving Alston the last laugh.

Recently and repeatedly parallels have been drawn between John McGraw and Billy Martin, but despite the superficial similarities they were quite different types. While both had explosive tempers, McGraw consistently used his temper to his own (and his team's) advantage. Even more so than today, hometown fans loved his battles with umpires and opposing players and flocked to the Polo Grounds to see them. Naturally, fans in other cities despised John J.—and flocked to the ball park to watch his Giants lose. Grantland Rice said that "McGraw's very walk across the field in a hostile town was a challenge to the multitude."

Since he was a part owner of the Giants, the Little Napoleon profited directly from his antics. George Steinbrenner has said that Martin also "puts fannies in the seats," but on and off the field his escapades bring only trouble. And that's the difference between them—self-discipline. McGraw suppressed and channeled his fiery nature to constructive purposes, whereas Martin often uses his head only to translate for his liver. To illustrate, when McGraw resigned as the Giants manager in 1932, he gave his job to Bill Terry, to whom he hadn't spoken in months and with whom he had tangled from the day they met. Furthermore, before hiring Terry he offered the job to ex-Giant Frankie Frisch—an ex-Giant because he jumped the club mid-season in 1926, fed up with McGraw's relentless and bitter criticism. Can you picture Martin turning over the reins to Reggie Jackson? Can you picture John McGraw, in the heat of a pennant race, leaving a pitcher in to take a beating just to spite the owner glaring down from his luxury box?

Speaking of leaving pitchers in, the two men couldn't have had more opposing philosophies of pitching. Martin delegated much authority to his pitching coach, usually Art Fowler, and he obviously believes in the complete game; in 14 seasons his teams have led the AL in complete games four times and been near the top several other times. On the other hand, McGraw called every pitch from the bench (except Christy Mathewson's) and juggled the staffs so that the Giants led the NL in complete games only twice in 32 years, and they finished last in CGs four times. In dealing with the umpires, too, there are contrasts. Both feuded with the umps to the limit and then some. But McGraw privately spoke highly even of his nemesis Bill Klem and often socialized with the men in blue. It should also be remembered that in those days the umpiring *was* bad, because with only one or two on the field they were frequently out of position, and they admitted as much. Not that McGraw was a saint, but do you remember Billy Martin in tears, accusing the umps of "throwing" the 1976 World Series? McGraw would never have done that.

What about on the field? Martin's record, as he reminds people, speaks for itself. He can take a team he's never seen before and make it a winner almost overnight. Some pundits have called him "the greatest one-season manager of all time."

In contrast to McGraw and Martin, Connie Mack was baseball's perfect gentleman. Ty Cobb, surely the stingiest of players with a compliment, said of him, "I played my last two years for Connie. I wish I had played all of them for him." As a catcher in the violent, often brutal game of the late 19th century, Cornelius McGillicuddy was merely tricky. As a manager from day one of the American League, he did a great deal to elevate the public image of baseball, both by personal example and by finding civilized, educated young men to play for his Philadelphia A's. Two of his teams, the 1911 and the 1929-30 clubs, must be mentioned when discussing the greatest champions ever.

Mack's managing style was not innovative or controversial; he stuck to the tactical basics, didn't platoon much, and in general shifted strategy as his talent dictated. Many a photo showed him positioning his fielders expertly from the bench with a rolled-up scorecard.

After Earl Weaver in the sixth slot, there's a big drop-off to Al Lopez and the rest of the field. Note that Weaver easily outpolls Martin, Whitey Herzog, Sparky Anderson, and Gene Mauch among the active managers. This could change, however, as Earl battles the law of averages and the others continue to succeed.

The Greatest Teams

		WON	LOST	PCT.
1.	1927 Yankees	37.9%	110	44	.714
2.	1961 Yankees	7.8	109	53	.673
3.	1975 Cincinnati Reds	5.4	108	54	.667
4.	1976 Reds	5.1	102	60	.630
5.	1926 Yankees	2.3	91	63	.591
6-7.	1973 Oakland Athletics	2.1	94	68	.580
6-7.	1928 Yankees	2.1	101	53	.656
8-10.	1929 Philadelphia A's	1.6	104	46	.693
8-10.	1930 Phil. A's	1.6	102	52	.662
8-10.	1934 St. Louis Cards	1.6	95	58	.621
11-14.	1962 Yankees	1.3	96	66	.593
11-14.	1936 Yankees	1.3	102	51	.667
11-14.	1931 Phil. A's	1.3	107	45	.704
11-14.	1932 Yankees	1.3	107	47	.695
15-17.	1950 Yankees	1.2	98	56	.636
15-17.	1956 Yankees	1.2	97	57	.630
15-17.	1941 Yankees	1.2	101	53	.656
18-19.	1942 Cardinals	1.1	106	48	.688
18-19.	1955 Brooklyn Dodgers	1.1	98	55	.641

Here's a more sensible way to read the responses:

1.	1926-1928 Yankees	42.3%
2.	1975-1976 Reds	10.5
3.	1960-1962 Yankees	10.1
4.	1929-1931 Philadelphia A's	4.6

5.	1972-1974 Oakland A's	4.2
6.	1949-1953 Yankees	3.9
7.	1936-1939 Yankees	3.1
8.	1969-1971 Baltimore Orioles	1.7
9.	1942 and 1946 Cardinals	1.5
10.	1956 Yankees	1.5

The Bronx Bombers place five mini-dynasties among the top 10. Surprise. In fact, all Yankee teams account for 65% of the votes—as impressive as it is expected.

When sizing up a club as an all-time great, one should ask several questions. What was their won-lost record? Did they win both the pennant and the world championship with relative ease? Did they repeat? Did they lead their league in runs scored or fewest runs allowed, or both? How many Hall of Famers did they have?

At their peak in 1927, the "Murderers' Row" Yankees won 110 games, one shy of the 1954 Indians' American League record. The Yanks of '27 finished 19 games in front of the runner-up Athletics of Philly, then destroyed the Pirates in four straight. They did indeed repeat in 1928, also winning the Series, again in four. Their 975 runs scored were a shocking 130 more than the next best total, and their 599 runs allowed were an equally astounding 109 fewer than second best. They also boasted five Hall of Famers, plus a few others close to that honor.

Cruising down the list, you'll see that all the teams make the grade on all or nearly all the aforementioned criteria. Don't overlook the 1942 Cardinals, by the way. Winners of 106 games, after a blistering pennant race with the Dodgers (who won 104), they dominated the heavily favored Yankees in the Series, four games to one. Those Redbirds also scored the most and allowed the fewest runs; their staff posted a sparkling 2.55 ERA, and they allowed nearly one fewer run per game than the rest of the National League. By the end of the season, only one pitcher had an ERA over 2.98 (and Sportsman's Park was far from a friend to the men on the mound). They hit only 60 home runs, 49 fewer than the league-leading Giants, yet still finished first in slugging average.

Since 1901, 29 teams have topped their leagues in both runs scored and least runs allowed. Most impressive in this regard were Joe McCarthy's 1936-39 Yankees, who did it four years in a row, winning four world championships and averaging 103 wins per 154-game season. That's dominance.

The Best Baseball Broadcaster		
1.	Vin Scully	20.0%
2.	Red Barber	15.7
3.	Mel Allen	15.1
4.	Joe Garagiola	4.6
5.	Harry Carey	4.2
6.	Ernie Harwell	3.8
7.	Jack Buck	3.2

8.	Dizzy Dean	3.0
9-10.	Bob Prince	2.7
9-10.	Curt Gowdy	2.7
11.	Tony Kubek	2.1
12.	Don Drysdale	1.6
13.	Bob Elson	1.3
14.	Russ Hodges	1.2
15-16.	Waite Hoyt	1.0
15-16.	Lindsay Nelson	1.0
17.	Jack Brickhouse	.9

Players' Choice: The 100 Greatest Players of All Time

In recent years at least four authors have published their opinions on the top 100 players in baseball history. One hundred is a nice round number, isn't it? We thought it might be instructive to compile such a list—the first ever, to our knowledge—from players' all-time all-star team voting. The writers and statisticians represent the consensus view of fandom. Let's see where we all disagree and agree with the guys who wore the uniform.

Because our ball player-participants voted *by position*—i.e., picking the best at each—this "100 Greatest" is perfectly balanced (which isn't necessarily the same thing as being perfect). We didn't bother to assign numbers. It's a little silly to say that Al Kaline is 33rd best, Bill Mazeroski 34th, etc., as one book does.

If we ran into a problem putting together this perfectly balanced list, it was what to do with relief pitchers. How many should make the top 100? Four, we decided. And the top four finishers in the voting were Goose Gossage, Rollie Fingers, Bruce Sutter, and Hoyt Wilhelm.

Without further ado, here are the 100 greatest of all time, in alphabetical order. Boldface type indicates that a ball player was chosen by the players *and* at least three of the four writers who have named their own top 100 recently. There are 72 such players. And by the way, these men are here because they are the 100 with the most individual votes. We did not eliminate anyone, aside from the #5 ranking relief pitcher, who received enough raw votes to be in the top 100.

Players' Choice: The 100 Greatest Ball Players of All Time

Hank Aaron	**Yogi Berra**	**Steve Carlton**
Grover (Pete) Alexander	**Lou Boudreau**	Gary Carter
Luis Aparicio	Ken Boyer	**Roberto Clemente**
Luke Appling	**George Brett**	**Ty Cobb**
Ernie Banks	**Roy Campanella**	**Mickey Cochrane**
Johnny Bench	**Rod Carew**	**Eddie Collins**

Dave Concepcion
Joe Cronin
Dizzy Dean
Bill Dickey
Joe DiMaggio
Bobby Doerr
Don Drysdale
Bob Feller
Rollie Fingers
Whitey Ford
Nellie Fox
Jimmie Foxx
Frankie Frisch
Lou Gehrig
Charlie Gehringer
Bob Gibson
Lefty Gomez
Joe Gordon
Goose Gossage
Hank Greenberg
Lefty Grove
Gabby Hartnett

Billy Herman
Gil Hodges
Rogers Hornsby
Carl Hubbell
Reggie Jackson
Travis Jackson
Walter Johnson
Al Kaline
George Kell
Harmon Killebrew
Sandy Koufax
Napoleon Lajoie
Bob Lemon
Mickey Mantle
Juan Marichal
Marty Marion
Eddie Mathews
Christy Mathewson
Willie Mays
Bill Mazeroski
Willie McCovey
Johnny Mize

Joe Morgan
Stan Musial
Graig Nettles
Hal Newhouser
Mel Ott
Pee Wee Reese
Allie Reynolds
Bobby Richardson
Cal Ripken
Robin Roberts
Brooks Robinson
Frank Robinson
Jackie Robinson
Phil Rizzuto
Red Rolfe
Pete Rose
Babe Ruth
Nolan Ryan
Mike Schmidt
Red Schoendienst
Tom Seaver
Al Simmons

St. Louis Cardinals

Red Schoendienst: Hall material?

George Sisler	Bruce Sutter	Hoyt Wilhelm
Ozzie Smith	**Bill Terry**	**Ted Williams**
Duke Snider	Pie Traynor	**Carl Yastrzemski**
Warren Spahn	**Honus Wagner**	**Cy Young**
Tris Speaker	**Paul Waner**	**Robin Yount**
Willie Stargell		

Only 51 of our *Players' Choice* greats were chosen by all four of the aforementioned writers, but some of the writers' omissions are so absurd that we defined "consensus view" as being named in three, not all four, of the books. What do we mean by absurd? In the *Hidden Game of Baseball*, the authors' formulas allow no room for Sandy Koufax, Roy Campanella, Ernie Banks, George Sisler, Luis Aparicio, Brooks Robinson, Bob Feller, or Robin Roberts. Picture these guys as a team, then pencil in Hot Rod Kanehl at second base and Horace Speed in the outfield, add Bo Belinsky and Mark Littell to the pitching staff, and they'd *still* win 110 games. So no matter what criticisms you care to levy at the players' choices, none of their omissions is anywhere near as serious as these, with the explainable exception of Mordecai "Three-Finger" Brown. There's little doubt that Brown belongs in the top 100, but he suffers in the voting from the heavy old-timer support for Walter Johnson, Cy Young, and Christy Mathewson.

You might well dispute the ball players for leaving out two superb players, Jim Palmer and Ralph Kiner. Palmer was overshadowed by flashier contemporaries like Nolan Ryan (and let's face it, Ryan threw five no-hitters). Palmer was harder to beat than Ryan, but Ryan was probably harder to face, hence the players' edge for him. As for Kiner of the Pittsburgh Pirates, he might just as well have played somewhere in Alaska for all the attention he got. He was admittedly no Gold Glover, but his home runs-per-at-bat ratio (one every 14 times up, and he was in the middle of a weak lineup) is second only to Babe Ruth!

In *The 100 Greatest Baseball Players of All Time*, authors Ritter and Honig omit Joe Cronin, Reggie Jackson, and Al Kaline; the players' response, in effect, is that Reggie is debatable, but that the others are not. In Bill James's *Historical Baseball Abstract*, there are two lists of the top 100, one for "peak value" and one for career contributions. The peak list leaves out Cy Young, Warren Spahn, Hank Greenberg, and Frankie Frisch, but they all made the career top 100 in James's book.

Should These Ball Players Be in the Hall of Fame?

Their peers think so. What follows is a list of players in the gang of 100 who haven't made it to Cooperstown (still-active players not included):

Phil Rizzuto	Gil Hodges	Allie Reynolds
Ken Boyer	Marty Marion	Bobby Richardson
Nellie Fox	Bill Mazeroski	Red Rolfe
Joe Gordon	Hal Newhouser	Red Schoendienst

Still, it's hard to figure how Frisch could fall short; during his five-year prime the Fordham Flash hit .336 and averaged 110 runs scored, not to mention his great defense at both second and third bases. The case for Greenberg making the James peak list is even stronger. He hit 63 doubles one year, 170, then 183 RBIs in two other years, followed by a year of 58 home runs—that's Lou Gehrig territory. Hank also finished first, second, and third in the MVP voting in a four-year period—that alone should put him comfortably in the top 100. The players themselves chose him eighth at first base, and all the other writers also placed him on their lists. Of all the authors, Maury Allen (*Baseball's 100*) is the only one who does not omit any player chosen by the consensus, possibly because he's the one writer closest to the diamond all season long.

On the other hand, mainly because of the built-in balanced distribution by position in our list, several infielders make the players' top 100 who weren't named by *any* of the above writers. They are Dave Concepcion, Travis Jackson, George Kell, Graig Nettles, Marty Marion, Bobby Richardson, Red Rolfe, and Ozzie Smith.

Before you throw up your hands in disbelief, consider the defensive contributions of these guys; in most analyses, glovework is mentioned as an afterthought, like basestealing. The players clearly disagree. There is no doubt that a player who saves hundreds of extra runs over the years should rank up there with some of the great sluggers. And though many sluggers were adequate at best in the field, all of the seven players' choices were or are at worst adequate with the bat, and usually well above average. To extend the analogy, as the sluggers usually play the less demanding positions, the glove men usually occupy the lower places in the batting order. It seems obvious (and most fans would agree) that defense is very important, but since fielding stats are less accurate, more subjective, less detailed, and less publicized than batting stats, defense is often forgotten when comparing, say, Ozzie Smith with Reggie Jackson. And if you don't think Ozzie will make the Hall of Fame, think again. Because judging from our survey, even if the baseball writers pass him by, the veterans committee will roll out the red carpet for Ozzie—and for Bill Mazeroski, for that matter.

Another point to consider, and a very telling one: except for batting champion George Kell, all seven of these infielders played for several pennant winners. In fact, the other six account for 27 pennants among them, as impressive a collection as nearly any other seven players one can name. And no one can deny that those pennants were won in part because of all the runs prevented by the defensive play of these men.

We're not saying that the players' top 100 should be carved in granite, because time can cause a player's reputation to rise or fall; too, some active players will undoubtedly displace some currently on the list. Nonetheless, our point in this book is to give voice to the forgotten experts, the professional players.

AFTERWORD

So there it is. The obvious, the esoteric, the unscientific but considered opinions of baseball playerdom—the men who answer the call to "Play Ball!" Anyone can disagree with any particular player's ballot, for a variety of more or less valid reasons. But that's not the point. The idea is to establish a consensus among living players, one we as fans can refer to when comparing stats or just jawing at the bar.

Player-Participants by Decade	
1910-1919	1%
1920-1929	6
1930-1939	14
1940-1949	18
1950-1959	20
1960-1969	20
1970-1979	16
1980-present	6

The average playing career for a participant is 5.1 years in the major leagues.

Player-Participants by Position

First basemen	53
Second basemen	67
Shortstops	74
Third basemen	84
Outfielders	129
Catchers	54
Pitchers	264

Survey Participants

Below is an alphabetical listing of every ball player who filled out a survey for *Players' Choice*. Some players participated anonymously; they are not listed, of course.

George Abrams
Tom Acker
Fritz Ackley
Bob Alexander
Ethan Allen
Matty Alou
George Altman
Wayne Ambler
Alf Anderson
Craig Anderson
Larry Anderson
Mike Armstrong
Rudy Arroyo
Earl Averill, Jr.
Bob Bailey
Ed Bailey
Jack Baker
Dave Baldwin
Dick Baney
George Banks
Lefty Barnes
E.V. Barnhart
Jim Barr
Bob Barton
Frank Baumann
Larry Bearnarth
Rich Beck
Clyde Beck
Joe Beggs
Ollie Bejima
Les Bell

Wally Berger
Ralph Betcher
Hank Biasetti
Paul Blair
Cy Block
Terry Bogener
Rob Boken
Milt Bolling
Ernie Bonman
Zeke Bonura
Ray Boone
Bill Bordley
Glenn Borgmann
Red Borom
Roger Bowman
Ted Bowsfield
William D. Bradford
Tom Bradley
George Bradshaw
Bobby Bragan
Jimmy Bragan
Ron Brand
Darrell Brandon
Jackie Brandt
Ed Bressoud
Ernie Broglio
Ike Brookens
Jim Brosnan
Joe Brovia
Bob Bruce

Jack Bruner
Warren Brusstar
Jim Bucher
Don Buddin
Mike Budnick
Jim Bunning
Larry Burchart
Ray Burris
Guy Bush
Craig Cacek
Bob Cain
Joe Camacho
Jim Campanis
Clarence Campbell, Jr.
Dave Campbell
Paul Campbell
Fred Cambria
Buzz Capra
Don Cardwell
Don Carrithers
George Case
Pete Castiglione
Bill Chamberlain
Cliff Chambers
Spud Chandler
Ed Charles
Walter Chipple
Harry Chozen
Gary Christenson
Larry Ciaffone

Dody Cicero
Jim Clark
Michael Clark
Otie Clark
Harlond Clift
Herman Clifton
Gil Coan
Andy Cohen
Syd Cohen
Jim Colborn
Dave Cole
Joe Coleman, Sr.
Dick Colpaert
Bill Conroy
Bobby Coombs
Jimmy Cooney
Henry Coppola
Gene Corbett
Ray Corbin
Jim Cosman
Ted Cox
Peter Craig
Pat Crawford
Frank Crespi
Dave Cripe
Jeff Cross
Frank Crosetti
Jack Cullen
Ray Culp
George Culver
Jack Curtis
Guy Curtright
Joe Cusick
Bruce Dal Canton
Bud Daley
Dominic Dallessandro
Bennie Daniels
Ray Daviault
Jerry Davie
Mark Davis
Otis Davis
Spud Davis
Ron Davis
Woodrow Davis
Paul Dear
Rod Dedeaux
Mike Degerick
Don Demeter

Don DeMola
Con Dempsey
Otto Denning
Jimmie DeShong
Steve Dillard
Charles Diering
Bob Dillinger
Ron Diorio
Robert DiPietro
Jack Dittmer
Leo Dixon
Art Ditmar
Bobby Doerr
John Donaldson
Pete Donohue
Dave Dowling
Al Downing
Howard Doyle
Walt Dropo
Gus Dugas
George Durning
Joe Dwyer
Jim Dyck
Arnold Earley
Rawley Eastwick
John Edwards
Mark Eichhorn
Harry Eisenstat
Pete Elko
Charlie English
Del Ennis
Aubrey Epps
Joe Erardi
Ed Erautt
Cal Ermer
Carl Erskine
Sam Esposito
Dutch Fehring
Don Ferrarese
Bill Ferrazzi
Tom Ferrick
Neil Fiala
Bill Fleming
John Flinn
Mort Flohr
Gene Fodge
Jim Foor
Whitey Ford

Roger Freed
Hershell Freeman
Tito Fuentes
Frank Funk
Alan Gallagher
Bob Garbark
Mike Garbark
Ford Garrison
Milt Gaston
Charlie Gehringer
Gary Gentry
Greek George
Rusty Gerhardt
Dick Gernert
Drew Gilbert
Dave Giusti
Danny Godby
John Goetz
Howard Gorman
Howard Goss
Dick Grapenthin
Randy Gumpert
Rich Hacker
Ed Halicki
Irv Hall
Buddy Hancken
Jay Hankins
Preston Hanna
Gerry Hannahs
Bob Hansen
Larry Hardy
Mike Hargrove
Chuck Harmon
Bill Harris
Sam Harshaney
Herb Hash
Buddy Hassett
Joe Hauser
Dave Heaverlo
Jack Heidemann
Val Heim
Babe Herman
Earl Hersh
Mike Hershberger
Jack Hiatt
Jim Hibbs
Glen Hobbie
Jack Hobbs

Frank Hoerst
Calvin Hogue
Al Hollingsworth
Bonnie Hollingsworth
Tommy Holmes
Sid Hudson
Terry Humphrey
Billy Hunter
Herb Hutson
Monte Irvin
Grant Jackson
Larry Jansen
Frank Jelincich
Jack Jenkins
Woody Jensen
Don Johnson
Silas Johnson
Bobby Jones
Darryl Jones
Buck Jordan
Dick Joyce
Mike Jurewicz
Don Kaiser
Arthur Karl
Bob Keegan
Robert Keely
Charlie Keller
Tom Kelley
George Kelly
Ken Keltner
Bob Kennedy
Vernon Kennedy
Bruce Kimm
Jerry Kindall
Nellie King
Thornton Kipper
Ernie Kish
Johnny Klippstein
Bob Knepper
Dick Kokos
Ernie Koy
Charles Kress
Bert Kuczynski
Harvey Kuenn
Rusty Kuntz
Bob Kuzava
Rene Lachemann
Al Lamacchia

Wayne LaMaster
Jim Landis
Don Landrum
Hal Lanier
Max Lanier
Dave LaPoint
Vance Law
Tim Leary
Bob Lee
Hal Lee
Roy Lee
Lefty LeFebvre
Ken Lehman
Jim Lentine
Eddie Leon
Buck Leonard
Ted Lepcio
Dennis Lewallyn
Allan Lewis
Glenn Liebhardt, Jr.
Johnny Lindell
Ed Linke
Phil Linz
Johnny Lipon
Ad Liska
Dario Lodigiani
Vic Lombardi
Dale Long
Eddie Lopat
Arthur Lopatka
Larry Loughlin
Fred Lucas
Jerry Lynch
Frank MacCormick
Mike Macha
Dave Machemer
Joe Jon Maciarz
Paul Macwhorter
Rick Mahler
Mal Mallette
Eddie Malone
Frank Malzone
Frank Mancuso
Gus Mancuso
Hal Manders
Cliff Mapes
Marty Marion
Roger Marquis

Cuddles Marshall
Doc Marshall
Walter Masterson
Mark Mauldin
Carmen Mauro
Jim McAndrew
John McCall
Dave McDonald
Gil McDougald
Dan McGinn
Don McMahon
Carl McNabb
Tim McNamara
Lloyd Merritt
George Metkovich
Charlie Metro
Russ Meyer
Ed Mickelson
Wayne Middleton
Brad Mills
Al Milnar
Rudy Minarcin
George Mitterwald
Vinegar Bend Mizell
Johnny Mokan
Bob Molinaro
Bill Monboquette
Bob Montgomery
Moe Morhardt
John Morlan
Dan Morogiello
Arnold Moser
Jerry Moses
John Moses
Les Mueller
Ray Mueller
Ford Mullen
Joe Mulligan
Frank Mullin
Frank Mulroney
Les Munns
Joe Munson
Amby Murray
Danny Musser
Al Naples
Cholly Naranjo
Jerry Narron
Cotton Nash

Phil Nastu
Jim Nelson
Jim Nettles
Steve Nicosia
Don Nottebart
Jim O'Bradovich
Joe Oeschger
Bob Oldis
Bob Oliver
Gene Oliver
Nate Oliver
Jim Ollom
Al Olsen
Wayne Osborn
Joe Ostrowski
Jimmy Outlaw
John Pacella
Tony Pacheco
Andy Pafko
Ed Palmquist
Jim Panther
Gene Patton
Mike Paul
Hal Peck
Homer Peel
Jack Perconte
Bob Perry
Johnny Pesky
Rusty Peters
Fritz Peterson
Ray Poat
Boots Poffenberger
Jay Porter
Lou Possehl
Vic Power
John Pregenzer
Pat Putnam
Billy Queen
Dick Radatz
Bill Ramsey
Bobby Randall
Eric Rasmussen
Paul Ratliff
Claude Raymond
Rudy Regalado
Bill Renna
Rip Repulski
Dino Restelli

Merv Rettenmund
Dusty Rhodes
Dennis Ribant
Bob Rice
Paul Richards
Harvey Riebe
George Riley
Andy Rincon
Walt Ripley
Ray Ripplemeyer
Phil Rizzuto
Tony Robello
Dave Roberts
Leon Roberts
Jerry Robertson
Jim Robertson
Bruce Robinson
Lee Rogers
Jim Romano
John Romonosky
Bob Roselli
Goody Rosen
Marv Rotblatt
Donald Rowe
Pete Runnels
Tom Saffell
Jim Saul
Bob Savage
Bob Saverine
Dan Schatzeder
Richie Scheinblum
Red Schoendienst
Dick Schofield (father)
Len Schulte
Bill Schuster
Tom Seats
George Selkirk
Ted Sepkowski
John Sevcik
Frank Seward
Joe Sewell
Luke Sewell
Rip Sewell
Walter Shaner
Rollie Sheldon
Bert Shepard
Neill Sheridan
Larry Sherry

Barry Shetrone
Charlie Silvera
Ken Silvestri
Fred Sington
Dave Sisler
Dick Sisler
Peter Sivess
Dave Skaugstad
Roe Skidmore
Enos Slaughter
Jim Small
Edgar Smith
Frank Smith
Hal Smith
Paddy Smith
Willie Smith
Eddie Solomon
Daryl Spencer
Tom Spencer
Jack Spring
Joe Spring
George Stablein
Gerry Staley
Tracy Stallard
Bobby Stevens
Chuck Stevens
R.C. Stevens
Ed Stewart
Ron Stone
Ray Stoviak
Bob Strampe
Brent Strom
Johnny Sturm
Charley Suche
Gus Suhr
Art Swanson
Ken Szotkiewicz
Chuck Tanner
Lee Tate
Eddie Taylor
Bud Teachout
Frank Tepedino
Zeb Terry
Nick Testa
Dick Tettelbach
George Thomas
Herb Thomas
Kite Thomas

Roy Thomas
Tommy Thomas
Gene Thompson
Shag Thompson
Les Tietje
Eric Tipton
Joe Tipton
Jim Todd
Specs Toporcer
Virgil Trucks
John Tsitouris
Robert Tufts
Scott Ullger
Tom Underwood
Dixie Upright
Glen Vaughan
Al Verdel
John Verhoeven
Sam Vick
Al Vincent
Ed Walczak
Bernie Walter
Billy Wambsganss

Jon Warden
Jimmy Wasdell
Dave Watkins
Ed Watt
Bill Webb
Skeeter Webb
Frank Weber
Phil Weintraub
Johnny Welaj
Eddie Wells
Dick Welteroth
Johnny Wertz
Sammy West
Dave Wickersham
Bob Whitcher
JoJo White
Sammy White
Burgess Whitehead
Fred Whitfield
Pinky Whitney
Bobby Wilkins
Bob Will

Don Williams
Matthew Williams
Stan Williams
Woody Williams
Hugh Willingham
Archie Wilson
Hugh Wise
Charles Wood
Spades Wood
Gene Woodling
Jim Woods
Floyd Wooldridge
Ab Wright
Ed Wright
Glenn Wright
Whitlow Wyatt
James York
Adrian Zabala
Chris Zachary
Don Zimmer
Jimmy Zinn
Frank Zupo

Ball Player Survey for <u>Players' Choice</u>

Please choose players from all eras, if possible. Feel free to use extra paper to expand your answers if you think that is necessary. This survey is for all active and former major-league ball players who wish to participate, as well as for past and present managers and coaches. It is three pages long, and we ask that you sign and date it on the bottom of page two. Thank you <u>very</u> much for your time and help.

Name your all-time All-Star Team. Then name your 2 all-time All-Star Team. Then name your all-time <u>defensive</u> team.

TEAM 1	TEAM 2
Outfield_____	Outfield_____
_____	_____
_____	_____
3B_____	3B_____
SS_____	SS_____
2B_____	2B_____
1B_____	1B_____
RH pitcher_____	RH pitcher_____
LH pitcher_____	LH pitcher_____
Catcher_____	Catcher_____
Relief pitcher_____	Relief pitcher_____

NAME YOUR ALL-TIME DEFENSIVE TEAM:

Outfield:_____, _____ and
_____.

1B:_____ 2B:_____ 3B:_____
SS:_____ RH Pitcher:_____ LH Pitcher:_____
Catcher:_____
===

1) Name the two or three most underrated ball players of all time: _____
_____

2) Who was the best clutch hitter ever?_____ Best pinch
hitter?_____ Best <u>pure</u> hitter?_____

3) What was the best SS-2B double-play combination ever?_____

4) You are the manager of a team in Game 7 of a World Series. What pitcher
would you pick to start the game?_____

5) Name the best manager of all time_____
The best team (including the year they played)_____

6) Which was your favorite stadium to play, manage, or coach in?_____
What city has the best fans?_____

7) Do you favor or oppose the designated hitter? OPPOSE___ FAVOR___

8) Name the pitcher who had: the best fastball_____
best curve_____ best sinker/drop_____
best screwball_____ best change-up_____
best spitball_____ best slider_____
best pickoff move_____

9) Who is the best base-stealer of all time?_____
Best bunter?_____ Best hit-and-run man?_____

10) Not including pitchers, who had the best throwing arm of all time?
_____

11) Who are/were the one or two most knowledgeable baseball broadcasters?
_____; _____

12) Best umpire you ever saw?_____

13) Name two or three ball players, if you care to, who you always thought for
one reason or another never played up to their potential:
_____; _____; _____

14) Who was the toughest pitcher you ever batted against?_____

15) Pitchers: What hitter did you find hardest to get out?_____

16) What ball player did the most to inspire his team?_____

17) Who is the best team owner you've known?_____

18) What baseball writer understood the game the best?_____

19) May we quote your answers and identify them as yours? YES___ NO___

20) Short of that, may we list you as a <u>participant</u>, while not quoting you?
    YES___ NO___

21) If you have photos from your playing days that you own rights to, and you
    don't mind letting us use them in the book, could you please give us your
    phone number?

    _____

22) Could you give us your phone number--and tell us the best time to call
    you--if you don't mind a possible follow-up interview?

    _____   _____
                                     (best time)

Please sign below, and to the right of your signature please print your name
and put the date. Thank you very much for your time.

Signature: _____   PRINTED name: _____
                                              date: _____

INDEX